The Understanding and
Management of Global Violence

The Understanding and Management of Global Violence

New Approaches to Theory and Research on Protracted Conflict

Edited by Harvey Starr

St. Martin's Press
New York

ISBN 0-312-21751-X

Library of Congress Cataloging-in-Publication Data

The understanding and management of global violence : new approaches
   to theory and research on protracted conflict / Harvey Starr,
   editor.
      p.   cm.
   Includes bibliographical references and index.
   ISBN 0312-21751-X
   1. International relations.   2. Crisis management.   3. Political
violence.   4. Crisis management—Case studies.   5. Political
violence—Case studies.   I. Starr, Harvey.
JZ5595.U53   1999
327.1'01—dc21   98–48412
                                                                            CIP

First published: April 1999

10   9   8   7   6   5   4   3   2   1

Contents

CHAPTER ONE

Introduction:
A Protracted Conflict Approach
to the Study of Social Conflict

Harvey Starr

Conflict into the Twenty-First Century

As scholars attempt to study and understand the global politics of the post–Cold War system, they must attend not only to changing structures of global order, but to the changing patterns of international, transnational, and domestic behavior. Conflict—and patterns of conflict—has not been immune to the transformations involved in the crossing of historical systems. In the post–Cold War period, the study of conflict must take such changes into account. Accentuating trends that began to emerge after the Second World War, patterns of conflict after the Cold War continue to de-emphasize cross-border, large-scale armed conflicts between two or more nation-states, and reflect the internal contention over the control of government, or the control of territory derived from separatist or secessionist movements (see, for example, Starr and Most 1985, Rosenau 1990, Wallensteen and Sollenberg 1997). While the end of the Cold War freed large- and middle-range powers to cooperate across a far more extensive range of issues, such as in the Security Council or in United Nations "peace keeping" operations (see Russett and Sutterlin 1991), it also provided the opportunity for ethnic conflict to reassert itself after decades of constraint. Much ethnic conflict had been contained both through authoritarian repression in the Eastern bloc, and through Western support for governments seen to be crucial in the Cold War struggle. In many areas of the world, this re-emergence of ethnic and separatist contention dominates regional conflict (see, for example, Gurr 1993, Gurr and Moore 1997, or Davis and Moore 1997).[1]

As we move into the twenty-first century conflicts based in ethnicity and/or territory will be increasingly linked to "enduring rivalries" or "principal rivalries" (Thompson 1995). That is, given certain dynamics over identity, territory, the stakes of conflict, and a cycle of escalation, quiescence, and re-emergence, we find certain "dangerous dyads" (Bremer 1992)—*recidivists* whose militarized relationship repeatedly erupts into violence. The study of conflict requires an investigation of the dynamics of such rivalries (see Goertz and Diehl 1995, Diehl 1998, and Huth 1996). In brief, we need models, concepts, and theories that will help us deal with conflict, especially violent social conflict, in the contemporary global system.

Looking at these factors in combination, the study of conflict in the post–Cold War world must then involve the analysis of domestic-foreign linkages, the analysis of the relationships between internal and external conflict, and employ models found in the array of two-level approaches to the study of conflict (see, for example, Putnam 1988, Starr 1994, Maoz 1996). The study of conflict, then, needs to focus on the investigation of the study of *conflict processes* that cut across levels of analysis. Despite the past difficulties in establishing systematic empirical relationships, continued concern with the internal-external relationship is justified because of a belief that it is possible to uncover the basic contours of *conflict processes* that apply at both levels. Indeed, Charles Tilly (1985, 522) has noted the necessity to look across levels of conflict and to show that "over much of history international and domestic conflict have been not merely similar but overlapping, even indistinguishable phenomena." Social conflict at any level is seen as a mechanism by which order is established, challenged, and re-established.

One approach to social conflict has great potential both for making contributions to each of these issues, and for further conceptual development by drawing upon the broad insights from the study of social conflict: the study of *protracted conflict,* as originally developed in the work of Edward Azar. Chapter 2 in this volume, "Protracted International Conflict: Ten Propositions," is a 1985 statement by Azar that summarizes the main features of his conception of "protracted conflict" or "protracted social conflict" (PSC).[2] However, while Azar created the concept of protracted conflict and presented it to the academic community in a number of articles, the concept was never fully specified and developed.[3] Drawing upon more recent theoretical and methodological developments, the chapters in this volume attempt to meet the challenge of clarifying this concept. They bring new thinking to the notion of protracted conflict. They elaborate on Azar's original ideas, expanding and specifying the concept of protracted conflict theoretically and methodologically, and applying it to a broad range of substantive cases. Protracted conflict is explicitly linked to two-level analyses, to the analysis of crisis, to the nature of identity groups, to enduring rivalries, and to a set of common conflict processes that cross levels of analysis. Protracted conflict is addressed and investigated using formal and spatial models, Markov models, chaos-related approaches, artificial-intelligence generated event-data analyses, standard statistical tools, and case studies. Analyses are presented that deal with Israel, the Palestinians, and Lebanon; the Phillipines and Nicaragua; Sri Lanka; India and Pakistan; and Northern Ireland. Each of the authors in this volume presents at least some basic notion of protracted conflict, and, as noted, some in part 1 spend considerable time clarifying and developing the concept. Nevertheless, in the next section I will present my own brief overview of protracted conflict. I will outline some of the core elements of social conflict and indicate where and how protracted conflict fits into the broader phenomena of social conflict as an analytic handle and/or a testing ground. More importantly, I will also indicate where PSC emerges as an exception—where it diverges from more general processes of social conflict, and thus why its study is so important. While I will refer to specific chapters included in this volume in the course of this discussion, I will also conclude with a brief characterization of the chapters that follow.

Introducing Protracted Conflict

In his classic work, Lewis Coser (1956, 8) defines social conflict as "a struggle over values or claims to status, power and scarce resources, in which the aims of the conflict groups are not only to gain the desired value but also to neutralize, injure or eliminate rivals." This definition also forms the core of Azar's conception of protracted conflict, but there is more. For Azar, protracted social conflict is long-term, ongoing conflict that permeates all aspects of society. Protracted conflict is apparently unresolvable, being unsusceptible to conventional conflict resolution methods because of the linkages between development and violence. Azar (1984, 85) notes that the term "protracted social conflict" was being used "to characterize those conflicts in which structural behavior (ethnic, religious, linguistic, economic) has affected overt hostile behavior (interaction), creating a complicated causal network that makes these conflicts difficult to 'solve.'" For Azar, protracted conflict accentuates issues regarding the identity and interests of the participants. As such, we agree with Rule (1988, 18) who notes that, "a full understanding of civil violence surely must deal with the *interests* of participants, and with participants' judgments as to how such interests are engaged in strife-torn situations."

Protracted Conflict and Two-Level Approaches to Conflict

In the chapter reprinted in this volume, Azar points to the salient characteristics of protracted conflict. Many of these characteristics force the analyst to think in terms of two-level approaches, as a conflict process that necessarily deals with conflict within and across polities. Two-level approaches are necessary given the factors Azar highlights. These include the effects of economic underdevelopment, the disintegrative effects of multi-ethnic and communal divisions, and the insecurity of identity group autonomy and survival.[4] Such factors lead Azar to lament the intractability of such conflicts—intractability that I see as based on the difficulty facing group leaders who must deal across groups and within their own groups, which is related to Putnam's concern with two-level games. Putnam's (1988, 427) "logic of two-level games," recognizes that "domestic politics and international relations are often somehow entangled but our theories have not yet sorted out the puzzling tangle."

Therefore, linkage, internal-external, and two-level approaches to conflict are all compelled to attend to, draw upon, and benefit from the insights that can be generated from the study of protracted conflict, and vice versa. All the chapters in this volume address this two-level issue in some way. It is important to use protracted conflict to help inform the study of internal-external conflict because this is an area of both long-standing concern, and an area that has presented considerable theoretical and empirical difficulties to scholars (see Starr 1994, Stohl 1980). As noted in Starr (1994), the paradox raised in many studies and reviews concerns the apparent inability of scholars to demonstrate in a systematic empirical manner relationships between internal and external phenomena that have been suggested by separate historical case studies, anecdotal material, or the gut feeling that a relationship must exist.

Various problems regarding the lack of theory in the area of internal-external linkage and a failure to achive integrative cumulation, as well as problems of research design, the lack of dynamic models, and the relevance of the topic to new global interdependence have all been raised and will be discussed in several of the chapters that follow. James Rosenau has specifically drawn attention to the weakness of the work on the internal-external nexus as an area of inquiry (1989, 5): "Work since the pace of global change quickened in the 1960s has resulted in islands of theory, but few bridges to connect them have been identified, much less built. Perhaps most notable in this regard is the persistent scarcity of theorizing addressed to the interaction of domestic and international politics." The contention of the contributors to this volume is that the concept of protracted conflict can be used to help fill this gap in our understanding, and that PSC as developed by Azar, and as extended and developed into several different models of analysis presented in this volume, can help us understand the theoretical and logical linkages between internal and external phenomena.

The utility of protracted conflict in the overall study of conflict derives from a belief that it is possible to uncover the basic contours of a conflict *process* whether or not that conflict is between nation-states or other types of actors at the sub-state level (see Starr 1994, Simon and Starr 1997). This view connects the activities of political scientists/international relations scholars with those of sociologists—in a desire to understand and map the phenomenon of social conflict. Along with James Rule (1988, 3) we are concerned with "the problem of order," in that social conflict is a mechanism by which order is established, challenged, and re-established. It is important to look at protracted conflict from this perspective, and to use protracted conflict as a way to understand how the conditions and context of conflict across two-levels, and with certain characteristics, might confound conflict theory developed for states in the international system, or any inter-group conflict between two territorially-based groups.

Protracted Conflict, Rivalries, and Escalation

We must also return to the notion of process and process theories of conflict. As Bremer (1995, 11) notes, citing the work of Mohr (1982), "process theories are stochastic, discrete, inherently dynamic theories of becoming."[5] Again citing Mohr, Bremer notes that in process theory, "time ordering among the contributing events is generally critical for the outcome" (1995, 11). Similar to Richardsonian arms race models, a process approach picks up the interaction of units, the continual interaction of units and context, and the evolution of new conditions of being. The discussion of the nature of interaction, and how to find patterns of such interaction, is central to the chapters by Thomas and by Schrodt. Their focus conforms strongly to the present notion of process.

Process therefore also implies an extended period of interaction between units. This becomes central to the idea of protracted conflict, because with PSC we are concerned with a long-term pattern of behavior between units in conflict. As discussed at length in Friedman's chapter, long-term patterns of conflict are also inherent in the notion of "enduring rivalry"—or simply a state of rivalry—between pairs of states. Here, a "rivalry" can be identified by some series of interactions (hostile/conflictual as defined/operationalized in different ways by different authors).[6] In chapter 2, as part of the characterization of protracted conflict, Azar indicates his concern with the "re-emergence of conflict in the same situation."

Note that in both protracted conflict and rivalry analysis it is not any single event that is of interest—but rather the flow of events, the sequence of events, or the historical context of any single event. Or, as Azar notes, "the set of events which we take as conflictual are always preceded and followed by a stream of events."

In both protracted conflict and rivalries we thus have an extended period of hostile/conflictual interactions—but *not* a perpetual series of ever expanding or intensifying hostile interactions. There are lulls as well as periods of "betterment" and "worsening" (Boulding 1962, 251). Therefore, we must also be concerned with process in the sense of the escalation and de-escalation of conflict between two entities, which is a concern in the chapters by Thomas, Kuchinsky, and Sharma. For many students of social conflict, the primary focus of analysis *is* the conflict process of escalation and de-escalation—how interactions lead to incompatibilities, which lead to disputes, which then may or may not escalate to the threat or use of force, and how and when this sequence might reverse itself.[7]

As noted in Starr (1995), from which this section draws, process models of conflict are crucial because they force the analyst to think in terms of escalation and de-escalation. The crucial point to be understood is that by using escalation to help conceptualize social conflict, we are in turn forced to think in terms of: the making of choices to behave in certain ways, the outcomes of *interdependent* interaction, the crossing of thresholds and the consequences of such movement (again, see the chapters by Thomas and Schrodt), and perhaps most critically, the possibility of *de*-escalation.

Rubin, Pruitt, and Kim in their conceptualization of escalation (1994, 70–1) discuss five types of "transformations" that can occur during conflict. Note that the development and continuation of protracted conflict involves *each* of these forms of escalation:

1. Light—>Heavy. "Light" influence techniques (such as promises and persuasion) move toward "heavy" ones (such as threats and violence). Protracted conflict is always characterized by the threat of "heavy" techniques.
2. Small—>Large. This dimension includes the increase in the number of issues involved, as well as the overall amount of resources each side devotes to the conflict. Azar (1984, 89) notes that "protracted social conflicts lack distinct termination points and spill over into all aspects of social life . . . and become all-consuming for the populations in question."
3. Specific—>General. The issues involved move from specific to general, from the small and concrete to the all-encompassing and vague. This form of escalation is also covered by the above quotation from Azar regarding the all-consuming nature of PSC.
4. Doing Well—>Winning—>Hurting the Other. This involves changes in the aims/goals of the parties (such as movement from Morton Deutsch's [1973] "individualistic orientation" to his "competitive orientation"). Again as Azar (1984, 89) notes: "In a protracted conflict situation, the conflict becomes an arena for redefining issues rather than a means of adjudicating them; it is therefore futile to look for any ultimate resolution because the conflict process itself becomes the *source* rather than the *outcome* of policy." In this form, it is not enough simply to have done well in terms of absolute gains, but to come out ahead in relative gains. And ultimately, as in Schelling's Dollar Game, relative gains may only mean that the other party's costs—hurt—are greater than one's own.
5. Few—>Many. The number of participants grows; this is also included in the societal pervasiveness of PSC.

Understanding the escalatory process and its various forms, and recognizing the possibility (at least in most types of conflict) of reversing that process, leads one back to some of the basic reasons to study conflict. In distinguishing between "constructive" and "destructive" conflict, Morton Deutsch (1973, 17) explicitly notes that the basic point of his work is "*not* how to eliminate or prevent conflict but rather how to make it productive." The study of escalation is a required component of such an approach. The nature of protracted conflict may, however, make de-escalation incredibly difficult, (and appearing to be impossible to many of the participants). How to make PSC *productive* similarly appears to have eluded both participants and third parties attempting to resolve or manage protracted conflict (see Friedman, chapter 3). Why this has often been the case is the issue to which we must turn.

Protracted Conflict and Conflict Resolution

While there are many similarities (and some important differences!) between protracted conflict and enduring rivalries, there has been little attention paid to them, and to how the work on each could help illuminate the other. It was noted above that "social conflict is a mechanism by which order is established, challenged and re-established." This view of conflict as an agent of change is consistent with a focus on conflict escalation and de-escalation, and argues for a closer comparison of protracted conflict and rivalry research. However, following Azar's view of protracted conflict, "change" in PSC's may be of a significantly different character than other forms of international conflict, and may thus account for the intractability of protracted conflict.

Protracted conflict is covered by, and consistent with, standard definitions of social conflict, such as that of Coser cited above, which include the ideas of struggle over resources or status, and bringing some form of harm to the other party. Protracted conflict involves Morton Deutsch's (1973) "incompatibilities" between parties, as well as the need for such incompatibilities to be seen and understood by the parties (Boulding 1962; Rubin, Pruitt, and Kim 1994).[8]

Thus, protracted conflict is also congruous with what Rubin, Pruitt, and Kim see as the basic source of conflict—divergent aspirations. Given that the major determinants of levels of aspirations include past achievement and comparisons with others (hence, involving relative deprivation and such phenomena as James Davies' "J-curve"), perceived power, and the formation of "struggle groups," protracted conflict is well within the parameters of general social conflict (Rubin, Pruitt, and Kim 1994, chap. 2). However, as noted above, there is "more," in terms of the degree and intensity with which these factors are found in protracted social conflict as compared to general social conflict.

In addition, in PSC situations there is an almost total absence of a set of "conditions that discourage conflict." These are conditions that when present helps create stability and dampen conflict (Rubin, Pruitt, and Kim 1994, 21–25). They include: consensus about norms; lack of information about the other party's attainments, and thus an absence of invidious comparisons; the ability to separate the parties physically and psychologically; social mobility (or at least the myth of social mobility); the ability to prevent the formation of struggle groups (through the co-optation or removal of potential leaders, and the prevention of outside support). Such "stabilizing" conditions are absent in situations of PSC, while at the same time, the destabilizing factors that increase levels of aspiration are unusually high.

Issues of development and especially identity associated with PSC work to make a conflict not only enduring, but one that totally permeates the attention and resources of the struggle groups. Because of these identity factors—and development factors that make conflict analogous to that of Galtungian structural theories and the generation of "structural violence" (1969)—we might be able to explain why protracted conflict appears to be less amenable to the standard modes of conflict resolution as Azar has claimed.

When looking at some of the classic works on social conflict—by Coser, Morton Deutsch, and more recently in the synthesizing formulations of Rubin, Pruitt, and Kim—we see that each presents typolgies of conflict (forms of conflict or orientations toward conflict) based on how the other party is perceived, how "realistic" perceptions of the other party and the situation might be, and the level of "rationality" that is involved in making choices about how to deal with the situation and the other party.

Rubin, Pruitt, and Kim (1994) begin their book with a discussion of five basic strategies for dealing with conflict (contending, yielding, problem solving, withdrawing, and inaction), and then concern themselves with what factors affect the *choice* of strategy for the parties. As noted above in discussing escalation, choice is a key issue for Rubin, Pruitt, and Kim. They develop two basic models for examining such choices.

In the "dual concern model" (Rubin, Pruitt, and Kim 1994, 29–37) the choice of strategy is based on the strength of concern for *one's own outcomes* and the strength of concern about *the other party's outcomes*. This concern might be "instrumental," where one is concerned because it advances one's own interests, or a "genuine" concern based on interpersonal bonds (as would be found in the responsiveness and community central to social communication models of integration). Thus, if one has a "high" concern about the other party, one would "yield" if concern about one's own outcomes was low; or one would engage in problem solving if concern about one's own outcome was also high. This corresponds directly to Morton Deutsch's "cooperative" orientation to conflict, where "the person has a positive interest in the welfare of the others as well as in his own welfare" (Deutsch and Shichman 1986, 224).

However, one key to the nature of protracted conflict is the existence of, or the perception of, distributive injustice because of structural violence—the conflict exists *because* the opponent exists. The zero-sum nature of protracted conflict is one way to indicate a total *lack* of concern (especially "genuine" concern) for the other party. Thus, protracted conflict looks more like Deutsch and Shichman's (1986, 224) "competitive" orientation, where "the person has an interest in doing better than the others and in doing as well as he can for himself." A competitive orientation is one of the central factors in the development of what Deutsch calls "malignant social conflict," which is the result of a malignant social process. Malignant conflict presents a direct analogy to protracted conflict:

> In a malignant conflict, the participants become enmeshed in a web of interactions and defensive-offensive manuevers that worsen instead of improve their situations, making them more insecure, vulnerable, and burdened. Pathological disputes have a tendency to expand and escalate so that they become independent of their initiating causes. In such a dispute, the conflict processes themselves serve to perpetuate and intensify the conflict. (Deutsch and Shichman 1986, 229)

Given that concern for the other is central to its applicability, the dual concern model would then seem an unlikely candidate for helping us to understand how parties to protracted conflict make strategic choices for dealing with conflict. Rubin, Pruitt, and Kim (1994, 37) present a second model for choosing strategies—the "perceived feasibility perspective," which is based on: "the extent to which the strategy seems capable of achieving the goals that give rise to it and the cost that is anticipated from enacting each strategy." Any choice must be seen as at least minimally feasible. This is clearly an approach based on some form of cost-benefit analysis. Indeed, by combining the stength of concern central to the dual concern model, and the probability of success central to the perecived feasibility model, the analyst arrives at a full-fledged model of expected utility.

Before turning directly to this rationality component, let us first look at other obstacles to the use of a perceived feasibility model that are generated by protracted conflict. To increase the probability or feasibility of problem solving, there must be a perceived common ground, and there must exist a level of trust in each party that the other party is prepared to engage in good-faith problem solving. As the existence of a common ground and trust are central to the feasibility of problem solving, the probability of problem solving as a strategic choice for PSC is practically nonexistent.[9]

Given the nature of protracted conflict, and the identity issues central to it, there would also be little feasibility in yielding, and thus also little feasibility in contending, which involves making the *other* party willing to yield. Given the nature of protracted conflict, including identity issues and structural violence, the perceived costs of continuing the status quo would be higher than those of *contending*. Therefore, the pressure in protracted conflict is to move to, and remain in, contention ("a strategy that involves an effort by Party to impose its preferred solution on Other," Rubin, Pruitt, and Kim 1994, 253). This is, indeed, the same conclusion we come to in the next section.

The Nature of Rational Choice

From this very cursory look at the nature of social conflict, and the role of choice in some basic models (see also Nicholson 1992), it might seem that models of purposive choice are inapplicable to protracted conflict. Such a conclusion would reinforce Azar's pessimism in regard to the management of protracted conflicts. I do not think this is necessarily the case. However, using standard models of international relations or standard models of intergroup conflict to specify a formal model of choice for a protracted conflict situation may be problematic.

The work of scholars dealing with social conflict noted above come at the conflict management or resolution problem with at least an implicit ordering of preferences for the parties involved. The avoidance of violence, death, and destruction—and possibly some meaningful joint resolution of the conflict situation because continuation increases the costs of conflict—appear to be at the top of the preference orderings used by the parties to calculate expected utility. The issue then is not really whether or not analytic models of choice can be applied to PSC, but what is the appropriate set of preference orderings for accurately protraying the situation involved. Based on the commentary by Azar—and by Friedman, Thomas, and Peleg in later chapters—protracted conflict calls for a different set of goals, some different dynamics, and clearly a different set of preference orderings.

This is clearly illustrated by Brams and Togman's analysis of the conflict in Northern Ireland. Brams and Togman (who never refer to "protracted conflict") employ Brams' dynamic game theoretic model of the "theory of moves" (TOM) in order "to demonstrate why certain steps were taken by each side" (1998, 32) in analyzing the possibility of conflict resolution. In actuality, they present moves that might, or should, lead from conflict to compromise. However, the values they present in the game matrix for the Sinn Fein/IRA player are flawed. These could be the values that the game theoretician might propose on the basis of standard conflict analysis (or even what a player from Great Britain might propose for the Sinn Fein/IRA)—but they are not the preference orderings that a student of protracted conflict would propose.

The best outcome that Brams and Togman propose for the Sinn Fein/IRA is "capitulation by Great Britain," and this is also what PSC would say. But after this the two orderings differ considerably. Brams and Togman say that the "worst" outcome for the IRA is "violent conflict" because "both British rule and the violence continue" (Brams and Togman 1998, 34). This ignores the identity issues of PSC, that is, how the conflict becomes part of the very identity of the struggle groups (see Peleg); how cooperation, or the end of the conflict, could constitute a "crisis" for a party such as Sinn Fein/IRA (see Thomas). Indeed, using a protracted conflict approach, I would place violent conflict as the *second-best* outcome. PSC would say that the worst outcome would be "capitulation by the IRA" (which Brams and Togman show as next to worst). The two orderings are presented in Table 1.1.

While Brams and Togman stress TOM and threats, the results are flawed because the Sinn Fein/IRA preferences are not ordered correctly. Using the preference orderings suggested by PSC, the payoffs that result from following a hard-line stance for Sinn Fein/IRA are either: British capitulation (best for IRA), or violent conflict (next best). Brams and Togman claim that Great Britain (thinking that their matrix is correct) sees the hard-line stance as a dominant strategy, and will stay there unless pushed to move. However, using PSC, the IRA also has a hard-line dominant strategy, and will stay there also.[10]

**Table 1.1 Sinn Fein/IRA Preference Orderings:
Brams and Togman vs. PSC Orderings**

	PSC (by Starr)	*Brams & Togman*
Best	Capitulation by GB	Capitulation by GB
	Violent conflict	Compromise
	Compromise	Capitulation by IRA
Worst	Capitulation by IRA	Violent conflict

Any basis for change on the part of Sinn Fein/IRA does not derive from threat. The positive movement taking place in the 1990s does not reflect the TOM analysis, but the nature of the two-level game being played *within* the parties in Northern Ireland, based almost entirely on the nature of economic development and the impact of the European Union (EU) on the economies of both Northern Ireland and the Republic. This dynamic of change is consistent with Azar's linkage of economic development and questions of structural inequalities to the manifestations of physical violence. It is not that we cannot use formal models, but that they must be more fully and accurately specified and constructed:

- Azar's concept of protracted conflict must be used in order to see that in certain conflicts identity issues are central and play a much stronger role than in standard conflict analyses. Thus, we must also pay more attention to identity groups—who they are and how they define themselves—as struggle groups.
- Azar's concept of protracted conflict must be used in order to see how a conflict can permeate an entire society. We must recognize how this affects the preference orderings that leaders of identity-based struggle groups bring to strategy and bargaining—that, as above, leaders and groups might prefer conflict to all but full capitulation by the opponent. In understanding this we have returned to the issues of escalation and de-escalation.
- Azar's concept of protracted conflict can help us understand how a crisis can be generated by improved relations among parties to a protracted conflict (a key point developed by Thomas).
- Azar's concept of protracted conflict, with its permeation of society and the crisis of bettering relations, is thus needed to fully understand the two-level nature of conflict. Tsebelis (1990) raised the question of why observers see some actions as sub-optimal. Tsebelis argues that the observer is attending to some "principal arena" while the actor is, indeed, playing games in multiple arenas. As with the Brams and Togman example above, protracted conflict forces the analyst not to ignore the complex games being played out internally within identity-based struggle groups. Deutsch and Shichman (1986, 230) point out that: "Malignant conflict persists because internal needs *require* the competitive process between the conflicting parties. . . . When an external conflict serves internal needs, it is difficult to give it up until other means of satisfying these needs is developed." (emphasis added)

In dealing with protracted conflicts we will need to identify those activities that diminish the focus on identity. We also need to reduce the all-consuming nature of the conflict. Finally, it is imperative to make the preference ordering facing the participants look more like that of a "normal" intergroup conflict. To do these things we need to return to Azar's arguments regarding economic development, structural inequality, and the recognition of identity claims.

The Chapters that Follow

Theoretically, the papers collected in this volume are important for the ongoing task of properly conceptualizing conflict in the contemporary system. Before the study of conflict can move forward, it is crucial to comprehend *exactly what it is* we are studying. Understanding types of conflict, the conflict process, the conditions under which conflict will escalate or can be ameliorated, are all crucial tasks for which the study of protracted conflict can provide useful contributions. Therefore, part 1 deals with theoretical considerations. It follows that, in methodological terms, these chapters will be useful in assisting the scholarly community to generate the proper research designs for the current study of social conflict. Four case studies are analyzed in part 2, "Empirical Investigation."

The first contribution to part 1 is a reprint of one of Azar's concise overviews of protracted conflict, which has been outlined in broad strokes above. In "Conceptualizing Protracted Conflict and Protracted Conflict Management," Gil Friedman goes into the concept in depth and masterfully demonstrates how protracted conflict helps us to understand contemporary modes of conflict. He links and contrasts protracted conflict to the concept and study of enduring rivalries, and uses this as a way to get at the difficult question of conflict management in situations of PSC. Drawing on Azar's propositions (such as three and eight), Friedman stresses that "imposed integration" is a central culprit and needs to be dealt with before effective conflict resolution can occur. But to do this explicit two-level modes of analysis must be employed. Thus, Friedman also provides a useful bridge between protracted conflict and two-level games.

In part 2, Sangeeta Sharma's chapter, "Protracted Conflict and Enduring Rivalry: India, Pakistan, and the Dynamics of Stalemate over Kashmir," returns to the linkages between protracted conflict and enduring rivalries. And, just as Friedman looks at the long-term nature of PSC as a concept centered on values and stakes, Sharma investigates factors related to PSC and rivalry, especially territory. She also picks up the theme of escalation, looking to see how stakes and values—territory—affect escalation. And, in line with comparisons between social conflict and protracted conflict, much of this analysis is placed within the context of status discrepancy theory.

Marc V. Simon's model-based case studies in chapter 7, "Protracted Conflict, Intervention, and Revolution: Case Studies of Nicaragua and the Philippines," is the empirical analysis that most explicitly picks up the theme of two-level analysis. As with Sharma, Simon is concerned with underlying patterns of escalation (or de-escalation) in protracted conflicts—in long enduring, *stalemated* domestic conflicts. The two-level relationships come with the incentives that each pattern of escalation holds for governments, internal oppositions, and potential external intervenors

The third chapter in part 1 is by G. Dale Thomas, "Conceptualizing and Identifying Crisis in Protracted Social Conflict." Thomas investigates exactly *how* the parties to a protracted conflict actually interact, which requires the measurement of interaction. In order to do so he is forced to reconceptualize the idea of "dyadic" behavior. He raises a variety of epistemological and logic-of-inquiry issues in regard to the very nature of protracted conflict, especially Azar's concept of a "normal relations range" between any two actors. Crisis models are used to help conceptualize protracted conflict (and vice versa), by thinking about how cooperative behavior as well as conflictual behavior could constitute a "crisis" given the normal relations range for a dyad involved in a PSC. Recognizing that such dyads comprise complex systems of PSC, Thomas uses several models of analysis, including chaos theory (as well as chaos-based metaphors), to understand crisis interaction within a protracted conflict system. The normal relations range of a protracted conflict is described metaphorically as a dynamic system with an "attractor."

A number of the same epistemological and methodological issues are raised in part 2 by Philip A. Schrodt in his chapter, "Early Warning of Conflict in Southern Lebanon Using Hidden Markov Models." Here, Schrodt applies hidden Markov models (HMMs) to the problems of early warning and forecasting outbreaks of conflict in a protracted international conflict. Schrodt's broader project, of which this chapter is but one part, uses HMMs to get at dynamic patterns of interaction—sequences of co-adaptation as measured by international event data. This project inspired Thomas to employ HMM models (and others) in his investigation of what protracted conflict interaction patterns are and what they mean. In addition, Schrodt focuses on the enduring and recidivist character of protracted conflict as well as many of the same issues of conflict management and resolution that Friedman introduces in chapter 3.

The final chapter in part 1 is Samuel Peleg's, "Who Participates in Protracted Conflicts and Why? Rediscovering the Group and Its Needs." Peleg continues the search for the theoretical and conceptual handles that will give us purchase on the central questions of part 1: why does protracted conflict occur and why does it persist? Peleg addresses these questions from yet another perspective, focusing on human needs and on "identity groups" (especially religious-based groups) as the key actors. His focus on communal cleavages and the identity group reflects Azar's propositions two and seven from the second chapter. Peleg also returns to a question of concern to Friedman—the intractability of protracted conflicts and the difficulties of conflict resolution. The nature of religious-based identity groups, as differentiated from states, cannot be ignored as a factor in PSC. As Peleg notes, "current conflict theories underestimate the importance of the aggrieved identity group and its contribution to the study of conflict." One scholar who does not ignore or underestimate the religious-based identity group is Michael Kuchinsky, as evidenced in his part 2 chapter, "Yielding Ground: Loss and Conflict Escalation in Sri Lankan Protracted Conflict."

In looking at the Sri Lankan PSC between Tamils and Sinhalese, Kuchinsky focuses on identity groups, religion, and group needs. Taking direct aim at the same Azar propositions (two and seven), Kuchinsky is concerned with the communal identity of an "ethnie," and related questions of the satisfaction of identity and other human needs. Again, akin to Friedman's discussion of forced integration, Kuchinsky investigates the Sri Lankan situation in terms of the legitimacy of governance within multicommunal and multicultural situations. Within this general theoretical context of his empirical investigation, Kuchinski also employs prospect theory as an important tool for analyzing the ways in which Tamils and Sinhalese perceive the conflict.

These chapters certainly do not constitute the final word on the meaning and nature of protracted conflict, nor do the analyses of these cases answer all our questions about PSC. However, given the advances in our thinking about conflict in the global system, such as models of conflict processes, enduring rivalries, two-level game approaches, it is time to see how Azar's original notions of protracted conflict both derive from and add to our understanding. The chapters in this volume go a long way in respecifying the notion of protracted conflict. They have helped PSC to re-emerge as an important tool in our thinking about conflict, and improved its ability to serve in this capacity.

Notes

1. We should be careful, however, not to view the re-emergence of such conflict as support for the argument by some that the post–Cold War world is more dangerous than ever. We must agree with John Mueller (1994, 358–359), who usefully contrasts perceptions of contemporary conflictual "messy-ness" with the Cold War period:

   Indeed, if the post-Cold war world resembles a jungle filled with poisonous snakes, the Cold War was a jungle filled with at least two dragons *and* poisonous snakes, some of whom were variously, changeably, and often quite ambiguously in devious complicity with one or the other of the dragons. It seems obvious which jungle is preferable—and less complicated.

2. As will be seen in the theoretical esays in part 1, Azar and others have used both terms—"protracted conflict" and "protracted social conflict"—for the phenomenon that is the subject of this volume. Generally speaking, the terms will be used interchangeably, while the acronym "PSC" will be used whenever the authors wish to employ abbreviations.

3. See the chapters in part 1 for an extensive set of references to the written work of Azar, both alone and with various collaborators.

4. The issue of economic development, the gap between groups, relative deprivation, and the effects of economic growth are touched on in the chapter by G. Dale Thomas. The importance of the "identity group" as a participant to conflict is stressed by Azar: "this is the key to research and conflict resolution." Samuel Peleg's chapter in part 1 and Michael Kuchinsky's chapter in part 2, deal with the identity group as unit of analysis.

5. As opposed to "variance theories," which are "deterministic, continuous, essentially static theories of being" (Bremer 1995, 11).

6. For definitions used most broadly in empirical research, see, for example, Goertz and Diehl (1993) and Thompson (1995).

7. Bremer's (1995) process model of war explicitly moves from context to the occurrence of militarized disputes, to the evolution of militarized disputes, to the occurrence and then evolution of interstate wars, as well as possible diffusion and growth effects of such wars. See also: Boulding (1962); the work of Bloomfield and colleagues, such as Bloomfield and Leiss (1969); Rummel's (1979, Part IV) discussion of the "conflict helix;" or overviews by social-psychologists, such as Rubin, Pruitt, and Kim (1994), who see social conflict as "escalation, stalemate, and settlement."

8. Rubin, Pruitt, and Kim (1994, 5) define conflict as a "perceived divergence of interest, or a belief that parties' current aspirations cannot be achived simultaneously."

9. Similarly, Deutsch's "cooperative" orientation requires an "open and honest exchange of relevant information, where each participant is interested

in informing and being informed by the other" (Deutsch and Shichman 1986, 225). Again, such a condition does not characterize a PSC, which is a competitive process that "tends to produce ineffective and impoverished communication" (Deutsch and Shichman 1986, 225).

10. A few excerpts from a May 1998 column by Maureen Dowd can exemplify my points and take the place of a long literature review of Northern Ireland as a protracted conflict:

> We are an unforgiving people. We believe in the Evil Eye. we like to fight. We don't like to compromise. We lie in wait for the worst. We lurk about the past . . ."There is security in the insecurity put forth by Ian Paisley," agreed Gary McMichael, a Unionist leader . . ."We're not happy unless we're fighting somebody. In his novel, *Trinity,* Leon Uris wrote, "In Ireland, there is not future, only the past happening over and over." And many find immense comfort in that." (Dowd 1998, 9)

References

Azar, Edward E. 1984. "The Theory of Protracted Social Conflict and the Challenge of Transforming Conflict Situations." In *Conflict Processes and the Breakdown of International Systems,* ed. Dina A. Zinnes. Denver, CO: Monograph Series in World Affairs, University of Denver, pp. 81–99.

Bloomfield, Lincoln P., and Amelia C. Leiss. 1969. *Controlling Small Wars.* New York: Alfred A. Knopf.

Brams, Steven J., and Jeffrey M. Togman. 1998. "Cooperation Through Threats: The Northern Ireland Case." *PS: Political Science & Politics* 31 (March): 32–9.

Boulding, Kenneth E. 1962. *Conflict and Defense.* New York: Harper & Row.

Bremer, Stuart A. 1992. "Dangerous Dyads: Conditions Affecting the Likelihood of Interstate War, 1816–1965." *Journal of Conflict Resolution* 36(June): 309–41.

———. 1995. "Advancing the Scientific Study of War." In *The Process of War,* ed. Stuart A. Bremer and Thomas R. Cusack. Philadelphia: Gordon and Breach, pp. 1–33.

Coser, Lewis. 1956. *The Functions of Social Conflict.* New York: The Free Press.

Davis, David, and Will Moore. 1997. "Ethnicity Matters: Transnational Ethnic Alliances and Foreign Policy Behavior." *International Studies Quarterly* 41(March): 171–84.

Deutsch, Morton. 1973. *The Resolution of Conflict.* New Haven, CT: Yale University Press.

——— and Shula Shichman. 1986. "Conflict: A Social Psychological Perspective." In *Political Psychology,* ed. Margaret G. Hermann. San Francisco: Jossey-Bass, pp. 219–50.

Diehl, Paul F., ed. 1998. *The Dynamics of Enduring Rivalries.* Urbana, IL: University of Illinois Press.

Dowd, Maureen. 1998. "Center Is Holding on Irish Question." *The State* (May 22, 1998): 9. Columbia, SC

Galtung, Johan. 1969. "Violence, Peace, and Peace Research." *Journal of Peace Research* 6 (3): 167–92.

———. 1993. "Enduring Rivalries: Theoretical Constructs and Empirical Patterns." *International Studies Quarterly* 37(June): 147–71.

———. 1995. "Taking 'Enduring' out of Enduring Rivalry: The Rivalry Approach to War and Peace." *International Interactions* 21(3): 291–308.

Gurr, Ted Robert. 1993. *Minorities at Risk*. Washington, DC: United States Institute of Peace Press.

——— and Will H. Moore. 1997. "Ethnopolitical Rebellion: A Cross-Sectional Analysis of the 1980s with Risk Assessments for the 1990s." *American Journal of Political Science* 41(October): 1079–1103.

Huth, Paul K. 1996. *Standing Your Ground: Territorial Disputes and International Conflict*. Ann Arbor, MI: University of Michigan Press.

Maoz, Zeev. 1996. *Domestic Sources of Global Change*. Ann Arbor, MI: University of Michigan Press.

Mohr, Lawrence. 1982. *Explaining Organization Behavior*. San Francisco: Jossey-Bass.

Mueller, John. 1994. "The Catastrophe Quota: Trouble after the Cold War." *Journal of Conflict Resolution* 38(September): 355–75.

Nicholson, Michael. 1992. *Rationality and the Analysis of International Conflict*. Cambridge: Cambridge University Press.

Putnam, Robert D. 1988. "Diplomacy and Domestic Politics: The Logic of Two-Level Games." *International Organization* 42 (3): 427–60.

Rosenau, James N. 1989. "Global Changes and Theoretical Challenges: Toward a Postinternational Politics for the 1990s." In *Global Changes and Theoretical Challenges,* ed. E.-O. Czempiel and James N. Rosenau. Lexington, MA: D.C. Heath, pp. 1–20.

———. 1990. *Turbulence in World Politics*. Princeton, NJ: Princeton University Press.

Rubin, Jeffrey Z., Dean G. Pruitt, and Sung Hee Kim. 1994. *Social Conflict,* 2nd ed. New York: McGraw-Hill.

Rule, James B. 1988. *Theories of Civil Violence*. Berkeley: University of California Press.

Rummel, R. J. 1979. *Understanding Conflict and War, Vol. 4, War, Power, Peace*. Beverly Hills, CA: Sage Publications.

Russett, Bruce, and James S. Sutterlin. "The U.N. in a New World Order." *Foreign Affairs* 70 (Spring): 69–83.

Simon, Marc V. and Harvey Starr. 1997. "A Two-Level Analysis of War and Revolution: A Dynamic Simulation of Response to Threat." In *Decison-Making on War and Peace,* ed. Nehemia Geva and Alex Mintz. Boulder, CO: Lynne Rienner, pp. 131–59.

Starr, Harvey. 1994. "Revolution and War: Rethinking the Linkage Between Internal and External Conflict." *Political Research Quarterly* 47 (June): 481–507.

————. 1995. "Advancing the Scientific Study of War: Commentary." In *The Process of War,* ed. Stuart A. Bremer and Thomas R. Cusack. Philadelphia: Gordon and Breach, pp. 233–40.

———— and Benjamin A. Most. 1985. "Patterns of Conflict: Quantitative Analysis and the Comparative Lessons of Third World Wars." In *The Lessons of Recent Wars in the Third World,* ed. Robert Harkavy and Stephanie Neuman. Lexington, MA: Lexington Books, pp. 33–52.

Stohl, Michael. 1980. "The Nexus of Civil and International Conflict." In *Handbook of Political Conflict,* ed. Ted Robert Gurr. New York: Free Press, pp. 297–330.

Thompson, William R. 1995. "Principal Rivalries." *Journal of Conflict Resolution* 39(June): 195–223.

Tilly, Charles. 1985. "Connecting Domestic and International Conflicts, Past and Present." In *Dynamic Models of International Conflict,* ed. Michael D. Ward. Boulder, CO: Lynne Rienner, pp. 517–31.

Tsebelis, George. 1990. *Nested Games.* Berkeley, CA: University of California Press.

Wallensteen, Peter, and Margareta Sollenberg. 1997. "Armed Conflicts, Conflict Termination and Peace Agreements, 1989–96." *Journal of Peace Research* 34(August): 339–58.

Part I

Theoretical Considerations

CHAPTER TWO

Protracted International Conflict: Ten Propositions[1]

Edward E. Azar

I wish to set down ten related propositions on protracted social conflicts. These propositions have been generated by monitoring conflictual and cooperative events in world society over a decade. I will then show how these propositions throw light on conflicts generally and, also, on the theory and practice of conflict resolution.

I am using the term "protracted social conflict" to suggest the type of ongoing and seemingly unresolvable conflict that is our current concern, whether it be a conflict such as in Lebanon or relations between the former Soviet Union and the United States. I am not concerned with low-level conflicts that are part of the normal processes of change, and adjustment to it, which all persons and societies experience in relationships with others.

1. Protracted social conflicts have typical characteristics that account for their prolonged nature. In particular, they have enduring features such as economic and technological underdevelopment, and unintegrated social and political systems. These conflicts do not lend themselves to solutions. They also have other features that are subject to change, but only when conditions allow for far-reaching political changes. These include features such as distributive injustice, which require the elimination or substantial modification of economic, social and extreme disparities in levels of political privilege

and opportunity. Any "solutions" that do not come to grips with these features are solutions that must rest on law enforcement, threat, or power control by the more powerful party to the conflict. Conflict is likely to erupt once again as soon as there is any change in the balance of forces, in leadership, or in some other significant ecopolitical conditions.

2. The following observable features provide the infrastructure for intractable conflict: multi-ethnic and communal cleavages and disintegrations, underdevelopment, and distributive injustice. The re-emergence of conflict in the same situation, a particular characteristic of protracted social conflicts, suggests to anyone monitoring events over a long period that the real sources of conflict—as distinct from features—are deep-rooted in the lives and ontological being of those concerned. Now and again this is confirmed in statements, as when some Turkish Cypriots once asserted that they were "nameless people" because they could not issue their own passports. Those involved in protracted social conflicts seem to have difficulty in articulating what it is that leads them to violent protest and even war.

    We are led to the hypothesis that the source of protracted social conflict is the denial of those elements required in the development of all people and societies, and whose pursuit is a compelling need. These are *security, distinctive identity, social recognition of identity,* and *effective participation* in the processes that determine conditions of security and identity, and other such developmental requirements. The real source of conflict is the denial of those human needs that are common to all and whose pursuit is an ontological drive.

3. It is difficult to detect, to define and to measure a sense of insecurity and distributive injustice and other such deprivations. On the other hand, ethnic and communal cleavages and the political structures associated with them, are more conspicuous. The fact that ethnic and communal cleavages as a source of protracted social conflicts are more obvious than others does not make ethnicity—used here to refer to identity groups that make up a polity—a special case. Ethnicity is an important case, though not a special one, because it draws our attention to a need that is fundamental. The study of ethnicity and the drive for ethnic identity enables us to understand the nature of conflicts generally. It is the denial of human needs, of which ethnic identity is merely one, that finally emerges as the source of conflict, be it domestic, communal, international, or interstate.

4. Situations of protracted social conflict in the world, of which there are more than sixty now active, are not unique events. To the participants—and to external observers who do not follow events over long periods—they appear to be unique, because local circumstances, histories, and attitudes give them individuality. In fact, they are not accidental combinations of circumstances, but have certain behavioral and structural characteristics in common. They are predictable for this reason. Some conflicts may be accidental and short-lived—though tracking events suggests that there are probably few. Protracted social conflicts universally are situations which arise out of attempts to combat conditions of perceived victimization stemming from: a denial of separate identity of parties involved in the political process; an absence of security of culture and valued relationships; and an absence of effective political participation through which victimization can be remedied.

5. Tracking conflict, negotiations, temporary settlements, and the outbreak of further conflicts (a sequence that is a characteristic of East-West relations no less than regional conflicts such as in the Middle East) draws attention to the reality that human needs and longstanding cultural values, such as those to which I have referred, will not be traded, exchanged, or bargained over. They are not subject to negotiation. Only interests that derive from personal roles and opportunities within existing political systems are exchangeable and negotiable. Agreements that come out of negotiations that may give certain advantages to elites, but do not touch upon the underlying issues in the conflict, do not last.

6. Conflictual and cooperative events flow together even in the most severe of intense conflicts. Cooperative events are sometimes far more numerous than conflictual ones even in the midst of intense social conflict situations. However, conflictual events are clearly more absorbing and have more impact on determining the consequent actions of groups and nations. Cooperative events are not sufficient to abate protracted social conflicts. Tension reduction measures may make the conflict more bearable in the short term, but conflict resolution involves a far more complex process than mere management of cooperative events.

7. The most useful unit of analysis in protracted social conflict situations is the identity group—racial, religious, ethnic, cultural, and others. It is more powerful as a unit of analysis than the nation-state. The reason is that "power" finally rests with the identity group. I

wish to deal with this proposition at some length, because in my experience this is the key to research and to conflict resolution. For the purpose of describing, explaining and predicting the dynamics of a protracted social conflict situation, the identity group is more informative than the nation-state. Most nation-states in our contemporary international system are unintegrated, artificially grouped or bounded, and totally incapable of inspiring loyalty and a civic culture, despite the strength of nationalism and the sophisticated strategies of communication. This is a reality with which we must come to terms. Since Westphalia, nation-states have been legal fictions of the international system. They perpetuate the myth of sovereignty and independence as instruments of control. There are times when national interest and group interest overlap, but these are becoming less obvious in the world.

Just as the rise of the nation-state since Westphalia has perpetuated the fiction that groups are not natural political units and will wither away and melt into the larger and more efficient "natural" unit, the nation, so has the rise of the individual in the last century perpetuated the fiction that all relevant political action deals with the satisfaction of all sorts of personal needs and wants of the discrete and smallest unit of social analysis, each separate individual. What is of concern are *the societal needs* of the individual—security, identity, recognition and others.

I realize that it is difficult for a student of international relations to get involved with empirical work on identity groups and their behavior. The international institutions and system are biased in such a way that we often cannot find reliable data on ethnic or religious groups, whereas we do find data on national variables. Because some states are made up of apparently homogeneous groups and others are not, one experiences disincentives for comparative analysis. Our focus on nation-states and their individual actions has deflected our attention from the study of ethnic, religious, and other identity group conflicts within these territorial entities.

The professional debate over the question of the appropriate unit of analysis has dwelt on the differences between focusing on the individual, state, or system and their implications (Waltz 1959; Singer 1961; Brody 1972). It has ignored the group totally. Our protracted social conflict research has impressed upon us the need to re-examine this issue of the unit of analysis and to correct this deficiency in the international politics literature.

The group appears to be a competitor to nation or system. Scholars in the field of international politics seem to have accepted the view that a legitimate role of the state is its historical role of suppressing the group. Furthermore, the group as a unit disturbs the neatness of the models at hand. We had no motivation to generate data and study the consequences of the actions of groups.

In my own work on events research and data banking, I took the most commonly accepted unit, the nation-state. My present familiarity with the phenomenon of protracted social conflict has led me to feel very strongly that we need to build data banks on ethnic, religious, cultural, and other groups if we want to understand better the phenomenon of needs, interests and motivations of parties in protracted social conflict situations.

8. All internal and external relations between states and nations are induced by the desire to satisfy such basic needs as I have been describing. The unit of analysis is the identity group that makes this possible, be it the state, the nation or some more intimate group. The origins of international conflict are, therefore, in domestic movements for the satisfaction of needs and in the drives of nations and states to satisfy the same needs. For this reason, distinctions made between domestic and international conflicts are misleading.

I have argued earlier that groups as actors in protracted conflict situations initiate plans, actions, reactions, and strategies in order to accomplish the goal of satisfying, individual societal needs or of reducing and eliminating need-deficiencies. For these purposes the domestic and the international are only arenas. In whatever arena the actors behave, they do so to satisfy their needs. The motivations for action are internal, not systemic or international.

Empirically, we have found that in protracted social conflicts actors seek to placate others, and seek alliances and do all the things they see as serving their interests as they set out to accomplish the task of satisfying their basic needs. Of course, there are many other variables that affect the behavior of groups and their leaders, but the basic motivation to act is internal, whereas the arena can be more extensive. In the conflict situations between 1979 and 1984 that I have examined, elites and their leaders show a serious contempt for international and regional arenas. They see these arenas as mere opportunities for scoring points with their own domestic constituencies. Self image and image of self by others are important needs to be satisfied, and, therefore, they can be a source for action and influence. In this sense, the regional and international environments are important, but only in a very limited way. Ultimately, actors behave in order to satisfy domestic social needs and not international ones.

To separate domestic and international is artificial—there is really only one social environment and its domestic face is the more compelling. Thus, there are international and national interests that actors manipulate and exchange in return for the opportunity of satisfying domestic needs, but not the other way around.

9. It follows that protracted social conflicts in multi-ethnic societies are not ameliorated peacefully by centralized structures. For conflict resolution to be enduringly resolved, appropriate decentralized structures are needed. These structures are designed to serve the psychological, economic, and relational needs of groups and individuals within nation-states.

Traditional and contemporary political theory is weak in this respect. We have few models of decentralization that would ensure the pursuit of human and societal needs. Western political theory, for example, favors the centralized state and its legitimate monopoly of violence. In recent years attempts have been made to address the needs of minorities by human rights guarantees, as in the original Cypriot constitution, and by "power sharing," as attempted by the British Government in Northern Ireland. Within the analysis I have made, neither could succeed. No compromises are possible when societal needs are at issue. We have to evolve non-power models.

The concept of a unified and centralized power entity has been mistaken for a socially integrated political unit. In protracted conflict situations, highly centralized political structures are sources of conflict. They reduce the opportunity for a sense of community among groups. They increase alienation and they tend to deny to groups the means to accomplish their needs.

Societies that have undergone decades of violence and hate retain very little trust for any sort of government—local or central and distant. They become cynical. They transform even benign systems into deformed political and economic entities and they show very little inclination to participatory politics. Decentralized political structures promise to provide the sort of environment that permits groups to better satisfy their identity and political needs. They promote local participation and self-reliance. They give the groups involved the sense of control over their affairs.

In general, decentralized political systems permit the local authority's control over their educational system and their social concerns. They increase the sense of identity, participation, and security in the broadest sense of these terms. Decentralized political systems have shortcomings such as parochialism; they foster autocratic rule; they do not address inequality across regions and groups and generally tend to be inefficient. But the benefits might outweigh the costs. Conflict resolution in protracted conflict situations necessitates an understanding of the importance of open, participatory, and decentralized political structures as opposed to centralized, dominant, and exclusive structures.

It is here that international relations theorists have a contribution to make. The international system is governed on a functional basis, and is remarkably orderly. There are a large number of function agreements observed even in times of high tension and war. They cover communications, navigation, health, and even the treatment of prisoners in war. It is this functional model that could be applicable to situations such as in Cyprus and Lebanon, where each community seeks the security of its identity and freedom, yet values its wider relationships within the state.

10. My tenth and final proposition is that, not only have we been mistaken in taking the state as the unit of analysis in international relations and have thus failed to perceive the continuity between domestic and international, but that we have, as researchers, failed to perceive the continuity over time of what appear to be discrete conflicts. I wish to communicate a perspective derived from monitoring events over a long period.

There is a strong tendency in international relations theory that leads us to regard conflict actions as discrete, delineated by time and space, and differentiated in terms of the actors, targets, and issues involved. Conflict is thus perceived as a phenomenon found in the natural unity of action events that can be empirically isolated, formalized, and studied. Each situation is a unique one. There are no patterns or common features that relate to common causes. The number of wars each year can be counted; but each one is a separate event to be studied separately.

This is a confused point of view. What happens is that we the observers select events that we call conflict events and others that are not. We devise intellectual criteria to represent conflict. Therefore, it is important to emphasize that the set of events that we take as conflictual are always preceded and followed by a stream of events. The start and end points are established by the external observer, generally, the researcher. Furthermore, those events we designate as conflictual are also part of a set of observable relationships, economic, social, and political "cooperative" ones as well. We draw the conclusion that conflict is the result of a mix of factors, accidental and inevitable, a part of human organization, about which little can be done.

Because conflicts fluctuate in intensity over time, we tend to make assertions about starting and end points that may be of limited utility for an understanding of the inertia embedded in some conflict situations. Fluctuations and stability of conflict curves over time, may lead us to a poor understanding of the role of intervention, management and conflict resolution.

This view of the natural unity of the flow of events has led to a systematic omission of the notion of protracted social conflict from the domain of empirical research. I did not pay attention to this phenomenon of protracted social conflict until I began, as mentioned earlier, to look for patterns and to deal with the existential experience of Lebanon and the Middle East situation. Such conflicts linger on for a substantial period of time, sometimes interrupted by relatively low-level co-existence and even cooperation. On the other hand, they play a significant role in reshaping the societies involved, and have a considerable spillover effect into the international society (Burton 1984).

We have thought that there are epoch-long changes involving social conflicts, and that the episodes that reflect the character of these changes are protracted social conflicts. However, when we try to formalize the beginning and end of these episodes that reflect the epoch-long phenomena, we find ourselves on very thin ice. Sorokin (1981) once noticed that the duration of conflict is not as self-evident as it seems. The difficulty arises when we try to determine the start and end points and what we consider continuous, discontinuous, or intermittent interactions. Does a conflict start at the moment of an act of aggression, at the installation of a conflict-structure, or only at the moment of violent interactions? The main thing that we are finding useful at this stage of our intellectual development is that in studying protracted social conflict situations, we benefit more from looking at historical sweeps of the episodes rather than from searching for specific start- or end-points. This historical outlook is lacking in the recent traditions of political, sociological and social-psychological research on empirically-based conflicts because of the dangers embedded in historiographic categories. Romantic overtones, which influence our impressions of these categories, have distanced social scientists from history.

Conclusions

What brief observations can be made on the handling of conflict situations from these propositions?

The outbreak of identity-related conflicts and crises has been on the increase since World War II, particularly in the Third World. Currently it is possible to identify more than 60 cases. Most are identity-related, that is they involve tribal and cultural rivalries that can be traced to colonial boundaries and to migrations. Examples are Lebanon, Sri Lanka, Northern Ireland, Ethiopia, Cyprus, Iran, Nigeria, and Zimbabwe. The "class struggle" is not a prime cause, though the existence of class itself creates conditions that promote identity struggles based on a common sense deprivation and injustice.

Each conflict invites the intervention of great powers, thus complicating even further the relationships of those powers, and complicating, also, the already difficult ethnic relationships of each situation. The result is that all of these seemingly intractable and protracted conflicts exhaust the resources of those directly and indirectly involved, further deform the economy, and thus accentuate underdevelopment. The increase of state sponsored terrorism and the disruption of trade and commerce are a by-product of these conflicts, thereby making their resolution all the more important.

These conflicts appear to start with one set of stated goals, primary actors, and tactics, but very quickly acquire new sub-actors, new goals, and new types of resources and behaviors. In Northern Ireland and in the Middle East, the protest movements broke down into many factions as new leaders come to the fore with slightly different emphases. Conflicts that commence as a clear confrontation between one authority and an opposition become complicated with many parties and issues that make the process of resolution all the more difficult.

How can some breakthrough be achieved? What can conflict and peace research contribute?

The Richardson thesis (1960) and the normative perspectives attached to it by Norman Alcock of the Canadian Peace Research Institute (1972), namely that war is a function of the availability of large stockpiles of arms in the hands of selfish and sometimes unstable leaders, who are bound to use them simply because they are there, is too simplistic. Certainly, the quantity and sophistication of arms have a lot to do with the maintenance and severity of conflicts, especially in Southeast Asia and the Middle East, and if the world could find a way to reduce the availability of arms, then nation-states might be able to do something about the perpetuation and spiraling of violent conflict. It is more likely, however, that the level of arms can be reduced only when they are no longer felt to be needed. The problems of perceived threat and of conflict have to be resolved first.

In the Third World, war and poverty combine to dermoralize entire populations and reduce their capacity to search actively for conflict resolution. War and poverty, which are dramatically obvious to the observer and the main cause of human physical suffering, are but symptoms of underlying structural conditions. The notion of protracted social conflicts provide a deeper insight into the issues of conflict-motivations; authority roles; political and social structures; behavior patterns, needs, and interests; and other aspects. It draws our attention away from the obvious and the superficial toward the underlying conditions that create conflict situations. It directs our attention, finally, to the means of resolution.

It follows from the above that conflict resolution requires a face-to-face exploration into the needs of the opposing parties and the ways and means of satisfying them. This analytical step appears to be the first and most essential in the resolution of protracted conflicts. Legal frameworks and negotiations over interests are useful efforts if they follow the analytical identification of needs and need-satisfaction mechanisms. Bargaining over interests should not be mistaken for the analytical phase of need-identification.

What has become clear is the need for structural change as part of the process of conflict resolution. One of the most devastating predicaments in the world today is the simultaneous occurrence of conflict and underdevelopment. These two processes feed on each other and make it difficult for societies to overcome. either condition alone. In protracted conflict situations, trying to resolve conflict without dealing with underdevelopment is futile. The two have to go together.

Reducing overt conflict requires a reduction in levels of underdevelopment. Groups that seek to satisfy their identity and security needs through conflict are in effect seeking change in the structure of their society. Conflict resolution can truly occur and last if satisfactory amelioration of the conflict of underdevelopment occurs as well. Studying protracted conflict leads one to conclude that peace is development in the broadest sense of the term.

Note

1. Reprinted from *International Interactions,* vol. 12, no. 1, pp. 59–70, with permission of Gordon and Breach, Science Publishers.

References

Alcock, Norman. 1972. *War Disease.* Oakville, Ont.: CPRI Press.

Azar, Edward. 1970. "Analysis of International Events." *Peace Science Reviews.*

———. 1972. *Making and Measuring the International Event as a Unit of Analysis.* Sage Professional Papers in International Studies, Vol. 1. Newbury Park, CA: Sage Publications.

———. 1978. "Major World Cooperation Events, 1945–1975." *International Interactions* 5 (2–3): 203–39.

——— and William Eckhardt. 1978. "Major Conflicts and Interventions, 1945–1975." *International Interactions* 5 (1): 75–110.

Brody, Richard A. 1972. "International Events: Problems of Measurement and Analysis." In *International Events Interaction Analysis: Some Research Considerartions,* ed. Edward Azar, Richard Brody, and Charles McClelland. Beverly Hills, CA: Sage, pp. 45–58.

Burton, John. 1984. *Global Conflict: The Domestic Sources of International Crisis.* College Park, MD: Center for International Development. Brighton, UK: Wheatsheaf.

Richardson, Lewis. 1960. *Statistics of Deadly Quarrels.* Pittsburgh, PA: Boxwood Press.

Singer, J. David. 1961. "The Level of Analysis Problem in International Relations." *World Politics* 14 (1): 77–92.

Waltz, Kenneth. 1959. *Man, the State, and War.* New York: Columbia University Press.

CHAPTER THREE

Conceptualizing Protracted Conflict and Protracted Conflict Management

Gil Friedman

Introduction

As the tragic courses of such struggles as those characterizing Israeli–Palestinian and Irish–English relations demonstrate, protracted conflicts have been responsible for much of the death, destruction, and stagnation witnessed by the modern world. Similarly, so-called enduring rivalries have provided the setting for over half of the interstate wars since 1816 and almost half of the international system's militarized disputes, and are several times more likely to experience a war than nonrivalrous dyads of states (Goertz and Diehl 1993, Goertz and Diehl 1995). Furthermore, 10 of the 12 most severe international wars in terms of battle deaths, including World Wars I and II, emerged from enduring rivalries (Bennett 1996). The normative impetus for scholarly analysis of protracted conflict is self-evident.

The work of Azar and his collaborators perhaps represents the most notable body of theoretical analysis of protracted conflict to date.[1] This literature might be most valuable for its contribution to the conceptualization of the phenomenon of protracted conflict and to modeling processes of protracted conflict management. Certainly, conceptualizing protracted conflict is the most integral element of any analysis of the phenomenon. And as protracted conflicts, indeed by definition, are intractable, the management of protracted conflicts represents the most crucial puzzle regarding the phenomenon.

Though insights from the literature on enduring rivalries certainly contribute to the analysis of protracted conflict, scholars of international relations and comparative politics have added little to Azar and his collaborators' thinking on protracted conflict. In light of the general division of labor between these two disciplines regarding the analysis of inter- and intra-state phenomena, the tendency of many cases of protracted conflicts to transcend nation-state boundaries might help account for the dearth of attention to protracted conflict. In any event, much work remains to be done to achieve compelling conceptualizations of protracted conflict and models of protracted conflict processes. Furthermore, consistent with the focus of Starr and his collaborators (Most and Starr 1989; Starr 1991a, 1991b, and 1994; Starr and McGinnis 1992; Simon and Starr 1994), a general conceptualization of protracted conflict enables the development of models that link international and domestic dynamics.

It is the objective of this chapter to contribute to this agenda. Drawing from literature on protracted conflict, enduring rivalry, and social conflict, this chapter conceptualizes protracted conflict as a conflict in which the issue(s) under contention are perceived by *both* adversaries to be *significantly linked* to *existential* group needs. Though caution must be used in the application of this conceptualization of protracted conflict to particular rivalries, such as positional rivalries, this conceptualization accounts for essential properties emphasized by rivalry theorists and protracted conflict theorists alike—the co-presence of rational and affective motivations in protracted conflicts, the predominance of territorial disputes in protracted conflicts, and the protracted nature of these conflicts.

The intractable nature of these conflicts, in turn, underlines the importance of the puzzle of protracted conflict management. The objective of conflict management, to encourage adversaries away from escalatory policies regarding the conflict, is especially troublesome in cases of protracted conflict. Internal stability is a crucial precondition for the effective management of external conflict. Intensive domestic opposition may undermine governmental preference for, and ability to implement, conciliatory foreign policies. Political instability, furthermore, can subvert governmental ability to prevent direct nongovernmental attacks on adversary targets. These dynamics, in turn, may erode the external rival's commitment to a conciliatory stand toward the focal polity, and, indeed, may intensify distrust, tension, fear, and thus hostility.

Governmental pursuit of a conciliatory foreign policy, however, may meet strong internal opposition, (see also Starr 1991a, 1991b, 1994). The probability of this negative linkage between external accommodation and internal stability is particularly high in cases of protracted conflict. Given that protracted conflicts threaten personal and national existential interests, exact high mobilization costs, and pervade socialization processes—given that protracted conflicts dominate the lives of their participants—the general issue of policy toward the external adversary likely represents an enduring axis around which intra-polity conflict groups emerge and are oriented. In other words, it is likely that members of polities embroiled in protracted conflict will allocate extensive resources, bear high costs, and take risks in pursuit of preferred polity-level outcomes regarding policy toward the protracted conflict adversary.

This chapter proposes, therefore, that effective protracted conflict management requires the *concomitant* achievement of adequate levels of external cooperation, on the one side, and domestic stability, on the other. The attainment of satisfactory if not optimal balances between these domestic and external imperatives, in turn, requires knowledge of the source and magnitude of opposition to particular policies. Such knowledge enables effective attempts to accommodate, coerce, persuade, and/or demobilize significant opposition.

Conceptualizing Protracted Conflict/Rivalry

It is useful to approach these foundational considerations with two dichotomous ideal-types of conflict in mind—Lewis Coser's (1956) "realistic" and "nonrealistic" conflict and Anatol Rapoport's (1960) "games" and "fights."[2] These general conceptualizations of conflict serve as templates against which to assess the literature on protracted conflict and rivalry reviewed below. Even more importantly, as Starr and his collaborators have emphasized, a universal conceptualization of conflict enables the development of models that link international and domestic conflict: "Developing a common structure for the conceptualization of violent conflict at either the domestic or interstate levels is necessary for clarifying the relationships between them" (Starr 1994, 484).

Protracted conflict, in fact, may be best viewed as a phenomenon that transcends the very boundaries differentiating internal and external systems. According to Azar (1990, vii), protracted conflict occurs between primary communal groups "defined by shared ethnic, religious, linguistic, or other cultural characteristics" and competing over basic collective needs. The state exists in Azar's approach as an apparatus controlled by one or a few communal groups. Though protracted conflicts are predominately *intra*-state processes, the possible transcendence of conflict group configurations of state boundaries entails that "distinctions made between domestic and international conflicts are misleading" (Azar 1985, 64).

The concepts "nonrealistic" and "realistic" conflict and "fights" and "games" subsume intrastate, interstate, and trans-state phenomena. Coser (1956, 49) differentiates between realistic and nonrealistic conflicts as follows:

> Conflicts which arise from frustration of specific demands within the relationship and from estimates of gains of the participants, and which are directed at the presumed frustrating object, can be called *realistic conflicts,* insofar as they are means toward a specific result. *Nonrealistic conflicts,* on the other hand, although still involving interaction between two or more persons, are not occasioned by the rival ends of the antagonists, but by the need for tension release of at least one of them. In this case the choice of antagonists depends on determinants not directly related to a contentious issue and is not oriented toward the attainment of specific results.

In addition to instrumental rationality, realistic conflicts involve choice over policy:

> In realistic conflict, there exist *functional alternatives to means.* Means other than conflict, depending on assessments of their efficacy, are always potentially available to the participants. In addition, it should be noted that in realistic conflicts there are also possibilities of choice between various forms of contention, such choice depending similarly on as assessment of their instrumental adequacy. In nonrealistic conflict, on the other hand, there exists only *functional alternatives as to objects.* (Coser 1956, 50; see also 54–5 and 156)

More specifically, Coser (1956, 42) notes that nonrealistic conflict may be (1) expressed directly against the individual or group responsible for the frustration; (2) displaced onto substitute targets; or (3) satisfied via tension release activity devoid of a target.

Rapoport's conceptualization of games shares much with Coser's definition of realistic conflict—conflict of interests and rational choice in the pursuit of favorable outcomes as concerns these interests. Conversely, fights, like nonrealistic conflicts, refer to affectively motivated efforts at harming the adversary. Rapoport (1960, 10) writes: "the essential difference between a fight and a game . . . is that while in a fight the object (if any) is to harm the opponent, in a game it is to outwit the opponent . . . a fight can be idealized as devoid of the rationality of the opponents, while a game, on the contrary, is idealized as a struggle in which complete 'rationality' of the opponents is assumed." Rapoport (1974, 180–1) elaborates:

In a fight, the opponent is perceived most clearly as an 'enemy,' as one who threatens one's own autonomy simply by being present or existing . . . Attention is focused on the enemy, and actions are guided by strong emotional impulses which frequently block rational analysis . . . Whereas the enemy is defined by associated emotions and attitudes (for example, as someone who is hated or feared), the opponent in a game is not. The attitude toward the *person* of the opponent may be neutral or even entirely friendly. The focus of attention is not on the presence of noxious stimuli in the person of the opponent but on the *situation,* which the opponent partially controls.

The following discussion demonstrates that scholars of both protracted conflict and rivalry emphasize, though to different extents, *both* types of conflict. More importantly, consonant with the rationalist hard core, this study conceptualizes protracted conflict as a conflict of interests viewed by both antagonists as (1) salient to the satisfaction of the group's basic needs and (2) zero-sum. Though caution must be used in the application of this conceptualization of protracted conflict to particular conceptualizations and cases of rivalry, such as positional rivalries, this conceptualization accounts in a compelling fashion for the essential properties emphasized by rivalry theorists and protracted conflict theorists alike. This conceptualization of protracted conflict accounts for the strong co-presence of rational and affective motivations in protracted conflicts, the predominance of territorial disputes in protracted conflicts, and the protracted nature of these conflicts, which underlines the importance of and complications involved in protracted conflict management.

Azar's View of Protracted Conflict

Azar's conceptualization of protracted conflict connotes elements of both fights and games. Azar attributes protracted conflict to contention over interests—over *basic* social needs: "the source of protracted social conflict is the denial of those elements required in the development of all people and societies, and whose pursuit is a compelling need in all. These are *security, distinctive identity, social recognition of identity, and effective participation* in the processes that determine conditions of security and identity, and other such developmental requirements" (1985, 60). The status quo resolution of issues, furthermore, is characterized by reinforcing cleavages in which one or more:

> communities are deprived of satisfaction of their basic needs on the basis of their communal identity . . . Political authority tends to be monopolized by

a dominant identity group or a coalition of hegemonic groups. These groups tend to use the state as an instrument for maximizing their interests at the expense of others. In the protracted social conflict context, these groups have manifested in communal terms. The monopoly of political authority by one or more groups denies the state a capacity for fair and successful governance. As a result, the means to satisfy basic needs are unevenly shared and the potential for protracted social conflict increases. (1990, 10, 12)

Azar concomitantly emphasizes the centrality of negative affect among protracted conflict groups. Protracted social conflicts:

> tend to generate, reinforce, or intensify mutual images of deception. They tend too to increase the likelihood of confusion in the direct and indirect communications between the parties and their allies. They increase the anxieties of the parties to the conflict, and they foster tension and conflict-maintenance strategies. In the protracted conflict situation, the conflict becomes an arena for redefining issues rather than a means for adjudicating them; it is therefore futile to look for any ultimate resolution. The conflict process becomes the source rather than the outcome of policy. (Azar et al. 1978, 51; see also Rapoport 1960 184–198, cited in Azar et al. 1978: 51)

As "animosity causes the conflict to spill over a broad spectrum of issues and to in and of itself push the rivalry outside the inter-state framework" (Azar et al. 1978, 55), Azar adds that these conflictual interactions lead to negative cognitive processes. Such processes include premature closure, misattribution of motives, stereotyping, tunnel vision, bolstering, and polarization, all of which tend to reinforce antagonistic perceptions and interactions (Azar 1990). The notion of "psychological ossification" captures the essence of the psychological motivation underlying protracted conflicts:

> Protracted social conflict entails a vicious cycle of fear and hostile interactions among the communal contestants. With the continued stress of such conflict, attitudes, cognitive processes and perceptions become set and ossified. War culture and cynicism dominate. Meaningful communication between or among conflicting parties dries up, and the ability to satisfy communal acceptance needs is severely diminished.[3] (Azar 1990, 17)

Despite the lack of explicit differentiation between realistic and nonrealistic conflict, however, Azar's conceptualization of protracted conflict embodies fundamental properties. First, the issues under contention are basic needs. Second, protracted conflict is characterized by reinforcing cleavages in which one of the protagonists dominates and the other is dominated. As a result, realistic and nonrealistic conflict interact and together, as will be elaborated below, undermine the prospects for protracted conflict resolution.

Rivalry

Most students of rivalry view rivalries primarily as realistic conflicts. Bennett (1996, 160) defines an interstate rivalry "as a dyad in which two states disagree over the resolution of some issue(s) between them for an extended period of time . . . [and] bargain over the issues at stake in an attempt to obtain a settlement favorable to themselves." Territorial control (Bennett 1996, Vasquez 1993, Thompson 1995, Huth 1996a and 1996b) and hegemonic ambitions (Thompson 1995; Williams and McGinnis 1988, 1992; McGinnis and Williams 1989) are primary issues driving rivalries. A given rivalry may revolve around more than one issue, and the issues around which it revolves, though meaningfully connected, might in fact vary over time (Goertz and Diehl 1993). Whatever their content, these issues are sufficiently salient to the antagonists that military force, or various substitutable forms of coercion, is a feasible option in the conduct of these conflicts.[4]

Though Vasquez (1993) acknowledges the realistic foundations of rivalry, his model closely associates rivalries with fights (see also Vasquez and Mansbach 1984). Vasquez suggests two ways of interpreting issues: along an actor dimension and along a stake dimension. He holds that rivalries are characterized by the interpretation of stakes according to the actor dimension: "The actor dimension results from a persistent disagreement and the use of negative acts which build up negative affect (psychological hostility)" (1993, 82). Furthermore, the actor dimension reduces all issues to a single overarching issue and encourages evaluation of concrete stakes as symbolic and/or transcendent stakes.

> Concrete stakes, because they are tangible and divisible, are more likely to permit compromise. Symbolic stakes make actors less flexible and more willing to stand firm because their symbolic nature leads to fears about losing a reputation for credibility or of establishing a bad precedent, if they entertain concessions necessary to bring about a compromise. Issues involving transcendent stakes are the most difficult to resolve, because they reflect fundamental differences over values, norms, and/or rules of the game. (1993, 78)

The actor dimension and emphasis upon symbolic and transcendant stakes are closely intertwined with hostility.

> The relationship is difficult to change because each side is involved in a vicious circle in which hostility makes actors define issues in ways that are intractable and threatening, and actors become hostile, in part, because of the way they have defined the issues that divide them . . . stalemate results and the issue festers. (1993, 82)

Vasquez in fact goes so far as to argue that nonrealistic motivation becomes more central than realistic motivation: "Frustration ensues, and a cost-benefit calculus of normal politics gives way to the feeling that *what is of primary importance is not one's own value satisfaction, but hurting the other side*" (1993, 82; emphasis added). It is the predominance of psychological hostility—of the view that "more emphasis is placed on hurting or denying something to the other side than on gaining something positive for oneself"—that distinguishes "rivalry from normal conflict" (Vasquez 1993, 76).

A thorough review of the proliferating literature on rivalry is beyond the scope of the present chapter. But it needs to be pointed out that while some models are more or less theoretically satisfying when it comes to the conceptualization of rivalry (for example, Vasquez 1993, Thompson 1995, and Bennett 1996), they are less satisfying when it comes to the postulation of relationships. For example, Vasquez (1993, 45) points out: "Few other issues between states produce armed conflict unless they are linked with territorial issues"(see also Huth and Russett 1993, Hensel 1996). To Vasquez (1993, 195), territory is clearly a catalyst: "One of the main factors that makes it less probable that war will be avoided is the intrusion of territorial disputes involving both rivals. Linking such violence-prone issues with the highly salient intangible issues fueling the rivalry makes it less likely that any of the issues separating the parties can be resolved in a mutually acceptable manner."

But Vasquez gives us little insight into *why* territorial disputes are so central. He does (1993, 78) suggest that territories are generally viewed by actors as symbolic and transcendent stakes: "human collectivities treat territory in symbolic and transcendent terms, infusing the concrete stake with all kinds of normative and ideological significance." But this does not explain why territory is especially contentious, but rather only *redefines* territory as an especially contentious issue. The question begged but not adequately addressed by Vasquez is why territory and not other issues?

Vasquez's (1993, 145) speculation—"The exact reason why human collectivities fight over territory rather than other issues remains a focus for future research, but it seems to be connected with genetic proclivities associated with territoriality, which in turn may be related to connection between territory and biological sustenance"—is unsatisfying.

Similarly, despite Thompson's (1995) emphasis on the intentional, rather than behavioral, foundations of rivalry, Thompson emphasizes in his discussion of conflict resolution empirical regularities at the expense of underlying causal relations. Thompson (1995, 206) suggests that: "spatial disputes are easier to resolve than are positional disputes. To resolve positional disputes, one side must convince its rival that its claims to leadership are superior. In the past, a considerable amount of force often has been required to bring about this end." The reason for this is that "the loser's resource base must first be exhausted either in a prolonged war, a series of wars, or in an attempt to remain competitive with its primary rival" (1995, 220). In addition, Thompson (1995, 219) states that: "Spatial rivalries tend to be less deadly and more common than positional rivalries." Not only is this proposition empirically rather than theoretically derived but, because of this lack of theoretical justification, Thompson and Vasquez harbor contradictory conclusions concerning the role of territorial disputes in rivalry dynamics, with Thompson claiming that spatial rivalries are easier to resolve than positional ones. In general, then, some scholarship on rivalry has resolved the dilemma of behavioristic rather than explanatory conceptualizations of rivalry only to turn to behavioristic argumentation in the postulation of hypotheses.

Finally, various problems exist with operational definitions of rivalry that emphasize more or less arbitrarily pre-specified frequencies of militarized disputes within a given time period. The primary deficiency in this approach is that it overemphasizes behavioral indicators at the expense of the motives, issues, and choices underlying variation of conflict escalation and de-escalation. Thompson (1995, 197) observes:

> Not surprisingly, emphasis on events data rather than actor choice processes leads to important inadequacies in population delimitation. If wars should not be plucked for analysis from their rivalry contexts, neither should one assume that all disputes are equivalent indicators that can be bundled into a rivalry threshold that holds equally well for all sorts of actors, arenas, and eras.

In light of this atheoretism, it is not surprising, as Thompson (1995, 197–200) points out, that an overemphasis on dispute frequencies has resulted in the erroneous treatment of particular cases as rivalries, in the eroneous exclusion of particular cases of rivalry from populations, and in the failure to recognize marked distinctions between different dyadic relationships exhibiting more or less continuous dispute patterns. At the least, it detracts from our ability to analyze cooperative phases of those rivalries that from a normative standpoint are most deserved of attention—the ones extant in the present system that have yet to be resolved.

Toward a General Model of Protracted Conflict

Protracted conflict outcomes, like all social outcomes, result from the intersection of particular individual choices and states of nature (see, for example, Starr 1978; Most and Starr 1989; Ordeshook 1986; Morrow 1988, 1994; Friedman and Starr 1997). Accordingly, it is useful to approach the problem of conceptualizing protracted conflict with a model of agency interpretation of the choice problem. Consonant with the realistic approach to conflict, the conceptualization of protracted conflict utilized herein emphasizes conflicts of interest revolving around one or more issues. This conceptualization emphasizes the elements of preference formation: the issues over which adversaries compete and the evaluation of particular resolutions of these issues according to a set of evaluation criteria. Accordingly, we can conceptualize the importance of conflicts of interest as a continuous quantity reflecting the extent to which (1) the issues under contention are linked to basic actor values; (2) the issues under contention have a large impact upon these basic values; and (3) this impact is significant relative to absolute levels of actor satisfaction of these basic needs. We can thus conceptualize protracted conflicts as those conflicts in which *both* adversaries perceive the issues under contention to be (1) significantly linked to basic values, and (2) constant-sum.

It should be pointed out from the outset that this conceptualization of protracted conflict excludes particular types of conflict treated by some scholars as rivalries. Perhaps most notably, this conceptualization of protracted conflict excludes contention over hegemonic status. Essentially by definition, positional rivalries do not capture the existential quality of protracted conflict issues. In Morrow's (1987) language, such struggles may be struggles for autonomy rather than security. Recalling Thompson's argument, positional rivalry may generally be more amenable to resolution through force than spatial rivalry precisely because positional rivalries by definition do not capture the existential quality of other protracted conflict issues. One must indeed consider the likelihood of strong states becoming embroiled in protracted conflict to be extremely slim, given that any two *strong* states are highly unlikely to be engaged with one another over one or more issues that significantly impinge upon the basic viability of both, given strong states' extensive satisfaction of basic needs. As such, this conceptualization of protracted conflict may be unsuitable for many scholarly concerns, and caution must be used in applying postulations regarding the intractability of protracted conflict and the implications of this intractability to legitimate cases of rivalry according to some definitions of that term.

But, more importantly, despite or perhaps in part because of the restricted denotation of this conceptualization, it captures properties emphasized by scholars of rivalry and protracted conflict alike. For one, this conceptualization helps account for the presence of negative affect in conflicts. Simply, negative affect is in large part a function of the fact that such conflicts represent enduring conflicts over incompatible and basic needs. In fact, it is precisely because of the intensity of the stakes involved in protracted conflicts that we should expect hostility to generally be more prevalent in protracted conflicts than in other forms of conflict.

Consonant with this view, Coser (1956, 68) maintains: "In groups that appeal only to a peripheral part of their members' personality, or . . . in groups in which relations are functionally specific and effectively neutral, conflicts are apt to be less sharp and violent than in groups wherein ties are diffuse and affective, engaging the total personality of their members." In other words, the disaffection in protracted conflicts emphasized by Vasquez and Azar is so prevalent in such conflicts precisely because they significantly impinge upon antagonists' basic and largely incompatible needs. At the same time, however, the conceptualization of protracted conflict presented above confirms Coser's proposition that hostility is neither a necessary nor sufficient condition for conflict.[5] Thus, this conceptualization of protracted conflict at once subsumes negative affect and nonrational values but represents a realistic conceptualization of conflict.

Indeed, a general advantage of beginning with a model of protracted conflict choice is that such a model draws attention to the important questions of the issues and values at stake that may lead toward protracted conflict scenarios. One important issue likely to be central in protracted conflicts but understandably downplayed by scholars of interstate competition is that of autonomy or sovereignty. Azar contends that successful resolution of a protracted conflict as defined by him requires allocation of significant political power to the dominated protagonist.[6]

Similarly, this conceptualization of protracted conflict accounts for the centrality of territorial disputes in protracted conflicts/rivalries, as territory refers to *basic* needs. Certainly, one potentially important value of territory is its contribution to geopolitical security. Huth (1996b), for example, has found support both for a positive relationship between the strategic location of bordering territory and involvement in territorial dispute, and the positive relationship between the prominence of strategic issues in territorial disputes and the probability that states will opt for coercive diplomatic and military policies to gain control of the disputed territory. Beyond its strategic value, territory may be valuable for its demographic composition, such as a large ethnic population related to that of one or more of the rivals; economic value; and symbolic significance. Similarly, to use Vasquez's terminology, the value of territorial as well as other issues under contention may derive from the issue's linkage to symbolic and transcendent as well as concrete stakes. Lastly, especially in light of the basic significance of territory, decisions concerning control over disputed territory may have important domestic political ramifications, (see for example, Starr 1991a, 1991b, 1994; Huth and Russett 1993; Huth 1996b). Thus, scholarship on the centrality of territory in protracted conflicts/rivalry generally confirms that territorial control is more closely associated with conflict escalation than are other issues because it generally exerts an important impact on actor satisfaction of basic needs relative to that of other issue-areas.[7]

Finally, the conceptualization of protracted conflict advanced here captures the enduring quality of these conflicts. It is precisely the conjunction of the mutual perception that basic values are at stake and that the issues are constant-sum that entails that the issues operative in protracted conflicts are largely unresolvable. In the terminology of formal theory of negotiation, issues in protracted conflict may be defined as those in which there is no overlap of reservation points among the protagonists (Raiffa 1982). As Azar (1985, 61) notes, "human needs and long-standing cultural values . . . will not be traded, exchanged or bargained over. They are not subject to negotiation." Furthermore, territorial issues, as well as other basic issues such as sovereignty, are complicated by *imposed integration*. "Imposed integration or incorporation of distinctive and often conflictual communities into one political entity retards the nation-building process, strains the social fabric and eventually breeds fragmentation and protracted social conflict" (Azar 1990, 7). In addition, differential structural positions, "such as economic and technological underdevelopment, and unintegrated social and political systems . . . do not lend themselves to solutions" (Azar 1985, 59).[8] It follows from the unresolvable nature of the conflict of interests characterizing protracted conflicts that protracted conflicts do not have clear, precise, and categorical beginning and end points. "While they [prolonged conflicts] may exhibit some breakpoints during which there is a cessation of overt violence, they linger on in time and have no distinguishable point of termination. . . . One cannot expect these conflicts to be terminated by explicit decision. Protracted conflicts . . . are not specific events or even clusters of events at a point in time; they are processes" (Azar et al. 1978, 50).

In fact, while explaining the *protracted* nature of these conflicts, this conceptualization of protracted conflicts points to the epiphenomenality of this property. In other words, consonant with the emphasis by scholars such as Bennett and Thompson on the causal mechanisms underlying rivalries, it is the conflict over issues rather than the protractedness of a protracted conflict that is central. It is the unresolvable quality of protracted conflicts that causally precedes, accounts for, and is thus more important than, the enduring quality of these conflicts.

Conceptualizing Protracted Conflict Management

The intractable nature of protracted conflict has a crucial implication for the study of conflict resolution and management. Dahrendorf (1959, 224) defined conflict *resolution* as follows: "There is one, and only one, sense in which one might say that a conflict has been resolved: the specific issues of a specific conflict . . . may be settled in such a way as not to reappear again." Given this definition, the intractability of protracted conflict places the entire enterprise of explaining protracted conflict *resolution* on shaky ground. Rather, the intractable nature of protracted conflicts entails that conflict management rather than conflict resolution becomes paramount.[9]

In regard to conflict resolution, there is one limitation intrinsic to the very concept of protracted conflict. Variation in levels of power and the prominence of immediate security in themselves have no impact whatsoever on the (dis)satisfaction of basic needs. In the words of Azar et al. (1978, 58–9): "struggles for recognition and acceptance . . . cannot be 'won' or 'lost' through protracted conflict." Thus, the distribution of threats and power across actors does not in itself contribute to an understanding of conflict termination and initiation. Instead, the distribution of capabilities is important in the analysis of variation in the policy preferences concerning conflict (de-)escalation and thus protracted conflict outcomes. A notable consequence is that we should expect protracted conflicts to become reactivated given shifts in structural properties that increase the opportunities (or possibilities) of the antagonist(s) significantly dissatisfied with the status quo.

Nonrealistic, Integrationist, and Realistic Approaches to Conflict Management

It is useful in the conceptualization of protracted conflict management to begin by distinguishing among three ideal-types of conflict management—nonrealistic, integrationist, and realistic. While adherents of each of these approaches recommends related if not overlapping types of tactics for conflict management, they can be distinguished in terms of their assumptions about the major problem underlying conflict and the corresponding solution.

The nonrealistic approach to conflict management is based on the premise that negative affect, hostility, distrust, fear, and so on, represent the primary problem for conflict management. Suffice it to say that to the extent that protracted conflicts are motivated by conflicts of interests, this approach will play little role in the conduct of the conflict. As Coser (1956, 47) eloquently puts it: "institutions that merely serve abreaction of feelings of hostility, thus leaving the terms of the relationship unchanged, may function as lightning rods but they cannot prevent a recurrent gathering of clouds."

The integrationist approach to conflict management is based upon two premises. The first is that conflict management conforms to what Dahrendorf refers to as the integrationist ontology of social systems. In the terms of Azar (1990), the primary premise of this approach is that politics is characterized by the promotion of consensus, cooperation, peaceful interactions, and so on, rather that by conflict over the distribution of scarce goods across competing actors. A subsidiary element of this second premise is that actors can learn to recognize the net advantages of cooperation. Accordingly, whereas the integrationist approach shares with a realist approach to international politics an emphasis on the primary role of interests as the glue of social interaction, it disagrees with the realist approach in maintaining that interests are generally compatible if not harmonious rather than incompatible.

Thus, adherents to the integrationist approach argue that a crucial component of conflict management is the cultivation among the antagonists of the belief that the conflict of interest is variable-, rather than constant-, sum. A manifestation of this approach, Track Two diplomacy,

> generally refers to the search for and promotion of peaceful relations between warring parties without reliance upon official efforts. Track One diplomacy, which emphasizes official contacts between representatives of sovereign entities, governments and other parties to a dispute within a bar-

gaining framework, lacks the necessary orientation to generate conflict resolution breakthroughs. A "bargaining" framework implies that the conflict is
about clearly defined goods which are in short supply, so that a "zero-sum"
outcome . . . is assumed. (Azar 1990, 19)

Similarly, the "problem-solving" approach to conflict management:

> is predicated on the belief that violent and prejudicial, or peaceful and co-
> operative, thinking and behavior are learned phenomena, and that what is
> learned therefore can also be modified. Problems of communication in con-
> flict situations obscure the common interests and potentials for mutual ben-
> efit which the protagonists share. (Azar 1990, 21)

The failure of the integrationist approach lies not in its neglect of the
configuration of interests but in its optimism concerning the relative importance of convergent rather than divergent interests. To elaborate on this
point it may be useful to rephrase the objective of the integrationist approach: Conflict management techniques commensurable with the integrationist approach may be viewed as aiming to redefine the relationships
between particular stakes and evaluation criteria. This might be achieved
through reduction, first, of the extent to which particular stakes at issue are
associated with existential concerns, and, second, of the extent to which an
agent values existential concerns. To promote issue-linkages, additionally,
the adversaries might be encouraged to somehow associate their existential values with different stakes. To the extent that conflicts revolve around
issues linked to the basic needs of the antagonists, however, the harmony
or compatibility of interests diminishes and the ability to persuade the antagonists to the contrary is tenuous.[10]

Given the conceptualization of protracted conflict as zero-sum competition over issues closely and substantially linked to the basic needs of both
rivals, any meaningful approach to conflict management must accept the
intractability and permanence of the conflict of interests relating the antagonists to one another. Dahrendorf (1959) is to be credited for emphasizing this premise of conflict management. Dahrendorf invokes the term
conflict "regulation" to refer primarily to efforts aimed not at resolving
conflict as defined above, but rather at controlling levels of violence that
become manifest in the course of the conflict.[11]

But at the same time that protracted conflicts require conflict regulation as defined by Dahrendorf, effective realization of conflict management so defined is especially troublesome in protracted conflicts. The

actors engaged in protracted conflict must not simply minimize levels of violence vis-à-vis the external adversary but rather must minimize some function of violence regarding the external adversary on the one hand and internal violence on the other. To explain this primary objective of protracted conflict regulation, it is useful to proceed deductively.

Two postulations in particular form the foundation of this deduction. First, recall that conflict regulation techniques aim to reduce the outbreak of violence among conflict groups, and to do so through measures that address rather than avoid or suppress the conflict of interests driving the conflict. Given this, the modeling of conflict regulation should focus on the incentive structures facing conflict groups in their choices between violent and nonviolent conduct of the conflict. Secondly, an important dimension of these incentive structures concerns consideration of internal political considerations.

These two suppositions, in turn lead to important implications for the study of protracted conflict regulation. Given political processes internal to protracted conflict groups, not only are leaders of these groups dissuaded from pursuing accommodationist bargaining strategies, but also such policies themselves may in fact sow the seeds that undermine the preconditions for successful application of regulatory techniques such as regimes, arbitration, and mediation. The bitter implication for conflict regulation of this state of affairs, in turn, is that the primary objective is not to minimize violence in absolute terms, as is sought in Dahrendorf's notion of conflict regulation, but rather to achieve an equilibrium between internal and external expression of violence.

The Viability Paradox and Nested Games

The viability paradox connotes that conciliatory bargaining strategies undermine the very willingness and opportunity to pursue effective conflict management. The basic premises of the viability paradox are that: (1) the issue of bargaining strategy regarding the external protracted conflict adversary simultaneously invokes domestic as well as external arenas of interaction; and (2) these arenas are negatively linked such that escalatory initiatives in one arena may lead to de-escalatory processes in the other, and vice versa. Two hypotheses can be deduced from these premises: (1) the domestic arena serves to dissuade decision makers from pursuing conciliatory external policies; and (2) conciliatory escalatory policies undermine the very preconditions for successful pursuit of the conflict regulation techniques emphasized by Dahrendorf. The viability paradox, then, is that conciliatory policy toward the external adversary itself sows the seeds for unsuccessful conflict regulation.

In the most general terms, the negative linkage between internal and external conflict is a manifestation of Tsebelis's notion of nested games:

> an optimal alternative in one arena (or game) will not necessarily be optimal with respect to the entire network of arenas in which the actor is involved. . . . The actor may choose a suboptimal strategy in one game if this strategy happens to maximize his payoffs when all arenas are taken into account. (Tsebelis 1990, 9)

While the seminal statement of this type of phenomenon in international relations is attributable to Putnam (1988), Starr and his collaborators (Most and Starr 1989, Starr 1994, Simon and Starr 1997) have given the greatest consideration to the negative linkage between internal and external *viability*. That is, governments' internal and external viability are negatively linked and, consequently, governments strive for balances between adequate levels of these types of viability. The present section suggests if only too briefly that the nested games approach emphasized by Starr and his collaborators is especially operative in cases of protracted conflict. The reason for this is that—because protracted conflict impacts the basic needs of its participants, engenders high mobilization costs, and is prevalent in socialization processes—the issue of bargaining strategy vis-à-vis the protracted conflict adversary becomes a locus around which domestic conflict groups are organized and mobilized.

Protracted conflict permeates various issue-areas of central concern to social actors. This is in part the case because the very issues under contention influence the lives of the members of society. That is, individuals may be living in disputed territory, dependent for their livelihood somehow on access to this territory, and so on. But the penetration of the protracted conflict into the lives of the members of society is also in part a consequence of the large costs of mobilization. International conflict requires a government to mobilize resources from its society (Organski and Kugler 1980, Tilly 1985). As Azar (1985, 68) notes, "all of these seemingly intractable and protracted conflicts exhaust the resources of those directly and indirectly involved, further deform the economy, and thus accentuate underdevelopment." Thus, in permeating social and economic as well as political institutions, protracted conflicts and attendant bargaining decisions implicate the basic needs not only of the rivals *qua* political and social organizations, but also of the individual members of and groups within these polities.

Furthermore, socialization dynamics reinforce the primacy of the external conflict in the psyches of the members of societies embroiled in these conflicts. For one, the protracted conflict is emphasized in the socialization of members of protracted conflict societies by the elites of these societies. The elites actively socialize the masses into the conflict in order to increase governmental extraction from and mobilization of societal sectors regarding the external conflict. Azar (1990), similarly, recognizes this and identifies the organization, mobilization, and effective leadership of communal groups as important factors in the unfolding of protracted social conflict.

In addition, the prominence of the conflict in the primary socialization of young cohorts is reinforced to the extent that the socializers of these young cohorts are themselves socialized into the conflict. This is so, as Berger and Luckmann (1966, 131) emphasize, because: "Every individual is born into an objective social structure within which he encounters the significant others who are in charge of his socialization. These significant others are imposed upon him. Their definitions of his situation are posited for him as objective reality." Thus, the duration of a protracted conflict is positively related to the proportion of a society's rulers of primary socialization who have been themselves socialized into the protracted conflict. As Inglehart (1990) suggests, political and cultural orientation are instilled in the formative years of life. Accordingly, the centrality of the conflict to the social orientation of the members of society is enhanced to the extent that the conflict was operative during the formative years of their lives. We may thus postulate a positive relationship between conflict duration and the proportion of the population influenced by the conflict in their formative years. In other words, given that the protracted conflict is central for significant others, later generations of individuals will be socialized by significant others for whom the external conflict is highly salient. This dynamic can be viewed as a function of the *protracted* property of the conflict.

Finally, to the extent that the external conflict permeates the various roles of individuals, individuals identify themselves in relation to the conflict. As Berger and Luckmann (1966, 73) elaborate, "the actor identifies with the socially objectivated typifications of conduct *in actu,* but reestablishes distance from them as he reflects about his conduct afterward. This distance between the actor and his action can be retained in consciousness and projected to future repetitions of the actions. In this way both acting self and acting others are apprehended not as unique individuals, but as *types.* By definition, these types are interchangeable."

For these reasons, the likelihood that the issue of bargaining strategy vis-à-vis the external adversary is highly salient for virtually all sectors of the society, that disagreement over the external adversary exists, and that actors feel strongly about these differences and are strongly committed to their positions is especially high in protracted conflicts. As a result, it is likely that actors will be willing to take high risks and bear high costs in pursuit of favorable policy outcomes; it is likely, in fact, that the very collective identities and ties of solidarity of the members of societies engaged in protracted conflict is configured around the debate concerning strategy toward the external adversary. In short, in protracted conflict, the social choice processes concerning the external adversary serve as enduring loci around which domestic-level conflict groups are oriented. Azar (1990, 121) goes so far as to write: "a community will not always have a unified leadership which can effectively speak for its constituents. The inability to institutionalize, or otherwise devise the means for the consistent expression of demands and interests, is one of the effects of protracted social conflict, and is most common in the case of victimized communities, which in a conflictive society are kept fragmented by the hegemonic group." Consequently, internal and external viability *are more likely* to be negatively linked in protracted conflicts than in more broadly conceived conflicts: efforts to dissolve international tensions increase domestic ones, and vice versa. The viability paradox is thus especially prevalent in protracted conflicts.

As mentioned above, one central implication for protracted conflict regulation derivative of this negative linkage is that government decision makers must take domestic viability considerations into account in decisions regarding external bargaining strategy and that they must often trade off some security at one level for added security at the other. Another central implication, which is herein referred to as the viability paradox, is that to the extent that conciliatory external policies undermine domestic conflict, they undermine both the willingness and ability of the rivals to engage in conflict management.[12]

The opportunity and willingness framework (Starr 1978, Most and Starr 1989)—or perhaps more accurately the pre-theoretic hypotheses that opportunity and willingness are jointly necessary conditions for social action—permits integration within the framework of a common logic and thus the general expression of various hypotheses accounting for decreases in willingness and opportunity to resort to conflict management stemming from domestic conflict in the focal society. As concerns willingness, domestic conflict in the focal country, state$_i$, can increase the willingness of state$_i$'s protracted conflict adversary, state$_j$, to escalate hostilities against state$_i$

by weakening state$_i$ and thus improving the expected utility of state$_j$ regarding an escalation of hostilities against state$_i$. In addition, successful revolution in state$_i$ may pose a threat to state$_j$, thus provoking state$_j$ to initiate hostilities against a victorious opposition$_i$ (see Starr 1991a, 1994).

Conversely, to the extent that domestic conflict in state$_i$ results from government$_i$'s pursuit of cooperative strategies vis-à-vis the external adversary, pending conflict within state$_i$ may increase government$_i$'s willingness to divert or dissolve domestic discontent by escalating hostilities against state$_j$. Thus, domestic political considerations may alter foreign policy preferences (or preference rankings). Short of such preference reversals, internal opposition can decrease government$_i$'s degree of commitment to accommodative external bargaining strategies. That is, the greater the domestic costs of an external de-escalation, the lower this foreign policy's utility is relative to other options.[13] Finally, successful revolt by opposition$_i$ may increase the willingness of government$_i$ to escalate the conflict with state$_j$ because a victory by opposition$_i$ may (1) strengthen state$_i$ and/or (2) increase state$_i$'s international ambitions.

Domestic political situations approaching multiple sovereignty, for example, the fragmentation of authority and the legitimate use of force, may undermine not only the willingness of rivals to resort to conflict management, but also their ability to do so effectively. First, multiple sovereignty provides opposition forces with the opportunity to pursue more or less independent strategies toward the external adversary, including the use of force. Given adequate levels of interaction opportunity, for example, geographical contiguity if not integrated populations (Starr and Most 1976, Most and Starr 1989, Siverson and Starr 1991), then, an internal opposition may be able to target the external adversary directly. Such action, in turn, would undermine general acceptance of a negotiated settlement and intensify hostility, distrust, fear, and thus tension.

To the extent that situations approaching multiple sovereignty undermine the ability of a protracted conflict rival to provide a unified negotiation team, such situations more directly undermine peace negotiations. As Coser elaborates, Simmel proposes that each conflict group is concerned "that the other live up to the rules even in conflict situations. This living up to the rules, however, requires unified and disciplined organization" (Coser 1956, 130). Dahrendorf also treats unified and organized conflict groups as a necessary condition for conflict regulation. "So long as conflicting forces are diffuse, incoherent aggregates, regulation is virtually impossible. . . . Guerrilla warfare is not susceptible of effective regulation" (Dahrendorf 1959, 226).

The Puzzle of Protracted Conflict Management:
Bargaining Strategy toward the External Adversary and Internal Conflict

The implication of the viability paradox for the management of protracted conflict is that deriving a balance between internal and external conflict serves not only the viability concerns of the focal government but also the effective achievement of conflict management regarding the external conflict. In other words, successful conflict management demands attention to the impact of de-escalatory external bargaining strategies upon the probability that domestic opposition groups will rebel. Balancing levels of internal viability in the focal country with external policies concerning the protracted conflict adversary is thus a central concern not only for focal country foreign policy elites but also for the focal country's external adversary. Certainly, the external adversary hopes that the balance its rival pursues favors the conciliation end in the international arena. But to the extent that the adversary wishes to successfully realize conflict regulation, it must be sensitive to the destabilizing effects within the focal country of progress in the international arena. It is in the adversary's interest that a situation of multiple sovereignty not arise within its rival's domain, especially when the former sovereign of that polity favored nonviolent strategies of external bargaining. Least of all does the adversary, state$_j$, want more aggressive forces coming to power in its protracted conflict adversary. Thus, notwithstanding differences in the desired balance between internal and external conflict in the focal country, the external adversary as well as the focal regime is concerned with mitigating the prospects of internal turmoil in the focal country.

It is important to note that actors may invoke various decision rules, or criterion functions, in the balancing of internal and external threats, and the function that an actor invokes directly influences the particular profile of threats that the actor faces, (Starr and McGinnis 1992, 13–5; Simon and Starr 1997). Criterion functions may vary according to the number of threats that they address and the balance of viability concerning these threats. In this regard, Starr and McGinnis (1992, 13) contend that "the nature of governments as complex organizations suggests that a more reasonable representation is to assume that these actors can only focus their attention on a small number of problems at a time, and perhaps only on their single most pressing security threat . . ." They elaborate:

> Accordingly, we base our criterion function on the idea that government i seeks to *minimize the maximum threat it faces*. That is, i acts to minimize

the maximum values of all Rj and Tk, or to minimize the value of z, defined as:

$$z = \max \{\max m\ pjwjcj, \text{mazk pkrksk}\} = \{\text{maxjRj, maxk Tk}\}$$

where p refers to i's interaction opportunities, or the relative frequency (p) with which i interacts with each external adversary, j, and domestic opposition, k,; w and r refer to the (subjective) probability of war or revolution arising from i's relationships with j and k, respectively; and c and s refer to the relative capability levels that in turn affect the probabilities (c,s) that j or k can defeat i in war or revolution.

Regardless of which criterion function is employed, however, a fundamental component of the achievement of desirable balances between internal and external viability is the assessment of the actual linkages between policy toward the external adversary and domestic conflict. The management of internal and external conflict, then, simultaneously requires consideration of the ways in which and the extent to which particular external bargaining strategies influence the prospects of domestic conflict.

This crucial element of effective conflict management can be stated in expected utility terminology as follows:

1. The relative importance of the impact the proximities/distances concerning policy preferences regarding the external protracted conflict adversary has upon domestic actors' utility for pursuing particular bargaining strategies in their internal competition.
2. The relationship of external bargaining strategy with other factors contributing to this utility score.
3. The impact of external bargaining strategy on probability of victory/power.

This set of puzzles may be viewed as a *second image reversed*[14] approach to the topic of domestic conflict in societies embroiled in protracted international conflicts. Accordingly, it is important to distinguish this approach from other hypotheses that likewise represent this general category.

It is important to compare this conceptualization with the research of Starr and his collaborators on two-level security management (Starr 1994; Starr and McGinnis 1992; Simon and Starr 1996, 1997). These studies focus on the strategies available to governments concerning the manipulation of *capabilities* at their disposal. More specifically, these studies begin with the assumption that governments have two distinct alternatives in the enhancement of their capabilities, resource allocation and extraction. Each of these strategies is in turn associated with a particular set of costs and benefits. Resource extraction and allocation can influence the expected utility calculations of the internal (and also external) adversary in two analytically distinct ways: (1) by reducing the probability that the adversary can defeat the government; and (2) by altering the relative utility of status quo and expected outcomes. The objective for the government decision maker becomes to enhance its capabilities in a way that maximizes its balance of internal and external threat. In the words of Starr and McGinnis (1992, 16–7): "The basic point that emerges from these analyses returns directly to the central purpose of this enterprise: that by its resource extraction efforts government$_i$ can, in effect, re-shape the profile of security threats it faces, making some actors more threatening while it makes others less threatening."

Differences between Starr and his collaborators' work and the present analysis concerning the dependent variable deserve mention. First, Starr and his collaborators are interested in the impact of extraction/allocation choices on the external position of state$_i$ (Simon and Starr 1997). More directly, extraction increases state$_i$'s exposure, or interaction opportunities, with other states in the system, which in turn contributes to external threat. In contrast, the present dicussion is interested in explaining outcomes in terms of conflict management or resolution. Externally, I am concerned with bargaining outcomes rather than the external position of the focal country. Secondly, and more importantly, domestic security is defined in the work of Starr and his collaborators in general terms of the probability of revolution by some opposition$_1$, itself a function of the status quo distribution and the utility of revolutionary outcomes, and the probability of defeat.

The most significant difference between the research of Starr and his collaborators and the present discussion of protracted conflict, concerns the independent variable(s). Whereas Starr and his collaborators focus on the pursuit of capability, this discussion focuses on the idea of particular bargaining strategies vis-à-vis a particular, external adversary. It is also useful to compare the present approach to protracted conflict to other studies linking internal and external conflict. The puzzle emphasized here, that is, the problem of balancing levels of internal and external viability, shares a notion of negative linkage—that domestic turmoil leads to external escalation—with diversionary war models. But the issue of balancing internal and external viability emphasized here differs from the diversionary hypothesis in that this escalation is motivated not to divert or distract but to satisfy international political interests.

The puzzle addressed here, moreover, diverges from the diversionary hypothesis in at least two other respects. First, in perhaps the most general of terms, the puzzle of protracted conflict management reverses the order of causality found in the diversionary hypothesis; that is, it emphasizes the direct impact of the external conflict on the internal conflict, rather than the reverse. Second, and most important, the discussion here rests on a premise that in effect contradicts or at the least problematizes the basic premise of the diversionary hypothesis. Simply, in the present analysis, the external conflict is itself treated as a source of internal conflict.

In addition, whereas most other literature on internal-external conflict linkages focuses on the impact of external *fights* on internal conflict, the present study may be characterized as attending to the impact of external *games* on internal conflict. That is, it models crisis over the social choice process of bargaining strategy as an important factor in domestic conflict.

Conclusion

This chapter has presented a conceptualization of protracted conflict that distinguishes these conflicts from interstate conflicts in their involvement of nonstate antagonists. Indeed, many of the stakes involved in imposed integration are by definition precluded by the assumption of nation-states as actors, and require arrangements for the *sharing* rather than division of goods. Some might thus contend that cases of protracted conflict, and the protracted conflict management puzzle, are not terribly relevant for scholars of international politics, or that they require models distinct from those used to explain interstate conflicts.

Accordingly, this chapter concludes by considering the relationship of protracted conflict to other conflicts studied by scholars of international politics: should protracted conflict be treated as qualitatively unique rather than quantitatively unique in relation to other conceptualizations of conflict? The response to this question may be based in turn on the answer to the following question: Does the conceptualization of protracted conflict entail qualitatively distinct puzzles and explanations?

These questions have been addressed, if generally, implicitly, and ambiguously, by the literature on rivalry. On the surface, much of this literature suggests that rivalry is a unique phenomenon. (for example, Goertz and Diehl 1996, 1993). Goertz and Diehl (1996, 304) propose that rivalry can be viewed as a necessary condition for a relationship or process, and as a "contextual model" (see Goertz 1994), in which properties of a continuously defined concept of rivalry interact with other factors central to models of international political phenomena. Alternatively, rivalry can be viewed "as the cause of the phenomenon, such as an arms race. Here the arms race 'intervenes' between the rivalry relationship and war."

Generally, however, the scholarship on rivalry itself does not suggest that rivalry is a qualitatively unique phenomenon. Consonant with reliance upon an operationalization of rivalry as a case selection device, the primary puzzles explored by rivalry scholars are the same as those explored by scholars of war and crisis. Of the various issues raised by scholars of rivalry or protracted conflict, two general ones garner primary emphasis: (1) rivalry initiation and termination: and (2) rivalry escalation to armed conflict and war.

Nor, have the questions raised by these issues been afforded answers different from those given to prior conflict explanations. That is clearly reflected in Goertz and Diehl's (1996, 293) suggestion of a direct translation of models of the causes of war to the explanation of rivalry:

> Research using the traditional causes of war framework tries to explain war as the result of certain hypothesized causes. . . . Scholars in this tradition search for the presence of the hypothesized causes shortly before or coterminous with the outbreak of war in a set of cases as well as in control groups in which no war occurs. Transferring these sorts of explanatory models into the rivalry framework leads us to look for the presence or occurrence of hypothesized events or conditions before the rivalry starts and just before it ends.

It is in the justification for reliance upon rivalry as a unit of analysis that the distinctiveness of this phenomenon, as much as it exists, is to be found. Reliance upon operationalizations of rivalry as a case selection device in the study of various extant puzzles of international relations, including power transitions (Geller 1993) and deterrence (Huth and Russett, 1993), is justified largely on the grounds that, as Goertz and Diehl (1993: 149) note, "the models tested assume a background of conflict and a reasonable likelihood of war or military conflict." This justification raises the question of whether or not "a background of conflict and a reasonable likelihood of war or military conflict" represents a qualitative or quantitative distinction between rivalry and other forms of competitive relationships. If it is the latter, then we must conclude that rivalries do not require qualitatively distinct explanations.

At the same time, however, this quantitative distinction between rivalry and other patterns of conflictual interactions suggests that the very context of rivalry serves to increase *probabilities* of particular outcomes. For example, the point suggested by Goertz and Diehl that we should expect power transitions in the distribution of capabilities to lead to conflict in the context of rivalry ultimately means that such transformations are most likely to lead to conflict when they are characterized by important conflicts of interests.

In this spirit, it may be best to treat the protracted conflict dichotomy as distinguishing between different probabilistically defined nice laws. That is, rather than the axiomatic statement of nice laws—for example, if a then b; if not a then not b—we have—if a then b with probability x; if not a then b with probability y. In other words, the probability that the relationship exists and the strength of the relationship may vary between a protracted conflict and other conflicts. In this spirit, the puzzle presented in this chapter may be best viewed as *especially* but not *exclusively* relevant to protracted conflicts. In other words, given that the impact of policy regarding the external adversary on the utility functions invoked in domestic conflict group strategic decisions is ultimately continuous—given, that is, that external issues can almost always impinge to some extent on domestic opposition groups—we must conclude that this puzzle is simply *especially* but not *exclusively* relevant to protracted conflicts.[15] In fact, as the conceptualization of protracted conflict developed above connotes some properties that are continuous, for example, the extent to which an issue impinges on basic needs, we may treat protracted conflict itself as a concept that applies in greater or lesser degree in different cases.

At the same time that the probabilistic/continuous uniqueness of protracted conflict makes this concept and its puzzles commensurable with more general models of conflict, it also undermines the external validity of findings concerning the magnitude and relative magnitude of bargaining strategy regarding a protracted conflict adversary in domestic conflict in relation to nonprotracted conflicts. Consonant with the subjectivist emphasis of spatial models of conflict—especially the emphasis on the case-specificity of the issues, preferences, and issue salience comprising conflict situtions—we should find variation in the relative magnitude of such linkages even across different cases of both protracted and other cases of conflict.

Regardless of whether or not scholars treat protracted conflicts as unique phenomena requiring unique models, to the extent that the international stage is inhabited by actors engaged in such struggles, and to the extent that these struggles transcend state boundaries, they require attention. This author does not believe, as Azar (1985, 63) himself has suggested, that the prevalence of protracted conflict threatens the predominance of the interstate system. Suffice it to say that this position founders upon Hedley Bull's (1977) point that the failure of states to monopolize organized violence does not undermine the dominant status of the state because nonstate actors wielding force generally do so precisely in their pursuit of statehood. On the contrary, as conflicts that have often invited the intervention of states, and as conflicts with direct implications for the sovereignty and territorial configuration of nations, protracted conflicts represent an important source of change *within* the interstate system. Furthermore, the study of protracted conflict is perfectly at home in a discipline devoted to inter*national* politics.

Notes

1. See the list of 11 items authored by Azar and various colleagues in the references to this chapter.

2. Each of these scholars explicitly acknowledges the ideal-typic nature of his concepts (see Coser 1956, 53; Rapoport 1974, 183). For the sake of convenience, the following discussion will interchangeably use the terms "realistic conflict" and "games," on the one side, and "nonrealistic conflict" and "fights," on the other.

3. Yet at other times Azar characterizes protracted conflicts as anomic situations: "In the long term, unmet psycho-political and socio-economic needs lead to dysfunctional cognitive and behavioral patterns that are not easily remedied by ordinary methods of diplomacy or the use of force" (1990, 2). Similarly, he emphasizes the importance of legitimacy crisis: "The domination of the state apparatus by one or few communal groups is achieved through the distortion of modes of governance. To sustain their monopoly of power, these dominant groups limit access to social institutions by other identity groups and thus often precipitate crises of *legitimacy*. Such crises exacerbate already existing competitive or conflictive situations, diminish the state's ability to meet basic needs, and lead to further developmental crises" (1990, 10–11). This brings to mind Durkheimian explanations of civil violence.

4. Altogether, Goertz and Diehl (1993: 154) attribute three basic properties to the concept of an enduring rivalry: competitiveness, time, and spatial consistency. Spatial consistency refers to enduring rivalries' inclusion of "a consistent set of states in their domain." Given the straightforward and noncontentious nature of this property, it is not discussed in the following discussion. The *enduring* element of rivalries will be discussed below.

5. Coser (1956, 59–60) writes: "Aggressive or hostile 'impulses' do not suffice to account for social conflict . . . Conflict can occur only in the interaction

between subject and object; it always presupposes a relationship. . . . Realistic conflict need not be accompanied by hostility and aggressiveness."

Coser in fact explicitly associates international conflict with realistic conflict. "Knowledge gained from the study of nonrealistic conflict is being applied to the field of international relations, overlooking the fact that conflicts in this field are primarily realistic conflicts of power, interests or values and that the nonrealistic elements which may be intermingled in the struggle are contingent and play, at best, a reinforcing role . . . a sociological study of international politics, although it may legitimately concern itself with tensions arising from various frustrations within national social systems, will not accomplish its main purpose unless it analyzes the realistic conflicts over scarce power around which the patterns of alliance and antagonisms form" (1956, 51–2).

6. Rapoport (1974, 189) also identifies autonomy as a basic need in perhaps a Durkheimian sense: "the need for autonomy . . . is fundamental because autonomy involves the identification of self, and, by extension, of an extended 'self' of a group with which the self identifies."

Azar (1985, 65) notes: "Conflict resolution in protracted conflict situations necessitates an understanding of the importance of open, participatory, and decentralized political structures as opposed to centralized, dominant and exclusive structures. . . . These structures are designed to serve the psychological, economic, and relational needs of groups and individuals within nation-states." Subsequent discussions by Rosenau (e.g., 1990) highlight the difference between states ("sovereignty-bound" actors) and nonstate actors that are not so bound; the key concern of the former is security, of the latter autonomy.

7. One fruitful test would be to distinguish territorial disputes related to basic needs from those not related to basic needs; we would expect, of course, that the former more closely approach protracted conflict and hypotheses pertaining to protracted conflict than the latter.

8. Recalling that though neither necessary nor sufficient, hostility reinforces proclivities toward conflict. It should be added that such hostilities take time to dissipate (see Azar et al. 1978, 59).

9. A related implication of the intractability of protracted conflict is that systemic and regional distributions of threat are significant not in the assessment of initiation or termination of conflict *per se,* but rather in modeling the bargaining strategies of actors *engaged within* protracted conflict. Some scholars have emphasized that rivalries are likely to terminate when one or more of the rivalry antagonists faces a significant threat from another state, because such a threat requires many of the resources that were previously engaged in the enduring rivalry and perhaps an alliance with the former rival (Bennett 1996, Huth 1996b). Other scholars have made the even stronger claim that wars between the rivals themselves is a primary method

of rivalry resolution. Vasquez (1993, 195), for example, writes: "For rivals, the road to war is a long one in which each side learns from its interactions with the other that force and ultimately war are the only way of resolving certain mutually salient issues."

10. One might even argue that with learning, or put differently with clarification of the parameters of the conflict emphasized in integrationist conflict management, meaningful resolution will become all the harder. Citing Simmel, Coser (1956, 59) elaborates that a mediator "helps to strip the conflict of its nonrational and aggressive overtones. Yet this will not in itself allow the parties to abandon their conflicting behavior since, even boiled down to the 'facts of the case,' the conflicting claims remain to be dealt with." Dahrendorf (1959, 225) concurs: "The attempt to obliterate lines of conflict by ready ideologies of harmony and unity in effect serves to increase rather than decrease the violence of conflict manifestations."

11. Conflict regulation so defined does not connote and must be distinguished from suppression. As Dahrendorf (1959, 224–5) maintains, "effective suppression of conflict is in the long run impossible . . . either suppression amounts to complete nonrecognition and exclusion of opposition, in which case revolutionary changes . . . are virtually bound to occur, or suppression of opposition is coupled with a careful and continuous scrutiny of the embryonic manifest interests of the potential opposition, and changes are introduced from time to time which incorporate some of these interests. In the latter case, suppression is not complete, and violent conflicts may simmer under the surface for a long time before they erupt."

12. Another general implication of negative linkage is that policies in one arena may be utilized to influence the situation in another arena. Starr (1994, 486) elaborates as follows:

> Two-level thinking with substitutability erases the neat distinctions between domestic and foreign policy which are so important to many Realist models of international relations. Revolution and war will be linked through the decision calculus of policymakers surveying multi-level problems and solutions. Substitutability, in particular, tells us *not* to expect clear one-to-one relationships between some stimulus and some response. For example, governments . . . require resources for continued survival or viability. Government leaders can identify alternative, more or less substitutable, sources— domestic and foreign. Hence, the single aim of survival, given alternative strategies for obtaining resources, might result in "apparently incommensurable behaviors." That is, revolution or war might occur, given from whom one tries to extract those resources.

In this spirit, it should be noted that policy toward internal opposition may become an important *international* issue.

13. This formulation/implementation divide can be viewed as providing the leaders faced with costly policies with a method of hedging their bets, that is, formally pursuing a policy yet reneging on its implementation.

14. Coinage of the term, itself a play on Waltz's "second image," is attributable to Gourevitch (1978). It should be pointed out, however, that though Gourevitch himself does emphasize domestic competition over the realization of policy objectives (see 1978, 905–7), and though he does note Skocpol's (1979) thesis of social revolution, he is not primarily concerned with the impact of external considerations upon overt domestic conflict.

15. Parenthetically, while the puzzle at hand is especially relevant in protracted conflict, the puzzles addressed by Starr and his collaborators concerning the manipulation of capabilities have greater external validity, since these studies do not emphasize extensive domestic concern with policy concerning the external adversary—which is the primary caues for the linkage emphasized here.

References

Azar, Edward E. 1979. "Peace Amidst Development." *International Interactions* 6 (2): 203–40.

———. 1982. "The Codebook of the Conflict and Peace Data Bank (COPDAB): A Computer Assisted Approach to Monitoring and Analyzing International and Domestic Conflicts." College Park, MD: Center for International Development and Conflict Management, University of Maryland.

———. 1984. "The Theory of Protracted Social Conflict and the Challenge of Transforming Conflict Situations." In *Conflict Processes and the Breakdown of International Systems,* ed. Dina A. Zinnes. Denver, CO: Monograph Series in World Affairs, University of Denver, pp. 81–99.

———. 1985. "Protracted International Conflicts: Ten Propositions." *International Interactions* 12 (1): 59–70.

———. 1986. "Management of Protracted Social Conflict in the Third World." *Ethnic Studies Report* 4 (2).

———. 1990. *The Management of Protracted Social Conflict: Theory and Cases.* Aldershot, UK: Dartmouth Publishing Company.

——— and J. W. Burton, eds. 1986. *International Conflict Resolution: Theory and Practice.* Sussex, UK: Wheatsheaf.

———, Paul Jureidini, and Ronald McLaurin. 1978. "Protracted Social Conflict: Theory and Practice in the Middle East." *Journal of Palestine Studies* 8 (1): 41–60.

——— and C. Moon, eds. 1988. *National Security in the Third World: The Management of Internal and External Threats.* Aldershot, UK: Edward Elgar.

——— and C. Moon. 1986. "Managing Protracted Social Conflicts in the Third World: Facilitation and Development Diplomacy." *Millennium: Journal of International Studies* 15 (3): 393–406.

Bennett, D. Scott. 1996. "Security, Bargaining, and the End of Interstate Rivalry." *International Studies Quarterly* 40 (June): 157–84.

Berger, Peter L., and Thomas Luckmann. 1966. *The Social Construction of Reality: A Treatise in the Sociology of Knowledge.* New York: Anchor Books, Doubleday.

Bull, Hedley. 1977. *The Anarchical Society.* New York: Columbia University Press.

Cohen, Stephen P., and Edward E. Azar. 1981. "The Transition from War to Peace between Israel and Egypt." *Journal of Conflict Resolution* 25 (1): 87–114.

Coser, Lewis. 1956. *The Functions of Social Conflict.* New York: The Free Press.

Dahrendorf, Ralf. 1959. *Class and Class Conflict in Industrial Society.* Stanford, CA: Stanford University Press.

Friedman, Gil, and Harvey Starr. 1997. *Agency, Structure, and International Politics: From Ontology to Empirical Inquiry.* London: Routledge Press.

Geller, D. S. 1993. "Power Differentials and War in Rival Dyads." *International Studies Quarterly* 37 (June): 173–93.

Goertz, Gary. 1994. *Contexts of International Politics.* Cambridge: Cambridge University Press.

Goertz, Gary, and Paul F. Diehl. 1993. "Enduring Rivalries: Theoretical Constructs and Empirical Patterns." *International Studies Quarterly* 37 (June): 147–71.

———. 1995. "The Initiation and Termination of Enduring Rivalries: The Impact of Political Shocks." *American Journal of Political Science* 39 (February): 147–72.

———. 1996. "Taking 'Enduring' out of Enduring Rivalry: The Rivalry Approach to War and Peace." *International Interactions* 21 (3): 291–308.

Gourevitch, Peter. 1978. "The Second Image Reversed: The International Sources of Domestic Politics." *International Organization* 32 (Autumn): 881–912.

Hensel, Paul R. 1996. "Charting a Course to Conflict: Territorial Issues and Interstate Conflict, 1816–1992." *Conflict Management and Peace Science* 15 (1): 43–73.

Huth, Paul K. 1996a. "Enduring Rivalries and Territorial Disputes, 1950–1990." *Conflict Management and Peace Science* 5 (1): 7–41.

———. 1996b. *Standing Your Ground.* Ann Arbor, MI: University of Michigan Press.

——— and Bruce Russett. 1993. "General Deterrence between Enduring Rivals: Testing Three Competing Models." *American Political Science Review* 87 (1): 61–72.

Inglehart, Ronald. 1990. *Culture Shift in Advanced International Society.* Princeton, NJ: Princeton University Press.

McGinnis, Michael D., and John T. Williams. 1989. "Change and Stability in Superpower Rivalry." *American Political Science Review* 83 (December): 1101–23.

Morrow, James D. 1987. "On the Theoretical Basis of a Measure of National Risk Attitudes." *International Studies Quarterly* 31 (December): 423–38.

———. 1988. "Social Choice and System Structure in International Politics." *World Politics* 41 (1): 75–97.

———. 1994. *Game Theory for Political Scientists.* Princeton, NJ: Princeton University Press.

Most, Benjamin A., and Harvey Starr. 1989. *Inquiry, Logic and International Politics.* Columbia, SC: University of South Carolina Press.

Ordeshook, Peter C. 1986. *Game Theory and Poltical Theory.* New York: Cambridge University Press.

Organski, A. F. K., and J. Kugler. 1980. *The War Ledger.* Chicago: University of Chicago Press.

Putnam, Robert D. 1988. "Diplomacy and Domestic Politics: The Logic of Two-Level Games." *International Organization* 42 (Summer): 427–60.

Raiffa, H. 1982. *The Art and Science of Negotiation.* Cambridge, MA: Harvard University Press.

Rapoport, Anatol. 1960. *Fights, Games, and Debates.* Ann Arbor, MI: University of Michigan Press.

———. 1974. *Conflict in a Man-Made Environment.* Middlesex, UK: Penguin Books.

Rosenau, James N. 1990. *Turbulence in World Politics.* Princeton, NJ: Princeton University Press.

Simon, Marc V., and Harvey Starr. 1994. "Extraction, Allocation, and the Rise and Decline of States: A Simulation Analysis of Two-Level Security Management." Presented at the annual meeting of the Peace Science Society, Champaign-Urbana, Illinois.

———. 1996. "Extraction, Allocation, and the Rise and Decline of States." *Journal of Conflict Resolution* 40 (June): 272–97.

———. 1997. "A Two-Level Analysis of War and Revolution: A Dynamic Simulation of Response to Threat." In *Decision-Making on War and Peace: The Cognitive-Rational Debate,* ed. Nehemia Geva and Alex Mintz. Boulder, CO: Lynne Rienner, pp. 131–59.

Siverson, Randolph M., and Harvey Starr. 1991. *The Diffusion of War.* Ann Arbor, MI: University of Michigan Press.

Skocpol, Theda. 1979. *States and Social Revolutions: A Comparative Analysis of France, Russia, and China.* Cambridge: Cambridge University Press.

Starr, Harvey. 1978. "'Opportunity' and 'Willingness' as Ordering Concepts in the Study of War." *International Interactions* 4(4):363–87.

———. 1991a. "Opportunity and Willingness and the Nexus between Internal and External Conflict." Presented at the annual meeting of the Western Political Science Association, Seattle, WA.

———. 1991b. "The Relationship between Revolution and War: A Theoretical Overview." Presented at the annual meeting of the International Studies Association, Vancouver, BC.

———. 1994. "Revolution and War: Rethinking the Linkage between Internal and External Conflict." *Political Research Quarterly* 47 (2): 481–507.

——— and Michael D. McGinnis. 1992. "War, Revolution, and Two-Level Games: A Simple Choice-Theoretic Model." Presented at the Twenty-Sixth North American meeting of the Peace Science Society, Pittsburgh, PA.

——— and Benjamin A. Most. 1976. "The Substance and Study of Borders in International Relations Research." *International Studies Quarterly* 20 (December): 581–620.

Thompson, William R. 1995. "Principal Rivalries." *Journal of Conflict Resolution* 39 (June): 195–223.

Tilly, Charles. 1985. "Connecting Domestic and International Conflicts, Past and Present." In *Dynamic Models of International Conflict,* ed. Urs Luterbacher and Michael D. Ward. Boulder, CO: Lynne Rienner, pp. 517–31.

Tsebelis, George. 1990. *Nested Games: Rational Choice in Comparative Politics.* Berkeley, CA: University of California Press.

Vasquez, John A. 1993. *The War Puzzle.* Cambridge: Cambridge University Press.

——— and Richard W. Mansbach. 1984. "The Role of Issues in Global Cooperation and Conflict." *British Journal of Political Science* 14 (September): 411–33.

Williams, John T., and Michael D. McGinnis. 1988. "Sophisticated Reaction in the U.S.-Soviet Arms Race: Evidence of Rational Expectations." *American Journal of Political Science* 32 (November): 968–95.

——— and Michael D. McGinnis. 1992. "The Dimension of Superpower Rivalry: A Dynamic Factor Analysis." *Journal of Conflict Resolution* 36 (March): 86–118.

CHAPTER FOUR

Conceptualizing and Identifying Crisis in Protracted Social Conflict

G. Dale Thomas

Introduction

Scholars and lay people alike have, during the twentieth century, become increasingly preoccupied by conflicts between states. Clearly, given the destructiveness of the two world wars and the intensity of superpower relations, this focus seems justified. However, other types of conflict, those based in nonstate identity associations, are historically more prevalent. Indeed, the destruction caused by religious wars—only one of many types of identity-based conflict—led to the establishment of the modern state system embodied in the Peace of Westphalia. While superpower politics resigned the study of nonstate identity-based conflicts to a darkened corner, the end of the Cold War has renewed interest in conflicts that have their foundations in social (or nonstate-identity) distinctions. Edward Azar's work on Protracted Social Conflict (PSC) preceded this latest swing toward studying social conflict and provides an excellent base on which to build. Furthermore, these conflicts can be studied with many of the same tools developed for the study of Cold War politics of which one of the most notable is the concept of crisis.

Crisis research, once a staple of the field of international relations, has gone into decline. A steady stream of articles that began appearing in the 1960s and continued well into the 1980s and even 1990 has now slowed to a trickle. Much of this literature can be divided into two major categories: decision-making and international interaction, or systemic analysis.

Charles Hermann's work has been among the most influential of the decision-making literature, which finds its primary contemporary scholar in Michael Brecher, while Charles McClelland's writing has formed the backbone of the international interaction literature. Edward Azar, Karen pler, and others have also written in the area of international interaction. he international interaction literature has been built primarily on the study of event data pioneered by McClelland and Azar and continued at the present by such researchers as Philip Schrodt.

The international interaction literature argues that crises are manifest in objective material form and can therefore be identified from data. However, a continuing problem within this school has been the difficulty of establishing an acceptable method for objectively identifying such crises. Initially, the problem derived from researcher preconceptions that crises result only from more conflictual behavior; however, as Azar and Stephen Cohen (1979) have pointed out, crises can result from unusual levels of cooperation between dyad members, particularly in cases of PSC. This realization has led to redefining crisis as a significant deviation from the normal behavior of a dyad. Thus, crisis becomes relative to the dyad in question, both in the quantity and quality of interaction.

The scuttling of any objective set of conditions that can be used across all cases for the identification of crises has prompted a search for nonetheless objective alternatives that can still be used to identify crises in their relative form. Azar and his research collaborators have relied on a statistical method of constructing a Normal Relations Range (NRR) by taking the mean of all scaled directed dyadic behavior and assuming that activity between one standard deviation above and below this mean appropriately captures the normal behavior of the dyad. Rasler (1984) has since followed a similar method in examining crises in Lebanon. Nonetheless, this method is based on an extraordinarily strong assumption of the normal distribution of events. Thus, while resolving the problem of the mistaken common objective nature of crises, researchers have created problems by imposing structure upon data through often unwarranted assumptions of normality.

This chapter proposes the use of three generalizable models with their respective methods that seek structure inherent in data in order to determine normal behavior for a specific dyad. The presence of structure may allow one to inductively establish the existence of crises. The first model assumes randomness—the only pattern in the dyadic interaction is a lack of pattern—and thus rejects social scientific "laws"; the second model reflects a deterministic and nonlinear understanding of reality deriving from the recent study of chaotic behavior in systems; and finally, the third model attempts to identify crises through pattern recognition using Hidden Markov Models (HMM). However, before exploring the three models, protracted social conflict and crisis must be clearly conceptualized.

Conceptualizing Crisis in Protracted Social Conflict

Azar and his coauthors argue that protracted conflicts have the following characteristics: "*duration* (protractedness) of a high-conflict NRR," "*fluctuation* in the intensity and frequency of interaction," "conflict *spillover* into all domains," "strong *equilibrating forces* that constrain interactions to remain within the existing NRR and force interaction trends back to the NRR when they go beyond its boundaries whether in conflict or cooperation," and the "*absence of a distinct determination*" (Azar, Jureidini, and McLaurin 1978, 53). PSC is a subset of protracted conflict and can be further specified by (1) multi-ethnic and communal cleavages and disintegrations, (2) underdevelopment, and (3) distributive injustice (Azar 1985). Additionally, Azar suggests that a PSC is a conflict "in which structural behavior (ethnic, religious, linguistic, economic) has affected overt hostile behavior (interaction), creating a complicated causal network that makes these conflicts difficult to solve" (Azar 1984, 85).

Coming from a different angle, Gurr operationally defines a protracted communal conflict (or PSC) "as three successive five-year periods in which group members took part in anti-state terrorism or rebellion to promote or defend their collective interests" (Gurr 1992, 5). Gurr captures the nature of a protracted conflict chronologically. However, what may be far more significant is that PSCs become, according to Azar, the "locus of identity" for participants (Azar 1984). The time that elapses from the beginning of the conflict until the conflict becomes the "locus of identity" is relative to each PSC; thus, there are problems with defining a PSC by its chronological time duration.

PSCs evolve into what appear to be "almost intransitive systems": "An observer might see one kind of behavior over a very long time, yet a completely different kind of behavior could be just as natural for the system. . . . It can stay in one equilibrium or the other, but not both. Only a kick from outside can force it to change states" (Gleick 1987, 169). Azar argues that trying to resolve a PSC in an area that is characterized by underdevelopment without alleviating the underdevelopment is *futile* [emphasis added]. He contends that "conflict resolution can truly occur and last only if satisfactory amelioration of the conflict of underdevelopment occurs as well" (1985, 69). Indeed, Azar suggests, "studying protracted conflict leads one to conclude that peace is development in the broadest sense of the term" (1985, 69).

Furthermore, Ross (1993) argues that any solution based on interests applied to conflicts in which the negative images of both sides held by the other make cooperation a less acceptable outcome than conflict will fail unless efforts are also made to change the psychocultural attitudes of the two groups. One must address not only interests but interpretations as well. In a review of the four major attempts at conflict resolution in Northern Ireland, Ross finds that in all the cases the attempts focused on either interests or interpretations but not both at the same time. Ross (1993) argues that all four consequently failed. Thus, the literature implies that the system in which a PSC takes place can only permanently escape the state of PSC, and thus its NRR, through a very specific shock to the system: underdevelopment must be eliminated and, concurrently, participants' images of "the other" must be modified. However, both images of "the other" and underdevelopment remain rooted in the multicausal structure identified by Azar.

Hermann defines a system as "a set of actors (e.g., nations, international organizations, and so on) interacting with one another in established patterns and through designated structures" (Hermann 1972, 8). Figure 4.1 extends Azar's conception of multiple causality (Azar 1985, 88) to include the structure of a four-principal-actor PSC system as found in Northern Ireland.[1] The roots of a PSC lie in Azar's structural behavior; however, following Hermann's lead, the system of a PSC includes the actors and their established patterns of interaction. With, one hopes, a clearer understanding of the nature of PSC, we can now turn to a discussion of crisis.

Crisis, once an indispensable term in international relations, has fallen into relative disuse. Yet, it continues to be a part of the popular vocabulary for describing certain political events. Indeed as McClelland (1961, 83) first wrote in 1961: "International crises tend to appear as first-order realities. They seem to be givens of history and, therefore, do not call for particular identification or definition. 'Everybody' knows when one happens." Perhaps, the familiarity of the term has contributed to its conceptual demise. Everyone knows what it means, but few seem to agree on a definition. Thus, as early as 1977, Parker documents four published discussions of the term's meaning that reviewed numerous competing definitions.

Nonetheless, the lack of a common meaning has not affected the shared belief in the importance of understanding crises. Parker (1977, 230) writes: "They all agree that conflict managers need to know when and why crises

Figure 4.1 The Structure of a Four-Principal-Actor PSC System with Actors (A, B, C, and D)

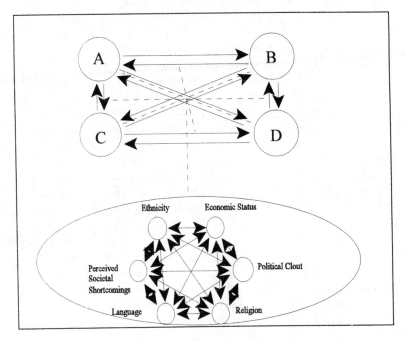

erupt and how these crises can be minimized. . . . They must thus have a model . . . , theory, or just tested propositions about crisis initiation, escalation, continuation, and abatement, as well as a set of predictive indicators."

Even so, confusion over the meaning of crisis might reflect an attempt to combine apples and kiwis. Raymond Aron comments: "It has not yet been proven that 'crisis situations' are all alike. It is possible that each crisis is unique or, if you prefer, has its own particular story" (cited in Hermann 1969, 410). Nonetheless, common elements seem to exist, since even in popular speech certain events are labeled crises. Indeed, Hermann (1969, 411) suggests, "if we *correctly* recognize a few critical properties of an international situation which identify it as a member of a general set of situations, we may establish many things about it even without examining many other qualities that make it unique."

Thus, international relations scholars have sought to identify these critical properties. The process has not been without difficulty. "Definitions are either extraordinarily specific and hence not widely applicable to a variety of situations, organizations, and subjects; or they are so broadly inclusive as to blur distinctions between crises and noncrises" (Robinson 1972, 22–23). In the 1970s and 1980s, reviewing, critiquing, and cataloging these definitional exercises became a cottage industry. Crisis definitions have been variously classified, including such schemes as substantive—procedural, rational—empiricist, micro—macro, and objective—subjective (Robinson 1972; Haas 1986). For example, whereas substantive definitions identify the specific content of a situation, procedural definitions apply to any situation. Weiner and Kahn give a list of 12 generic characteristics, such as "crisis is often a turning point in an unfolding sequence of events and actions . . . crisis is a threat to the goals and objectives of those involved" et cetera (cited in Robinson 1972, 21). However, the most comprehensive categorization scheme is proposed by Haas, who suggests a tree of metaphysics, epistemology, and levels of analysis (Haas 1986). Although Haas' ordering is not important, he addresses the primary divisions in crisis research.

Haas differentiates a "rationalist" versus an "empiricist" epistemology. Rationalism involves an arbitrary definition based on self-evident or logical grounds. It is important that Haas (1986, 43) asks, "But how are we to classify a situation as a 'crisis' or as a 'non-crisis'? If we rely on intuition alone we are using a rationalist approach. But if we insist that we must see data before we can classify a situation as a crisis, we are engaging in an empirical exercise." Indeed, he suggests an a priori approach prevents one from researching the term's meaning:

> It should be noted that it is a contradiction to justify a rationalist definition on the basis of empirical research. To pretend that empirical efforts can be used to exclude one possible factor (surprise) as a component of otherwise nonempirically-derived definitions is to beg the question of why several dozen possible components, used in other formulations, are excluded without any such evidence. The variety of definitions . . . in . . . idealist metaphysical conceptions is perhaps the most impressive *reductio ad absurdum* argument against rationalism: as definitions multiply, intuition cannot be used as a reliable standard. *A priori* definitions can only establish that they are self-evident when scholars are in universal agreement. (Haas 1986, 43)

Alternatively, the empirical method "seeks precise measurement of the phenomenon. The empirical approach involves a researcher in the task of assembling variables that are claimed to be direct measures of 'crisis'; an empirical study is then undertaken to see which measure best taps the phenomenon" (Haas 1986, 26–27).

The rationalist-empiricist division coincides well with the more widely recognized categories of the decision-making versus the systemic study of crisis, which have been apparent from the 1960s on (Hermann 1969). As Parker explains: "Those who have written in the tradition of McClelland have tended to describe or explain crises at the nation or systemic levels, and those following Hermann have studied the behavior of individuals" (Parker 1977, 227). The decision-making-systemic distinction reflects both different ontological positions as well as levels of analysis, but various attempts have been made to reconcile the two lines of analysis. Haas writes: "For Phil Williams . . . another way of stating the micro-macro distinction is that a *foreign policy crisis* concerns just one country, whereas an *international crisis* has two or more countries in confrontation" (Haas 1986, 27). The Williams distinction seems somewhat accepted and appears in a recent survey of the field of crisis, conflict, and war literature (Brecher 1996a). Indeed, decision-making crises and systemic crises have become identified with foreign policy crisis and international crisis respectively. Finally, the decision-making-systemic distinction has also been labeled monadic-dyadic. "'Monadic' studies analyze the behavior of a single actor within a crisis environment; 'dyadic' studies ignore internal attributes and focus primarily on the sequence of transactions between actors during a crisis" (Rasler 1984, 428).

The decision-making analysis of crisis has received the greatest attention. A review of a recent undergraduate text in international relations turned up only a decision making perspective on crisis (Goldstein 1994). Significantly, a relative consensus has developed around Hermann's definition of crisis as "a situation that (1) threatens high priority goals of the decision-making unit, (2) restricts the amount of time available for response before the decision is transformed, and (3) surprises the members of the decision making unit by its occurrence" (Hermann 1969, 414; Kegley and Wittkopf 1993; Brecher 1996b; Brecher and Wilkenfeld 1982). One of the basic points of the decision-making school is that: "The decision-makers behave according to their interpretation of the situation, not according to its 'objective' character as viewed by some theoretical omnipotent observer" (Hermann 1969, 413). Thus, the decision making approach reflects a subjective ontology. However, as decision makers act upon their interpretation of a situation, the crisis can become objective.

In sum, a foreign policy crisis arises from the highest decision makers' images of pressure(s) to cope with externally focused stress. It also marks the beginning of an international crisis. Herein lies the analytical link between the two levels of crisis. An international crisis erupts when there is behavioral change by one or more states leading to more hostile interaction; the change in A's behavior triggers a foreign policy crisis for B, first through B's perception of threat and, later, of time pressure and heightened likelihood of war. Thus perception and behavior, state level and system/interactor level, foreign policy crisis and international crisis, are interlinked. (Brecher 1996a, 128)

Less consensus exists within the systemic school. At least three subschools exist: Young's analysis of system stability, McClelland's interaction approach, and Azar's Normal Relations Range (NRR). Hermann not only defines a system as "a set of actors (e.g., nations, international organizations, and so on) interacting with one another in established patterns and through designated structures," but continues by saying that "in any given international political system, critical variables must be maintained within certain limits or the instability of the system will be greatly increased" (Hermann 1972, 10). Young writes: "An international crisis, then, is a set of rapidly unfolding events which raises the impact of destabilizing forces in the general international system or any of its subsystems substantially above 'normal' (i.e., average) levels and increases the likelihood of violence occurring in the system" (cited in Hermann 1969, 412). Similarly, Young suggests the following:

> Crisis refers to situations which have important implications for the stability for some pattern of interaction, system, or subsystem. Crises are in no sense limited to situations which actively jeopardize the stability of the international system, but they do raise certain considerations concerning stability. To begin with, stability refers here to the ability of a system or pattern of interactions to undergo a disruptive sequence of events without breaking down or suffering qualitative changes of nature. (cited in Hermann 1972, 8)

Young's understanding of crisis when coupled with the work of the two major interaction-approach scholars provides a solid basis for conceptualizing crisis in PSC.

The interaction approach first suggested by McClelland in 1961 examines the exchanges of words and the deeds of actors. The approach is systemic in that it studies the external behavior of actors: "Those who concentrate on crisis decision making problems deal mainly with *intra-unit* situations and processes whereas the students of international systems primarily investigate *inter-unit* phenomena" (McClelland 1972, 85–86). One of McClelland's major contributions has been his procedure for studying such activity, that is the World Event-Interaction Survey (WEIS), a method for counting and recording events. McClelland has also called these "interactions," hence the "interaction" approach. "Interactions are, by our definition, single action items of a nonroutine, extraordinary, or newsworthy character that in some clear sense are directed across a national boundary and have, in most instances, a specific foreign target" (McClelland and Hoggard 1969, 713).

On the basis of the interaction approach, McClelland asks: "Can a 'change of state' be detected in the activities of a system in the transition from a non-crisis period to a crisis period?" (McClelland 1968, 161). McClelland's analysis finds that changes in measures of both volume and variety mark crises. Subsequently, McClelland and Hoggard compare crises with violent weather:

> Flurries of international activity appear suddenly and then recede. Most of these flareups are easily connected with the strong conflicts that are called international crises. Such conflicts are analogous to storm fronts and appear to override the usual pattern of international action and response. These fronts are marked by sharp increases in interaction including the cooperative types of behavior. (721, 723)

Although McClelland seems to prefer the "change of state conception" of crisis, he also examines crises as "turning points in conflicts" (see Boulding 1962; Weiner and Kahn cited in Robinson 1972), "preludes to war," "and averted approaches to war." He further states: "Crises are most commonly thought of as interpositions between the prolongation of peace and the outbreak of war" (McClelland 1972, 83; 1961; 1968).

Normal Relations Range

Other systemic writers appear to have built upon McClelland's foundation. "Richard Beal . . . , similarly, has developed several ingenious measures of 'crisis' in terms of event acceleration, such as event flow, event reliance, event uncertainty, and event volume" (Haas 1986, 33). Edward Azar follows a line of reasoning similar to McClelland's suggesting that crises reflect an alteration in interaction. Comparing the two: for McClelland, crisis is an ontologically objective phenomenon:

> From a systemic standpoint, a reasonable definition of international crisis is that it is a particular kind of alteration of the pattern of the interflowing

actions between conflict parties. The change takes place in a short time and is large enough to be recognized. Thus the uptrend stage of a crisis (if there is such) should establish a change from the noncrisis condition to the crisis condition and the downtrend should be another change of state in the interaction flow, perhaps different from both the uptrend and the noncrisis situations. (McClelland 1972, 97)

Similarly for Azar:

Over a period of time any two nations establish between them an interaction range which they perceive as "normal." This *normal relations range* (NRR) is an interaction range (on a scale from very friendly to very hostile) which tends to incorporate most of the signals exchanged between that pair and is bound by two critical thresholds—an *upper and a lower threshold.* The upper critical threshold is that level of hostility above which signals exhibited by either member of the interacting dyad are regarded as unacceptable to the other. Interaction above the present upper critical threshold (or present upper tolerable limit) for more than a very short time implies that a crisis situation has set in. The lower critical threshold on the other hand is that level of friendliness beyond which signals between the members imply that some integrative shift in their relations—the inverse of a crisis—has occurred. (Azar 1972, 184–185; Azar and Cohen 1979; Azar 1978)

Azar is clearly arguing an objective ontology for crisis[2] but contending that crisis is relative the dyad in question: "each pair of nations in the international system has a different NRR and different levels of critical thresholds depending upon their past history, cultural congruity, tolerable and expected modes of communication and the like" (Azar et al. 1977, 197). This is an important point also supported by Hermann: "A conflict between parties that continues at a relatively constant level of intensity would not constitute a crisis, but a sudden shift in the level of hostilities—most notably from peace to war—would be a crisis at least for the subsystem comprised of the combatants" (Hermann 1972, 10). The conception of crisis resulting only from more hostile behavior remained unchallenged until a ground-breaking article by Azar and Stephen Cohen in 1979.[3]

Not only does movement above the upper critical threshold constitute a crisis, but, we want to propose, so does a downward movement into abnormally cooperative interaction. In either case, the normal range of responses will seem inadequate, and a threat to the consensual definition of national identity and solidarity will occur. When the upper limit is crossed due to conflictive events of unexpected intensity, the threat is that serious material and human damage could be done the state. When on the other hand, it is the lower limit which is crossed and the crisis is due to an unusually cooperative event, a response may be evoked that appears equally threatening to the national consensus and the delicate balance of national solidarity. Perhaps because to the superpowers conflictive crises have appeared to pose the major danger—they require considerable outside intervention and present considerable external threat, international relations researchers have focused on the dynamics of those crises which are conflictive. It must, however, be realized that either type of crisis is a serious matter for national decision makers. . . . It is the crossing of the threshold on the side of unusual cooperation that provokes the real shock of surprise. (166–67)

To summarize, actors tend to establish a range of activity—varying somewhere between extreme cooperation and extreme hostility—that becomes accepted as normal for the participants. Deviations from this normal range, either toward greater hostility or cooperation, represent the onset of crises. Sloan, a co-contributor to some of Azar's research, follows essentially the same definition of the NRR. However, he extends its possible use to domestic domains (Sloan 1978). Indeed, Rasler successfully applies the NRR to her study of the 1976 Lebanese crisis (Rasler 1984). Consequently, one can reasonably utilize the NRR concept for identifying crises in PSC, such as in Northern Ireland.

The interaction approach, and more specifically the use of an NRR, to identify crisis can be criticized for black-boxing decision makers. However, considerable justification seems to exist for doing so. McClelland addresses the point as follows:

Since the strategy of interaction analysis is to exploit a different sector of this unceasing and spiraling process, the investigator of interactions will prefer to deal with approximations and generalizations about the traits of participating actors that would be too inexact and too hypothetical for the purposes of the student of decision making. In other words, the research bet of an interaction approach is that a large amount of the work of decision making study can be by-passed safely in arriving at explanations of international behavior. The contention is that the performances of the participants—the interaction sequences—are reliable indicators of active traits of participating actors. Hence, we are free to build hypothetical constructs concerning these pertinent actor traits and to make tentative statements about the patterns of interaction to which the traits are coupled. (1961, 194)

Alternatively, he contends that "behind the welter of events there is a large amount of repetition and rule-bound behavior in international politics. It is the tendency toward some consistency of action that gives the promise that the international system may be managed" (1968, 165). Although Mc-Clelland's arguments are a priori, they appear to receive similar support from the most active contemporary decision making crisis analyst, Brecher:

> Stress is a shared challenge, an indicator of impending harm and danger. States have common traits that outweigh their diversity, especially the need to survive and minimize harm from external foes. And foreign policy decision makers, in coping with crisis-generated stress act as humans do in all comparable situations of impending harm. In essence, the commonality of statehood, stress and human response to expected harm, or gain, overrides all variations among specific states and generates a near-identical pattern of coping in an external crisis. (1996b, 229)

A priori arguments aside, Rasler's research findings support the argument "that dyadic indicators can be sensitive measures of complex political behavior" (Rasler 1984, 443).

As a counterpoint, Rasler's findings also suggest that researchers must nonetheless remain sensitive to decision maker's perceptions. Event data alone without a contextual background can mislead:

> Because events which trigger crises ultimately depend on how they are perceived by the participants, low intensity events of political significance may have the same effect as high intensity events. These subtle and sometimes intangible shifts in political factors are difficult for any early warning indicator to capture. To allow behavioral deviations from some norm to signal the onset of a crisis increases the risk of misidentifying interaction sequences as crises when they are not regarded as such by the decisionmaker. (Rasler, 1984, 442)

Thus, although not going as far as Haas' dualist metaphysical position,[4] Rasler's analysis does lend overall support to the use of an NRR to identify crises while emphasizing the importance of referencing other sources to provide, as accurately as possible, the decision-making contexts of crises. Nonetheless, how can one calculate an NRR?

According to the literature, an NRR can in theory be operationalized in three ways: empirically, historically, and statistically. In Azar's initial formulation of the concept, he argues an NRR can be operationalized empirically by "content analyzing statements of key decision-makers as they express acceptable or tolerable limits which their target nations can behave towards them without a need for a reassessment of the existing relations between them" (Azar 1972, 189). Alternatively, a researcher can attempt to identify the mix of events that have led to situations that are perceived as crises in the literature. Nevertheless, although Azar contends that the first two methods can be used, neither has actually been employed in NRR research.[5]

The third technique originally mentioned by Azar is the only one used in practice. This involves an arbitrary construction based on taking the mean of scale values for all signals exchanged in a dyad and moving away from the mean by one standard deviation in each direction. In Azar's research, the actual values of the NRR upper and lower parameters are one Conflict and Peace Databank (COPDAB) scale point above and one COPDAB scale point below the given values (Azar 1972). Sloan also uses the same procedure "placing a confidence interval of one standard deviation around the mean of Lebanese domestic conflict behavior" (Sloan 1978, 150). Although Andriole and Young (1977) do not explicitly use the term NRR, they are interested in deviations from a band of normal behavior. Similar to Azar's work, their analysis uses Z-scores to characterize crisis situations. Rasler explicitly uses an NRR based on Andriole and Young's work using Z-scores to characterize crisis and precrisis situations (1984).

Although not entirely static, an NRR is not expected to change very rapidly. In his early work, Azar assumes that "a dyad's NRR will not change significantly during a relatively short period of time, such as six months to one year" (1972, 184). Azar (1978, 228) also suggests that: "the level and width of the NRR of a pair of nations does change over time, but the process is a long one. Changes are usually due to significant shifts in a nation's economy, technological capacities, political system, or military capabilities." Sloan (1978, 149) concurs, saying: "Changes in a dyad's NRR may result (albeit slowly) from changes in each actor's domestic or international conditions, attributes, or behavior."

Is an NRR merely a description based on arbitrary research assumptions? In other words, do researchers assume an NRR exists and therefore observe or, in fact, create one? One can clarify the issue by returning to the ways in which an NRR can be constructed: empirically, historically, and statistically. Theoretically, analyzing statements of key decision makers could allow one to establish the range of predictable and acceptable behavior in a dyad. However, although a decision maker might specify certain types of behavior that would require a change in policy and attitude toward greater hostility or cooperation within a dyad, a researcher cannot easily determine if the information reflects the decision maker's actual position or is a ploy for political gain.

Inventorying the mix of events preceding acknowledged crisis periods can allow one to establish possible boundaries, but only in special cases. Given the possibility of an NRR shifting through time, these boundaries may change. Therefore, one would need a number of crises both toward greater hostility and greater cooperation to occur within a relatively short period of time to establish an NRR. However, crises are by definition supposed to be unusual events and therefore too few in number to reasonably fix the critical thresholds of an NRR. Thus, for most situations this method seems inappropriate. Nonetheless, as Schrodt (1997b) has recently pointed out, protracted conflicts lead to co-adaptive behavior between organizations thereby establishing a set of standard operating procedures (SOPs) that neither side can move away from without a loss of utility. Therefore, although this method does not seem applicable to all situations, a survey of events preceding crises may be an excellent alternative in the study of PSC.

Consequently, in most cases, one is left only with the statistical method for fixing the upper and lower thresholds of the NRR. Yet in the literature, this method has deprived the NRR of any objective existence due to the arbitrary placement of upper and lower thresholds. Researchers have based their decisions regarding the placement of thresholds on the premise that event data are normally distributed. However, in Azar's own pioneering 1972 article in which he introduces the concept of an NRR, all three of his dyads involving Egypt show definite bimodal distributions with the mean falling on a scale value without any corresponding events in two out of the three dyads. Furthermore, in establishing an NRR in this manner, a researcher creates a circular argument. An NRR exists because one can create a confidence interval of one standard deviation around a mean and call it a normal relations range. Means are sensitive to outlying observations and, moreover, the supposedly most "normal" behavior may not even exist. Thus, real problems exist with the statistical construction of an NRR.

Nevertheless, a normal range of relations seems intuitively reasonable and, furthermore, such a concept can be useful in characterizing crisis in PSC. Building on Young's conception of crisis as a situation that threatens the stability of a system, crisis in PSC can be defined as a situation that threatens the stability of the system through either a possible change of actors or a modification of the NRR between any of the system's dyads. Crises resulting from a possible change of actors include a break up of a principal actor into two or more new actors or the consolidation of two or more principal actors in the system. The first appears more likely and can occur particularly during a shift toward greater cooperation among the principal actors leading to threats to group cohesion. Any event or series of events that causes actors to seriously re-evaluate their normal pattern of relations, or NRR, with the other system actors also constitutes a crisis. Situations do not have to result in long-term changes in the system in order to be a crisis. However, crises are key events that clearly threaten the stability of the system.

Identifying Crisis in Protracted Social Conflict

In order to identify a crisis in PSC one must specify both the principal actors and the NRRs among these actors. The principal actors at a particular point in time can readily be identified through a variety of secondary sources; however, as has previously been shown, operationalizing the NRR poses considerable difficulty. Consequently, this section details three proposed methods for identifying the NRRs of a PSC. The first section examines the reasonableness of looking for law like regularities in the behavior intensity of the conflict. The second section uses "chaos theory" to look at PSC as an iterative process. Finally, the third section discusses Schrodt's work on pattern recognition using Hidden Markov Models (HMM) (1997a, 1997b) to identify crisis situations in PSC.

Randomness

A vociferous debate has raged in social science journals at different times during the second half of the twentieth century between those who assert the similarity of the social and natural sciences and those who object, contending that man is by nature self-defining and therefore distinct from objects of study in the natural sciences. The fundamental question: do laws governing human behavior exist, and if so, can researchers successfully identify them?

Although an extreme position rejects even the possibility of understanding another's action, a more moderate stand suggests that one can identify reasons why an individual has acted a certain way at a certain time but without asserting a general law. Brian Fay identifies this as the "singularity thesis of human action" (Fay 1994). Or, in other words:

> reason-explanations invoke principles of action (as opposed to empirical laws) to explain human behavior . . . the relationship between principles and their outcomes is not essentially one of a recurring pattern, but is rather one in which the outcome (in this case the action) is intrinsically

(logically, conceptually) connected with the principle itself. Reasons give the grounds for which the action is a consequent, and, since the relationship between ground and consequent is logical rather than empirical, . . . reason-explanations do not require general statements linking a kind of reason with a kind of action. (Fay 1994, 92)

Although Fay rejects the singularity thesis, he notes additional support for the thesis in the essential-nature argument: "good explanations are those which ultimately rest on an account of the nature of the basic entities involved. Knowing that the essence of an entity is to act in a certain manner means that the operation of this entity does not require further explanation in terms of some general law under which one could subsume its fundamental dispositions" (Fay 1994, 94).

Alternatively, the argument is often made that social scientific laws are at best impractical and at worst impossible simply due to the complexity of the phenomena under study. Almost all social systems are open in some sense, allowing for an almost endless supply of contributing factors. How can one identify a causal mechanism—"a series of events governed by lawlike regularities that lead from the explanans to the explanandum" (Little 1991)—in such a morass? For many scholars, you simply cannot. Nonetheless, even in physics, the epitome of natural science, many fundamental discoveries have been made not by studying closed systems but by focusing on factors deemed relevant.[6] Thus, the question becomes, how much can one safely ignore.

While both the singularity thesis and the complexity arguments are open for study, an additional factor—the arrow of time—further complicates the situation. The unidirectionality of time is a fundamental belief underlying virtually all natural and social research. Given open systems, verification of lawlike regularities can be nightmarish; the same or even similar conditions may be difficult or impossible to find.

The outlook for social scientific laws seemingly looks bleak, but one can reasonably ask if researchers in the natural sciences can ignore astrophysics when calculating classical mechanics equations, cannot scholars in the social sciences make similar choices. Although the answer may be subject specific, an answer can easily be found. If lawlike regularities do not exist or cannot be readily identified due to system complexity, then, in the presence of any variation, the only pattern in one's data should be a lack of pattern—for example, the progression of events, or the symbols used to represent them, should approximate a random sequence.

Even though one would not expect interaction intensity to be essentially random, this remains a possibility, however unlikely. Therefore, one of the first steps in assessing the underlying dynamics of dyadic interaction should be to test the hypothesis that no discernable relationship exists between events: the probability of an event at time $_t$ is independent of the outcome of event $_{i<t<i}$.

The absence of a pattern suggests that the best hope of a researcher in such a situation is a detailed case study. Alternatively, if events within the sequence show dependent probabilities, then, depending upon the degree of relatedness, the system can be treated as closed, and infinite complexity can be rejected.

In the absence of *ceteris paribus*, an NRR assumes a relatively closed system. To illustrate, the actions of farmers in Uganda are normally assumed to be irrelevant to events in Northern Ireland. Although an NRR may change, it is believed to do so relatively slowly as a function of technological, economic, and social changes within dyad members. Consequently, the objective ontological position of an NRR, and thus crisis, is undermined in the absence of a relatively closed system. Furthermore, in the absence of structure, any event is as likely as any other. Therefore, crisis as commonly understood in the systemic literature would not exist, since there could not be deviations from a nonexistent underlying pattern.

Chaotic Behavior in Systems

Complex modernizing societies are regularly beset by so many chronic problems that there is a normal propensity to become preoccupied only with those which erupt in an acute form. Then, certain instrumental values take control so that it is assumed that the "reasons" for the problem should be exposed, the causes should be removed, and the needed remedies and reforms should be instituted. The problem-solving blanket is thrown over the flames of conflict in the expectation that they will be smothered. Underlying is the faith that no problem can fail to have a relevant solution. The devoted pursuit of causes and remedies will succeed.

—Charles McClelland

The new science of chaos is reordering the way in which many perceive the world. Deterministic chaotic behavior has been found lurking in the shadows of many systems formerly perceived to be stable, and an eerie order has been found in what were believed to be "random" systems. The philosophical and theoretical foundations of Newtonian science, which has undergird innovation not only in the natural sciences but the social sciences as well, have been weakened by repeated attacks in the twentieth century. As one physicist has suggested: "Relativity eliminated the Newtonian illusion of absolute space and time; quantum theory eliminated the Newtonian dream of a controllable measurement process; and chaos eliminates the Laplacian fantasy of deterministic predictability" (cited in Gleick 1987, 6). Given the interrelatedness of Enlightenment thought in both the natural and social sciences, many social theorists had already begun challenging the fundamental assumptions that prediction and control are possible for all social systems.

Questions of what we know, under what conditions will our knowledge remain valid, and what can we do with what we know, have been given new life and considerable vigor from "chaos theory."[7] Sociologists have been at the forefront of an effort to reconstruct theoretical understandings of social organization and collapse in light of nonequilibrium research. Specifically, recent articles have appeared in *Sociological Inquiry,* the *Social Sciences Journal, Behavioral Science, Human Relations,* and the *American Journal of Economics and Sociology* (such as, Loye and Eisler 1987; De Greene 1990; Young 1991; Baker 1993; Gregersen and Sailer 1993; Smith, D. 1995; Khalil 1995). Three major arguments of chaos theory are (1) "change isn't necessarily linear; that is, small causes can have larger effects," (2) "determinism and predictability are not synonymous—deterministic equations can lead to unpredictable results—chaos—when there is feedback within a system," and (3) "in systems that are 'far-from-equilibrium' (i.e., chaotic), change does not have to be related to external causes. Such systems can organize at a higher level of organization" (Robertson 1995, 12–13).

As Loye and Eisler (1987) have pointed out, even within the natural sciences, two main streams of thought are evident. The first form of chaos research developed out of the study of dynamics and is highly mathematic and well developed, whereas the second line of research is more metaphorical and can be found in biological evolution research and chemistry, as well as other areas. Similarly, within the social sciences two main trends can be found mirroring those of the natural sciences. One is modeled on the mathematical study of dynamics and uses techniques developed in physics to search for hidden underlying structure in time series data, while the other reflects a more general metaphorical application of chaos research.

Sociologists have been the major proponents of the second type of work, but the majority of articles using the mathematics of dynamical systems outside of the natural sciences are currently found in economics (for example, Brock 1986, Deneckere 1986, Frank and Stengos 1989, Frank et al. 1988, Grandmont and Malgrange 1986, Kelsey 1988, Mirowski 1990, Ramsey et al. 1990, Rosser 1990, Serletis 1996, White 1990). Furthermore, both mathematical and metaphorical chaos models are appearing in psychology. For example, Goertzel (1995a; 1995b) argues that belief systems are attractors and has attempted to construct a cognitive law of motion. In the meantime, more mathematically oriented international relations scholars have been pursuing the formal application of dynamic system modeling as in Saperstein's collaboration with Mandelbrot and Wisdom to examine chaos and the outbreak of war (Mandelbrot et al. 1984). Saperstein has also written two more recent articles on the utility of chaos as a tool in studying international relations (1994; 1995). Richards (1990; 1992; 1993) provides additional examples of dynamic system modeling. She finds support for chaotic models both in power concentration in the international system and in strategic decision making.[8]

Application of these methods should not be on the basis of trial and error but should be guided by theory In this respect, much of the early work in chaos is informing: scientists looked for analogous systems. Nonetheless, the following warning is relevant:

> There is a danger, however, in this new fascination with dynamic theory. The danger lies in the temptation to naively adopt a new terminology or set of metaphors, to merely redescribe the phenomena we have been studying for so long, and then conclude that we have explained them. Because dynamic concepts and theory are seductive, we may mistake translation for explanation. As a first step in going beyond mere redescription, we should apply the theory to particular phenomena and pursue the application in as rigorous of a fashion as we can, without trying to sidestep the theory's mathematical foundations. But the application should not be blind. We must demonstrate at each step that the phenomenon exhibits the characteristics assumed or predicted by the theory. In this process we must acknowledge the constraints imposed by our level of analysis (e.g., overt behavior) and by limitations in the quality and quantity of our measurements. Ultimately, the goal should be to build a dynamic model of the mechanism controlling the observed phenomenon from which new observable properties can be deduced and subjected to experimental test. (Robertson et al. 1993)

Although the roots of a PSC are supposedly located in structure, Azar's conceptualization of PSC is deeply rooted in the study of *process*.[9] Movement of a PSC through time defines many of its underlying characteristics. Azar argues that these types of conflicts,

> do not permit change in the fundamental grievances and continually reduce the chances for dealing with settlement issues. . . . In a protracted conflict

situation, the conflict becomes an arena for redefining issues rather than a means for adjudicating them; it is therefore futile to look for any ultimate resolution because the conflict process itself becomes the source rather than the outcome of policy. (1984, 89)

Furthermore, as Pruitt and Rubin have noted, a social categorization effect exists: "People like better, think more highly of, and discriminate in favor of other people with whom they are classed, regardless of the basis for the classification" (Pruitt and Rubin 1986, 70). As PSCs become the "locus of identity" for their participants, each side views itself more favorably than the other. Indeed, Azar and Cohen argue that "protracted conflicts tend to deepen and reinforce as they go on and to fix ever more firmly held mutual images of deception and hate" (Azar and Cohen 1979, 162). Consequently, a PSC should be conceptualized as an iterative process, a system moving through time, or a system involving motion.

Given that events represent discrete states, and therefore, that the system does not change continuously, a PSC system may perhaps be mathematically modeled using a first order difference equation:

(1) $$\Delta x \equiv x_{n+1} - x_n = G(x_n, c)$$

or

$$x_{n+1} = F(x_n, c)$$

where c are control parameters ($c \in R^k$) and n is a discrete time measure. A stimulus-response sequence can be seen in figure 4.2. Control parameters for a first-order difference equation modeling a stimulus-response sequence would, theoretically, include environmental constraints, or, more elaborately, could be expanded to include filters for perception and slippage in moving from intention to action. Such an expanded model would then be an environmentally situated mediated stimulus-response-model.[10]

The dynamics of such a system can also be viewed as a sequence of mappings, $F: x_n \rightarrow x_{n+1}$ (Jackson 1990). A PSC dynamical system is dissipative, in that resources, money, munitions, lives, and so on, expended in the conflict do not translate directly into gains, alternatively, one might argue that the system is both damped and driven. Jackson, speaking of dissipative systems generally, comments, "'dissipation' in the present sense does not necessarily imply that all states 'die,' but rather that there is an attraction toward some final, generally dynamic, set of states, called an *attractor*" (Jackson 1990, vol. 1, 143).

Figure 4.2 **Modeling a Stimulus Response Sequence with a First-Order Difference Equation**

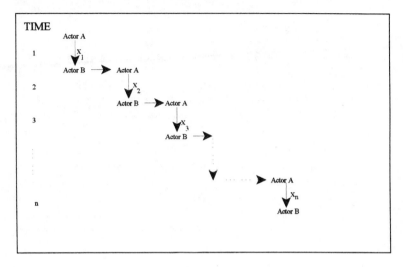

Schaffer and Kot (1985) have identified a taxonomy of motion that includes: point attractors, limit cycles, toroidal flow, strange attractors, and turbulence. "Loosely speaking, an attractor is something that 'attracts' initial conditions from a region around it once transients have died out" (Schaffer and Kot 1985, 342).[11] First, point attractors are similar to a pendulum that is damped by friction. "If we plot displacement (from the vertical) of the pendulum against its velocity, we observe oscillations that decay. Thus, there is an attracting point (zero displacement, zero velocity) to which almost all initial conditions converge" (Schaffer and Kot 1985, 342). Next, limit cycles, rather than decaying to a point, remain in a fixed loop. On the other hand, in a toroidal flow, the motion is on a donut. This can be created by taking a system that has a limit cycle and subjecting it to a periodic outside push. "The motion can be periodic, where the orbit winds around the torus an integer number of times before repeating itself. Or the motion can be quasi-periodic; the orbit never repeats itself, and in fact, covers the torus's entire surface" (Schaffer and Kot 1985, 342). Following Stewart, periodic behavior in a toroidal flow results from the combination of flows having periods whose ratio is a rational number. A quasi-periodic flow results from a ratio that is irrational (Stewart 1989).

Strange attractors are neither periodic nor quasi-periodic, but have orbits confined to a low dimensional surface. Schaffer and Kot continue:

> Motion on a strange attractor is often chaotic in the sense that it is impossible to forecast the system's long-term behavior in the presence of even the smallest amount of observational error; for practical purposes, these systems are stochastic. Nevertheless, over certain time scales, regularities may emerge, leading to the expression order in chaos. . . . To the extent that these regularities can be detected in real world data, it follows that fluctuations heretofore believed due to chance are in fact deterministic. (342)

The Poincaré-Bendixon Theorem says that for a typical structurally stable system in the plane, only two types of attractors exist: point and limit cycle attractors. Changing to a $2 + -$ *dimensional space* opens up the possibility for a strange attractor. *"The system may settle into a long-term behavior that is neither a point nor a limit cycle but is nonetheless an attractor in that it exhibits regular, albeit difficult to forecast beyond the immediate future, behavior"* (Stewart 1989).

Finally, turbulence involves highly erratic behavior like that found in boiling water. "One can say only that there is a distribution of positions and velocities to which the molecules as a whole converge" (Schaffer and Kot 1985, 342). Turbulence is the domain of statistics due to system complexity. If one wishes to determine the position and velocity of particular elements, they will appear as random and structureless even though these values are the result of a deterministic process. The complexity argument has been a major factor in the use of statistics in the social sciences.

However, as Froehling and his collaborators have argued: "it is possible that weakly turbulent fluid flow, which in principle must be considered as an infinite-dimensional system, can be modeled by a system with relatively few phase-space dimensions" (1981, 605). This is not to suggest that all phenomena can be described with few variables. Indeed, they continue: "Many natural phenomena . . . exhibit aperiodic behavior that can only be explained by a model with a very large number of dimensions." Thus, one must distinguish between systems with low- and high-dimensional aperiodicity. In the face of high-dimensional aperiodicity, statistical analysis appears to be the appropriate solution. Yet, if social phenomena can be shown to have low-dimensional aperiodicity (dynamic systems with strange attractors), then the processes can be modeled deterministically.

Metaphorically, the NRR of a PSC appears to be an attractor. To support this, here is a lengthy comment from Azar:

Any threats to the tolerable and predictable behavior between states (i.e., any threats to the level of interactions within the boundaries of the NRR) will mobilize domestic and international forces to restore the status quo or the return to within the NRR. When states are in a protracted social conflict NRR, these forces will act so as to push the violators of the norms back to within the acceptable and familiar limits. Thus, when the upper critical threshold of the NRR of two conflicting states is crossed, the conflict events would be of extraordinary intensity and would be evaluated as posing such serious material and human damage as to reduce the states' vitality. This situation might mobilize the international community in an extraordinary way to move the conflict toward the status quo (i.e., the present NRR).

When the lower critical threshold is crossed, the crisis is due to an unusually cooperative event (such as, in the Middle East, Sadat's visit to Jerusalem). Such an event would demand an answer that would constitute a threat to the national consensus as defined in the protracted conflict, and therefore tend to destroy the delicate balance of national solidarity. This is why the status quo, with intermittent rising tensions and instability, is the most probable and most predictable future of nations that are locked into a protracted social conflict. (Azar, Jureidini, and McLaurin 1978, 52–53)

Similarly, Azar contends PSCs are inertial systems:

Systems with high inertia levels such as protracted social conflicts are much less affected by environmental interventions than those with low inertia levels. These high inertia systems are ultra-stable; that is, they resist change, even when the deviations from equilibrium are fairly strong and frequent. . . . The inertia of these conflicts is what allows a familiar routine and "normal" internation interaction to materialize. If it were not for this property, normal international relations ranges would not be distinguishable. The higher the inertia of a conflict, the lower the entropy of the normal relations range and the sharper that it will look. (Azar 1984, 92–93)

Thus, metaphorically one can describe the NRR of a PSC as a dynamic system with an attractor that is occasionally perturbed by environmental factors but which remains robust. "The interconnected nature of the various structural factors (political, economic, ethnic, religious, linguistic) is what makes protracted social conflicts so devastatingly unresolvable. It is impossible to isolate each issue and resolve it separately, because each issue/sector of the conflict is linked to the others at a number of different levels" (Azar 1984, 92). This reflects Azar's and others' research concerning why an NRR changes, normally as a result of structural changes in the economy, political system, or military and technological capabilities. The

interwoven nature of these structural factors in a PSC severely circum-
scribes opportunities for shifting the NRR and, when coupled with a
PSC's inherent psychological factors, leads to a relatively tight and robust
attractor. Although metaphorically useful, evidence is emerging to suggest
that this attractor may be characteristic of a model that appropriately captures the nature and behavior of PSC.

A growing body of literature suggests that dynamic systems approaches
have strong explanatory value in studying cognitive development. In a very
explicit attempt to take the dynamical systems perspective beyond
metaphor, Robertson et al. find strong evidence for an attractor governing
cylic motor activity, a type of activity observed in a variety of species including the human neonate (Robertson et al. 1993). Other evidence of
strange attractors has been found in motor skill activity, language, and states
of consciousness (Smith and Thelen 1993, Elman 1995, Petitot 1995,
Combs et al. 1995). By assessing children's responses to novel words, Smith
has demonstrated that knowledge does not come in the form of a
"canned" solution, rather:

> Each real-time problem has its own special properties, its own needs. . . .
> Dynamical systems theory offers a new solution . . . there are no knowledge
> structures, just process. Thus, children's novel-word interpretations exhibit
> both a global structure and a local adaptability because these interpretations
> emerge in context as the result of a nonlinear attention system that creates
> new solutions from past experiences and the particular properties of the per-
> ceptually present. Stability and variability emerge as the joint products of
> real-time process. (L. Smith 1995)

This is similar to Gleick's reconstruction of Feigenbaum's reflections on
color. "Redness is not necessarily a particular bandwidth of light, as the
Newtonians would have it. It is a territory of a chaotic universe, and the
boundaries of that territory are not so easy to describe—yet our minds
find redness with regular and verifiable consistency" (Gleick 1987). Thus,
although most of the research in cognition is preliminary, the initial results
suggest that attractors may govern a variety of cognitive processes. This
forms one of the three justifications for searching for a strange attractor as
the foundation for a PSC NRR.

On the basis of the definition of an NRR, one could expect to find an
attractor in (1) dynamics occurring individually in the minds of the decision
makers, (2) in the dyadic interaction without consideration of the environment, and (3) in the dyadic interaction as influenced by structural factors in

the environment. Examining group interaction in pscyhotheraputic sessions, Burlingame et al. have found a strange attractor embedded in ten dimensions, which is to say that the interactive process can be mathematically modeled with a minimum of ten different variables. They also find that group maturation has a significant impact on the variability of the fractal dimension (for example, the number of variables necessary to fix the system in phase space at any single point in time) with "nearly two-thirds as much variability exist[ing] in the underlying order of interactions during the early life of the group than in the latter" (Burlingame et al. 1995, 98). Although the domains are certainly different, this strongly reflects the verbal description of the behavior of a PSC NRR. Remember: "Protracted conflicts tend to deepen and reinforce as they go on and to fix ever more firmly held mutual images of deception and hate" (Azar and Cohen 1979, 162).

Newtson's preliminary analysis of dyadic behavior with each actor anchored in an environment suggests that dynamic, coupled systems can generate "highly patterned behavior in two systems that interrelate in a stable way. At the same time that these strange attractors exist in interaction of the two systems, the behavior of the two component systems is chaotic" (Newtson 1993, 261). This is also an apt characterization of an NRR. Although each side of the dyad may at different times vary its activity, the NRR tends to remain globally stable due to the interconnections between the parties. Schrodt's work (1997a) also supports this point by arguing that protracted interaction leads to co-adaptive SOPs that neither side can change without a loss of utility.[12]

In conclusion, a dynamical systems perspective and, more specifically, an attractor appears to be an appropriate metaphor for describing an NRR. Yet, emerging literature from cognitive psychology suggests that the basis for an attractor governing the NRR may be much more than metaphorical. An attempt should be undertaken to reconstruct the phase space[13] of an NRR attractor. If such an attractor exists, then the number of underlying dimensions in what appears to be highly complex interactions can be characterized with a relatively small number of variables. If a high number of dimensions are found to be necessary to describe the attractor, then this would cause one to be highly skeptical of arguments that focus on only one or two dimensions—such as: "Conflict resolution can truly occur and last only if satisfactory amelioration of the conflict of underdevelopment occurs as well," and "Peace" may, in fact, be "development in the broadest sense of the term" (Azar 1985, 69).

If on the other hand the attractor can be located in only a few dimensions, this would lead to a re-evaluation of the "infinite" complexity of dyadic interaction and, more important, provide a method for inductively identifying the NRR of a PSC dyad. Once such an NRR attractor has been identified, crises would then appear as significant—sustained for at least a few time units and far enough away from the attractor that one would not consider the graphical deviation to be due solely to chance or measurement error.

Hidden Markov Models

Schrodt's recent work on pattern recognition provides an outstanding alternative to the linear models that dominated much of the early event data research (1997a; 1997b). Schrodt convincingly argues that the prognosis for linear models in crisis forecasting is quite bad—in fact, event data research went into a severe decline due to the poor performance of linear based early warning systems. However, HMMs provide a relatively new method of recognizing patterns in relatively irregular nominal time series data with a stochastic component (Schrodt 1997a).

Pattern recognition has a distinguished background in political studies often appearing in the guise of case studies and historical analysis. Furthermore, decision makers often reason by analogy—the lessons of history—whether it is appropriate or not.[14] However, pattern recognition is not always appropriate. Schrodt cites the implications of "Van Creveld's Law" as undermining the usefulness of historical analogy:

> War consists in large part of an interplay of double-crosses [and] is, therefore, not linear but paradoxical. The same action will not always lead to the same result. The opposite, indeed, is closer to the truth. Given an opponent who is capable of learning, a very real danger exits that an action will not succeed twice *because* it has succeeded once. (Van Creveld cited in Schrodt 1997a, 5)

With adaptive agents, historical analogy is of limited utility. However, as mentioned earlier, rational agents engaged in a protracted relationship with a relatively stable payoff structure may exhibit co-adaptive behavior.[15] This is particularly true in the case of organizations that function on the basis of SOPs. In such cases, the SOPs of the organizations will eventually reach a Nash equilibrium with neither side being able unilaterally to modify its SOPs without a loss of utility (Schrodt 1997a).

HMMs are particularly interesting in the study of event data used to characterize and analyze PSCs, in that they avoid many of the troubling data problems that tend to appear in the traditional treatment of such data. Researchers frequently scale data using either Azar's scale (1980) or Goldstein's more recent scale developed for the WEIS categories (1992) and then aggregate the resulting numbers into monthly or yearly totals. Such efforts move the data further away from its original form and introduce unnecessary error. If crises seem to be composed of similar patterns of nominal events, these can be directly identified using an HMM, which Schrodt explains as follows:

> As with a conventional Markov chain, a HMM consists of a set of discrete states and a matrix $A = \{a_{ij}\}$ of *transition probabilities* for going between those states. In addition, however, every state has a vector of *observed symbol* probabilities, $B = \{b_j(k)\}$ *that corresponds to the probability that the system will produce a symbol of type k when it is in state j. The states of the HMM cannot be directly observed and can only be inferred from the observed symbols, hence the adjective "hidden."* (Schrodt 1997a, 12)

Although Schrodt tests only a "left right" (LR) model in his early 1997 piece, he extends on this by using a "left right left" (LRL) model in his subsequent piece. The latter allows the system to return to a previous state, while the former has an absorbing state with a recurrence probability of one. Speech recognition and similar applications use LR models because the ordering of word sounds is unidirectional. However, an LRL model seems more appropriate for the study of event data in that it allows for the escalation and de-escalation of crisis.[16]

The transition matrix, A, of an LRL model is of the form

$$
\begin{matrix}
a_{11} & 1\text{-}a_{11} & 0 & 0 & \dots & 0 \\
a_{21} & a_{22} & a_{23} & 0 & \dots & 0 \\
0 & a_{32} & a_{33} & a_{34} & \dots & 0 \\
\dots & & & & \dots & \dots \\
0 & 0 & 0 & 0 & \dots & a_{n-1,n} \\
0 & 0 & 0 & 0 & \dots & a_{nn}
\end{matrix}
$$

where a_{11} represents the recurrence probability of the starting state, $1\text{-}a_{11}$ represents the transition probability to the second state, a_{21} represents the transition probability to the first state from the second state, a_{22} represents the recurrence probability of the second state, a_{23} represents the transition probability to the third state from the second state, and so on. An element of the model can be seen in figure 4.3. An LRL model is simply the combination of [I] elements.

Schrodt bases the number of states in his model, six, on the concept of crisis "phase" found in a number of other researchers' work (Butterworth 1976; Bloomfield and Moulton 1989, 1997; Sherman and Neack 1993). However, he has also tested as many as 12 states. Crisis in PSC remains an understudied phenomenon, and the number of phases has not been empirically determined. Therefore, one might use six to begin with as did Schrodt (1997a, 1997b). The transition probability matrix may suggest fewer hidden states if the recurrence probabilities are very low in one or more states. This suggests that two or more of the states may be combined.

Figure 4.3 Elements of a LRL Hidden Markov Model

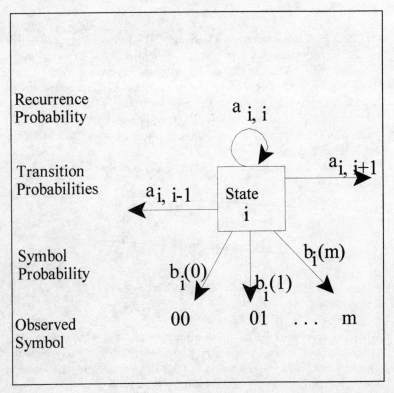

Source: Schrodt 1997a, 13.

The model would be "trained" on several sequences of events that represent the phenomenon under study—for example, 20 speakers might say the word "off"—which would be a PSC crisis in this case. Schrodt (1997b) examines crises that lead to war versus those that do not; he has also examined the periods preceding multiple tit-for-tat (TFT) exchanges of violence (1997a). In the second case, Schrodt randomly selects event sequences from his data to train a "background" model. Having two models trained for recognizing different phenomena, war versus nonwar crises and TFT versus background noise, allows one to assess the relative success of the model at coding its training cases. For example, if a nonwar crisis has a better likelihood of having been produced by the war HMM than a war-crisis, then the war HMM has misidentified the sequence.

A suggested design would follow Schrodt's original split sample design (1997b) and divide those sequences of events that can be clearly identified as crises in PSC into two groups. This would allow one to test the ability of a HMM model to distinguish, first, its training cases from background noise and, second, crises from the other half of the data. Then, if a PSC crisis HMM can correctly identify not only its training cases but also additional cases of crisis, the chances of crisis simply being a product of researcher assumptions are quite small. Hidden Markov modeling is a substantially inductive process and avoids many of the problems associated with former constructions of an NRR. Although, if successful, the Hidden Markov Model technique eliminates the need for an operationalized NRR, the background noise model would seem to be able to perform such a function if necessary.

Conclusion

PSC offers a conceptually rich way of approaching many of the nonstate-identity conflicts that seem to dominate the post–Cold War political scene. Nonetheless, important conceptual links remain with Cold War scholarship. Crisis research offers a needed window to the escalatory and de-escalatory tendencies that these conflicts seem to exhibit.

After reviewing the PSC concept as found in Azar's work, this chapter has attempted to integrate the Cold War scholarship concept of crisis in a way that avoids the pitfalls found in previous "interaction" research. As a result, three different philosophical positions and their resulting modeling strategies have been explored in an effort to inductively establish the existence of PSC crises. The existence of a variety of event data sets makes it possible for each of the three models to be tested in a number of contexts.

Although the suggested modeling strategies do not exhaust possible research options in this area, they do allow one to avoid the circular argument that an NRR exists because scholars can create a two standard deviation bands of behavior around a mean and call it an NRR. Indeed, until further research has been conducted on the distribution of events in particular conflicts, inductively identifying crisis situations appears to be the best option.

Notes

1. The commonly identified actors (groups) in the Northern Ireland conflict are (a.) Unionists (Protestant), (b.) Nationalists (Catholic), (c.) the British government, and (d.) the government of the Republic of Ireland. However, experimental research has also shown that although the minority Catholic— Nationalist identity shows unity, the identity labels of Protestant and Unionist may have different domains within the majority (Gallagher 1989).

2. "The concept of a NRR thus implies a conceptualization of inter-nation relations as an aggregate of acts or events" (Azar 1978, 227).

3. This remains true even in Azar's work as late as 1977: "Thus when the relations between two nations cross the upper critical NRR threshold, then the two nations have entered into a strategic crisis" (Azar et al. 1977).

4. "A dualist metaphysical position is that neither mental nor physical phenomena can be reduced to each other, so the two conceptions are equally valid, logically distinct, and thus must both be represented in any definitional exercise" (Haas 1986, 26).

5. Schrodt's work on pattern recognition (Schrodt 1990; Schrodt 1997a; Schrodt 1997b) follows the second procedure; however, he does not use the NRR concept.

6. Although every mass exerts a gravitational pull on all other masses, Galileo still calculated Earth's gravitational constant without knowing the mass of surrounding objects.

7. No single theory exists, rather chaos theory reflects a variety of strands of thought growing out of diverse disciplines and converging in the mid- to late-1970s.

8. The validity of Richard's findings has since been questioned (Huckfeldt and Williams 1993) because of the sensitivity of the spatial correlation test (Grassberger-Procaccia algorithm; Grassberger and Procaccia 1983) to measurement error and stochastic disturbances. However, a more appropriate criticism is that Richards shows a disregard for the ever-present warning in natural science literature that for the test to work properly one must have 10^D data points, where D is the dimension of the underlying attractor. In testing Modelski and Thompson's (1988) sea-power data

(n=500), Richards reports an attractor dimension of 3.5. The accuracy of this result is questionable with less than 10,000 data points and inappropriate to report without substantial qualification with only 500 data points.

9. Azar (1984, 89) contends, PSCs "are not specific events at distinct points in time; they are processes." Furthermore, Brecher pointedly argues that crises are dynamic processes: "The concepts of international and foreign policy crisis denote dynamic processes over time, with separate phases/periods: onset/re-crisis, escalation/crisis, de-escalation/end-crisis, and impact/post crisis" (Brecher 1996a, 127).

10. See Cashman (1993) for a discussion of stimulus-response and mediated stimulus-response models in the study of crisis.

11. Or: "More precisely, an *attractor* is a compact set, A, with the property that there is a neighborhood of A such that for almost every* initial condition the limit set of the orbit as n or t $\to$ $+\infty$ is A. Thus, almost every trajectory in this neighborhood of A passes arbitrarily close to every point of A. The *basin of attraction* of A is the closure of the set of initial conditions that approach A" (Farmer et al. 1983, 154).

12. In the case of a duopoly, a Nash equilibrium results from a Cournot equilibrium when both players' strategy is optimal given the strategy chosen by the other player.

13. The phase space of a system refers to the n-dimensional space required to describe the motion of a point (Jackson 1990).

14. Some of the obvious cases in the twentieth century are Munich, the Cuban Missile Crisis, and Vietnam. Russell Leng's (1988) research suggests that a reliance on "lessons" in which the former outcome was unsatisfactory due to a "failure to show resolve" leads to escalative initial strategies that are likely to reduce payoffs in crisis-learning games.

15. A Thomas Schelling comment on bargaining reflects a similar line of thought:

> Each party's strategy is guided mainly by what he expects the other party to accept or insist on; yet each knows that the other is guided by reciprocal thoughts. The final outcome must be a point from which neither expects the other to retreat; yet the main ingredient of this expectation is what one thinks the other expects the first to expect and so on. Somehow, out of this fluid and indeterminate situation that seemingly provides no logical reason for anyone except what he expects to be expected to expect, a decision is reached. These infinitely reflexive expectations must somehow converge on a single point, at which each expects the other not to expect to be expected to retreat. (cited in Russett and Starr 1996, 142–43)

16. Nonetheless, a hidden assumption in moving to an LRL model is that the arrow of time is irrelevant to a specific crisis. Crisis may be generic in the

sense that the word "helpless" as pronounced by 20 speakers maintains its meaning. However, an LRL model assumes that crisis stages preceding and following the apex of a crisis are indeed comparable. To paraphrase Aron (cited in Hermann 1969), it has not yet been proven that all crisis stages are alike (ABCBA which in reality may be ABCB'A').

References

Andriole, Stephen J., and Robert A. Young. 1977. "Toward the Development of an Integrated Crisis Warning System." *International Studies Quarterly* 21 (March): 107–50.

Azar, Edward. 1972. "Conflict Escalation and Conflict Reduction in an International Crisis: Suez, 1956." *Journal of Conflict Resolution* 16 (June): 183–201.

———. 1978. "An Early Warning Model of International Hostilities." In *Forecasting in International Relations: Theory, Methods, Problems, Prospects,* ed. N. Choucri and T. Robinson. San Francisco: WH Freeman, pp. 223–38.

———. 1980. "The Conflict and Peace Data Bank (COPDAB) Project." *Journal of Conflict Resolution* 24 (March): 143–252.

———. 1984. "The Theory of Protracted Social Conflict and the Challenge of Transforming Conflict." In *Conflict Processes and the Breakdown of International Systems,* ed. Dina A. Zinnes. Monograph Series on World Affairs. Denver, CO: Graduate School of International Studies, University of Denver, pp. 81–99.

———. 1985. "Protracted International Conflicts: Ten Propositions." *International Interactions* 12 (1): 59–70.

———and Stephen Cohen. 1979. "Peace as Crisis and War as Status-Quo: The Arab-Israeli Conflict Environment." *International Interactions* 6 (2): 159–84.

———, Paul Jureidini, and Ronald McLaurin. 1978. "Protracted Social Conflict: Theory and Practice in the Middle East." *Journal of Palestine Studies* 8 (1): 41–60.

———, R. D. McLaurin, Thomas Havener, Craig Murphy, Thomas Sloan, and Charles H. Wagner. 1977. "A System for Forecasting Strategic Crises: Findings and Speculations About Conflict in the Middle East." *International Interactions* 3 (3): 192–222.

Baker, Patrick. 1993. "Chaos, Order, and Sociological Theory." *Sociological Inquiry* 6 (Spring): 123–49.

Bloomfield, L. P. and A. Moulton. 1989. *CASCON III: Computer-Aided System for Analysis of Local Conflicts.* Cambridge, MA: MIT Center for International Studies.

———. 1997. *Managing International Conflict.* New York: St. Martin's Press.

Boulding, Kenneth. 1962. *Conflict and Defense: A General Theory.* New York: Harper and Brothers.

Brecher, Michael. 1996a. "Introduction: Crisis, Conflict, War—State of the Discipline." *International Political Science Review* 17 (April): 127–39.

———. 1996b. "Crisis Escalation: Model and Findings." *International Political Science Review* 17 (April): 215–30.

———— and Jonathan Wilkenfeld. 1982. "Crisis in World Politics." *World Politics* 34 (April): 380–417.

Brock, W. A. 1986. "Distinguishing Random and Deterministic Systems Abridged Version." *Journal of Economic Theory* 40 (October): 168–95.

Burlingame, Gary M., et al. 1995. "Group Therapy as a Nonlinear Dynamical System: Analysis of Therapeutic Communication for Chaotic Patterns." In *Chaos Theory in Psychology,* eds. Fredrick David Abraham and Albert R. Gilgen. Westport, CT: Greenwood, pp. 87–105.

Butterworth, R. L. 1976. *Managing Interstate Conflict, 1945–1975: Data with Synopses.* Pittsburgh, PA: University of Pittsburgh Center for International Studies.

Cashman, Greg. 1993. *What Causes War? An Introduction to Theories of International Conflict.* New York: Lexington Books.

Combs, Allan, et al. 1995. "Psychology, Chaos, and the Process Nature of Consciousness." In *Chaos Theory in Psychology,* ed. Fredrick David Abraham and Albert R. Gilgen. Westport, CT: Greenwood, pp. 129–37.

De Greene, Kenyon. 1990. "The Turbulent-Field Environment of Sociotechnical Systems: Beyond Metaphor." *Behavioral Science* 35 (January): 49–59.

Deneckere, Raymond. 1986. "Competitive Chaos." *Journal of Economic Theory* 40 (October): 13–25.

Elman, Jeffrey L. 1995. "Language As a Dynamical System." In *Mind as Motion: Explorations in the Dynamics of Cognition,* eds. Robert F. Port and Timothy van Gelder. Cambridge, MA: MIT Press, pp. 195–225.

Farmer, J. Doyne, et al. 1983. "The Dimension of Chaotic Attractors." *Physica* 7D: 153–80.

Fay, Brian. 1994. "General Laws and Explaining Human Behavior." In *Readings in the Philosophy of Social Science,* eds. Michael Martin and Lee C. McIntyre. Cambridge, MA: MIT Press, pp. 91–110.

Frank, Murray and Thanasis Stengos. 1989. "Measuring the Strangeness of Gold and Silver Rates of Return." *The Review of Economic Studies* 56 (October): 553–67.

Frank, Murray, et al. 1988. "International Chaos?" *European Economic Review* 32 (October): 1569–84.

Froehling, Harold, et al. 1981. "On Determining the Dimension of Chaotic Flows." *Physica* 3D: 605–17.

Gallagher, A. M. 1989. "Social Identity and the Northern Ireland Conflict." *Human Relations* 42 (October): 917–35.

Gleick, James. 1987. *Chaos: Making a New Science.* New York: Penguin Books.

Goertzel, Ben. 1995a. "Belief Systems As Attractors." In *Chaos Theory in Psychology and the Life Sciences,* eds. Robin Robertson and Allan Combs. Mahway, NJ: Lawrence Erlbaum Associates, pp. 123–34.

————. 1995b. "A Cognitive Law of Motion." In *Chaos Theory in Psychology and the Life Sciences,* ed.s Robin Robertson and Allan Combs. Mahway, NJ: Lawrence Erlbaum Associates, pp. 135–53.

Goldstein, Joshua S. 1992. "A Conflict-Cooperation Scale for WEIS Events Data." *Journal of Conflict Resolution* 36 (June): 369–85.

———. 1994. *International Relations.* New York: HarperCollins.

Grandmont, Jean-Michel, and Pierre Malgrange. 1986. "Nonlinear Economic Dynamics: Introduction." *Journal of Economic Theory* 40 (October): 3–12.

Grassberger, Peter, and Itamar Procaccia. 1983. "Characterization of Strange Attractors." *Physical Review Letters* 50 (5): 346–49.

Gregersen, Hal, and Lee Sailer. 1993. "Chaos Theory and Its Implications for Social Science Research." *Human Relations* 46 (July): 777–802.

Gurr, Ted. 1992. "The Internationalization of Protracted Communal Conflicts Since 1945: Which Groups, Where, and How." In *The Internationalization of Communal Strife,* ed. Manus Midlarsky. New York: Routledge, pp. 3–26.

Haas, Michael. 1986. "Research on International Crisis: Obsolescence of an Approach." *International Interactions* 13 (1): 23–58.

Hermann, Charles. 1969. "International Crisis As a Situational Variable." In *International Politics and Foreign Policy: A Reader in Research and Theory,* ed. James Rosenau. New York: Free Press, pp. 409–21.

———. 1972. "Some Issues in the Study of International Crisis." In *International Crises: Insights from Behavioral Research,* ed. Charles Hermann. New York: Free Press, pp. 3–17.

Huckfeldt, Robert, and John T. Williams. 1993. "Empirically Discriminating between Chaotic and Stochastic Time Series." Presented at the annual meeting of the American Political Science Association, Washington, D.C.

Jackson, E. Atlee. 1990. *Perspectives of Nonlinear Dynamics,* vol. 1 and 2. New York: Cambridge University Press.

Kegley, Charles W., Jr., and Eugene R. Wittkopf. 1993. *World Politics: Trend and Transformation,* 4th ed. New York: St. Martin's Press.

Kelsey, David. 1988. "The Economics of Chaos or the Chaos of Economics." *Oxford Economic Papers* 40 (March): 1–31.

Khalil, Elias. 1995. "Nonlinear Thermodynamics and Social Science Modeling: Fad Cycles, Cultural Development, and Identificational Slips." *American Journal of Economics and Sociology* 54 (October): 423–38.

Leng, Russell. 1988. "Crisis Learning Games." *American Political Science Review* 82 (March): 179–94.

Little, Daniel. 1991. *Varieties of Social Explanation: An Introduction to the Philosophy of Social Science.* Boulder, CO: Westview.

Loye, David, and Riane Eisler. 1987. "Chaos and Transformation: Implications of Nonequilibrium Theory for Social Science and Society." *Behavioral Science* 32 (January): 53–65.

Mandelbrot, Ramsey, Marcus Wisdom, and Alvin Saperstein. 1984. "Chaos—A Model for the Outbreak of War." *Nature* 309: 303–5.

McClelland, Charles A. 1961. "The Acute International Crisis." *World Politics* 14 (October): 182–204.

————. 1968. "Access to Berlin: The Quantity and Variety of Events, 1948–1963." In *Quantitative International Politics,* ed. J. David Singer. New York: Free Press, pp. 159–86.

————. 1972. "The Beginning, Duration, and Abatement of International Crises: Comparisons in Two Conflict Arenas." In *International Crises: Insights from Behavioral Research,* ed. Charles Hermann. New York: Free Press, pp. 83–105.

———— and Gary D. Hoggard. 1969. "Conflict Patterns in the Interactions among Nations." In *International Politics and Foreign Policy: A Reader in Research and Theory,* ed. James Rosenau. New York: Free Press, pp. 711–24.

Mirowski, Philip. 1990. "From Mandlebrot to Chaos in Economic Theory." *Southern Economic Journal* 57 (October): 289–307.

Modelski, George, and William Thompson. 1988. *Seapower.* Seattle: University of Washington Press.

Newtson, Darren. 1993. "The Dynamics of Action and Interaction." In *A Dynamic Systems Approach to Development Applications,* ed. Linda B. Smith and Esther Thelen. Cambridge, MA: MIT Press, pp. 241–64.

Parker, Richard W. 1977. "An Examination of Basic and Applied International Crisis Research." *International Studies Quarterly* 21 (March): 225–46.

Petitot, Jean. 1995. "Morphodynamics and Attractor Syntax: Constituency in Visual Perception and Cognitive Grammar." In *Mind as Motion: Explorations in the Dynamics of Cognition,* ed. Robert F. Port and Timothy van Gelder. Cambridge, MA: MIT Press, pp. 227–81.

Pruitt, Dean, and Jeffrey Rubin. 1986. *Social Conflict.* New York: Random House.

Ramsey, James, et al. 1990. "The Statistical Properties of Dimension Calculations Using Small Data Sets: Some Economic Applications." *International Economic Review* 31 (November): 991–1020.

Rasler, Karen. 1984. "A Comparative Analysis of Monadic and Dyadic Perspectives on the 1976 Lebanese Crisis." *International Studies Quarterly* 28 (September): 427–46.

Richards, Diana. 1990. "Is Strategic Decision Making Chaotic?" *Behavioral Science* 35 (July): 219–32.

————. 1992. "Spatial Correlation Test for Chaotic Dynamics in Political Science." *American Journal of Political Science* 36 (November): 1047–69.

————. 1993. "A Chaotic Model of Power Concentration in the International System." *International Studies Quarterly* 37 (March): 55–72.

Robertson, Robin. 1995. "Chaos Theory and the Relationship Between Psychology and Science." In *Chaos Theory in Psychology and the Life Sciences,* eds. Robin Robertson and Allan Combs. Mahway, NJ: Lawrence Erlbaum Associates, pp. 3–15.

Robertson, Steven S. et al. 1993. "Behavioral Chaos: Beyond the Metaphor." In *A Dynamic Systems Approach to Development: Applications,* ed. Linda B. Smith and Esther Thelen. Cambridge, MA: MIT Press, pp. 119–50.

Robinson, James. 1972. "Crisis: An Appraisal of Concepts and Theories." In *International Crises: Insights from Behavioral Research,* ed. C. Hermann. New York: Free Press, pp. 20–35.

Ross, Marc. 1993. *The Management of Conflict*. New Haven: Yale University Press.

Rosser, J. 1990. "Chaos Theory and the New Keynesian Economics." *The Manchester School of Economic and Social Studies* 58 (September): 265–91.

Russett, Bruce, and Harvey Starr. 1996. *World Politics: The Menu for Choice*, 5th ed. New York: WH Freeman and Company.

Saperstein, Alvin. 1994. "Chaos as a Tool for Exploring Questions of International Security." *Conflict Management and Peace Science* 13 (2): 149–77.

———. 1995. "War and Chaos: Complexity Theory May be Useful in Modeling How Real-World Situations Get Out of Control." *American Scientist* 83 (6): 548–57.

Schaffer, William, and Mark Kot. 1985. "Do Strange Attractors Govern Ecological Systems?" *BioScience* 35 (6): 342–50.

Schrodt, Philip A. 1990. "Parallel Event Sequences in International Crisis." *Political Behavior* 12 (2): 97–123.

———. 1997a. "Pattern Recognition of International Crises Using Hidden Markov Models." Presented at the annual meeting of the International Studies Association, Toronto.

———. 1997b. "Early Warning of Conflict in Southern Lebanon Using Hidden Markov Models." Presented at the annual meeting of the American Political Science Association, Washington, D.C.

Serletis, Apostolos. 1996. "Is There Chaos in Economic Time Series." *Canadian Journal of Economics* 29 (April): S210–12.

Sherman, F. L., and L. Neack. 1993. "Imagining the Possibilities: The Prospects of Isolating the Genome of International Conflict from the SHERFACS Dataset." In *International Event- Data Developments: DDIR Phase II*, ed. R. L. Merritt, R. G. Muncaster, and D. A. Zinnes. Ann Arbor: University of Michigan Press, pp. 87–111.

Sloan, Thomas J. 1978. "Dyadic Linkage Politics in Lebanon." *Journal of Peace Science* 3 (Fall): 147–58.

Smith, David. 1995. "The Inapplicability Principle: What Chaos Means for Social Science." *Behavioral Science* 40 (January): 22–40.

Smith, Linda B. 1995. "Stability and Variability: The Geometry of Children's Novel-Word Interpretations." In *Chaos Theory in Psychology*, eds. Fredrick David Abraham and Albert R. Gilgen. Westport, CT: Greenwood, pp. 53–72.

——— and Esther Thelen, eds. 1993. *A Dynamic Systems Approach to Development Applications*. Cambridge, MA: MIT Press.

Stewart, Ian. 1989. *Does God Play Dice? The Mathematics of Chaos*. Cambridge, MA: Blackwell.

Young, T. R. 1991. "Chaos and Social Change: Metaphysics of the Postmodern." *The Social Science Journal* 28 (3): 289–305.

White, R. W. 1990. "Transient Chaotic Behavior in a Hierarchical Economic System." *Environment and Planning* 22 (October): 1309–21.

CHAPTER FIVE

Who Participates in Protracted Conflicts and Why? Rediscovering the Group and Its Needs

Samuel Peleg

Protracted Conflicts: Why Now?
The Prevalency of Protracted Conflicts

A very prominent form of conflict in the last decade of the twentieth century has been called "protracted" (Azar 1979, 1986) and "deep-rooted" (Burton 1987). The name suggests an ongoing and prolonged nature, along with a sense of ineluctability. This type of conflict, which symbolizes an intricate and a highly interdependent world, has no well-defined boundaries of duration nor sharp delimitations on scope and intensity.

Such conflicts display enduring features, such as multiple reinforcing cleavages, perpetuated grievances, and intolerable inequality and injustice. Such conflicts are usually not discrete and, hence, cannot be studied in isolation. They persist as long as the underlying predicament continues, but their outbursts are periodic. Protracted conflicts are set apart from any other social conflicts mainly because they are harder to resolve. Their intractability accounts for the persistence of about 60 of them since 1945 (Azar 1986, 30).

There are several explanations why hard-to-resolve, deep-rooted conflicts are so prevalent in the modern world. One reason is that the struggle against colonialism promoted awareness of group rights and identity. This placed many ethnic, religious, and nationalistic groups on a collision course with their oppressors. The immensely discrepant interests were not amenable to reconciliation. The demands of the deprived grew with the refractory attitudes of the privileged. Recalcitrance battled intransigence to an impasse, giving rise to bitter wars of attrition in places such as Northern Ireland, Ethiopia, the Sudan, Lebanon, Sri Lanka, Bosnia, and the various republics of the former Soviet Union.

A second reason, and stemming from the historical explanation, is a structural-systemic explanation. In a complex interdependent global arena there are multiple actors with a plethora of issues to promote (Keohane and Nye 1977). In many cases, the military capabilities of the larger powers are ineffective and irrelevant. Small nations equipped with adequate economic resources and diplomatic experience fearlessly challenge the old guard of ruling nations. Affairs of states are intermixed and confrontations between broad alliances or large-scale wars are less frequent. The modern overt confrontation is *limited but relentless,* subnational in character but not lacking in firepower or zeal. The colonial legacy left third world nations and ethnic groups arbitrarily divided by artificial boundaries drawn by Europe. The desire to reunite along natural boundaries, coupled with the incapacity to militarily confront the industrial powers inspires low-intensity conflicts (White 1991, 15) like guerrilla warfare and terrorism, which have become the means for intermittent, sporadic, but unswerving political struggles.

Systems analysis, with its emphasis on relationship and legitimacy, extends the structural explication of intractable conflict. According to this approach, there is an inescapable clash between the practical and functional system and the artificial and obstructive state. Thus "conflict in this case arises, first, out of the fact of territorial boundaries that interrupt transactions, and second, out of the function that authorities have of allocating values and resources" (Burton 1968, 81).

It is also an altercation between legitimized and nonlegitimized relationships. States are administrative structures presiding over people who dwell within their legal jurisdictions, that is, their borders. Such legality does not render this rule legitimate. Especially in a fragmented society, such as a multinational one, large portions of the population might not accept the authority of the government or its policies. Systems, on the other hand, can be voluntary. Actors join systems on their own accord, hence their authority is more legitimate. The universal status quo is perpetuated by states and is marked by power politics and unequal distribution of capabilities. As such, it is not legitimized by the initiators of protracted contentions.

A third explanation of the persistence of these types of conflict is sociological and it pertains to the dynamics of the group. Group cohesion and identity fortification processes are stimulated by denigrating the rival (Williams 1994). For the group to crystallize, foes are required. Internal dissension is quelled by a common outside threat (Coser 1956, 110). Furthermore, animosity and hostility toward the enemy are encouraged because they help build ferocity and stamina among the group members. Such an attitude bolsters the position of each antagonist and diminishes the option of mutual reconciliation.

Azar admits that "group identity formation and protracted social conflicts are inextricably linked" (1984, 90). He presents ethnicity—"the structural awareness that there is a bond between people of similar culture, language, religion, beliefs, customs, habits and . . . life perspectives (1984, 90)—as an example of an identity core that agitates and fans rancor to buttress its existence. Accommodation and mollification might spell disintegration, thus the group must engage in persistent conflict. The insistence on sharpening stances and differentiating attributes leads to both attitudinal and social polarization that hastens "the division of the community into two socially and attitudinally separate camps, each convinced it is absolutely right" (Coleman 1957, 13). The acute split spurs each party into more vigorous and extreme positions to draw attention and sympathy to their side. As the two parties distance themselves from each other, their lines of communication elongate and their ability to understand reciprocal messages declines. Hatred and reluctance to propitiate are amplified due to resulting misperceptions.

A fourth explanation for the widespread ineluctable conflict is rational-strategic in nature and reminiscent of resource mobilization theory. It is founded on the dynamic action-reaction sequence between challengers who want to change the status quo and incumbents who want to preserve it. According to this scenario, the challengers, or the underdogs, initiate the conflict because they suffer from a "fear of extinction" (Horowitz 1985, 175) in the face of a dominant culture, religion, or nationality. The situation escalates and becomes difficult to control when the perceived inferiority is institutionalized in the political and economic structures of the country. Then, the notion of victimization is activated—the deliberate and systematic deprivation of a whole constituency. This idea is central to Azar's research on protracted conflict, as he argues: "structural victimization is perceived to affect some groups disproportionately or to benefit other groups. It is at this juncture of actual physical and psychological deprivation that structural victimization bursts into hostile and violent actions and interactions" (1984, 90).

The institutionalization of dominance provokes a mobilization process by the deprived. Soon after, "threatened members of the dominant group respond by countermobilization which escalates the violence and undermines the negotiation process necessary to resolve group differences" (Crighton and MacIver 1991). This mobilization-countermobilization (MCM) dynamic augments social conflicts by increasing the stakes in each round (Peleg 1996). Like two zealous bidders in an auction, each side is prompted to raise its price by the offer of the contender. Neither side wants to back down now that the stakes have been raised and the prize is so coveted. Gurr (1970, 1994), Oberschall (1973, 1995) and Tilly (1978, 1995) reiterate the importance of mobilization on both sides as aggravating an initial incompatibility. They all see elements such as a regime's legitimacy, its inaccessibility to challengers, external support, and a political culture conducive to violence, as intervening variables between the structural origins of conflicts and collective action.

The higher the stage of mobilization and the more costly the resources needed to maintain the group, the more daring the demands raised. Hewitt (1977, 158), for example, finds a correlation between increased ethnic violence and demands for fundamental constitutional change, while Crighton and MacIver (1991, 1) profess that hard-to-solve conflicts are those that involve "demands for substantial redefinition of the political system." Similarly, Morton Deutsch surmises that conflict is enlarged when it is over a substantive issue rather than a marginal one and "over principle rather than the application of a principle" (1969). Finally, Oberschall presents a rational choice option for a lingering conflict. During a confrontation each side chooses an alternative that maximizes the expected net benefit, or the balance of benefits minus costs. His model suggests that rival groups insist on continuing the conflict despite low prospects of success because they are convinced that abandoning it would be costly and certain to result in high penalties (1995, 106).

In light of the aforementioned, it is becoming more and more apparent that on the verge of the new millennium the protracted kind of conflict is the most prevalent. It is an alarming and discomforting observation since it is neither an efficient nor a constructive type of conflict, one which consolidates societies, that is surviving the twentieth century but a lingering and a costly one, which destabilizes and disintegrates. Azar's ten propositions regarding the nature of protracted conflicts were highly elucidating. They captured and epitomized the burgeoning phenomenon. With the benefit of 15 years hindsight, I would reinspect two of them: the second proposition that underlines human needs as the source of grievances and the seventh proposition that calls for a new level of analysis to grasp protracted conflicts-the identity group.

Protracted Conflicts: Why at All?
Human Needs as the Engine of Protracted Conflicts

The motivation and rationale for international, as well as domestic, politics are epitomized in the idea of men striving for human needs. The quest for these needs propagates sociopolitical dynamics such as individuals joining political associations, the consolidation of identity groups, and the ensuing clash between such groups and institutions of the state. Understanding the essence of these interactions better entails elaboration on the meaning, function, and the theoretical contribution of the human needs approach.

The point of departure is the inevitable tension between a society that aims at integration and individuals who want to maintain their uniqueness. The two basic assumptions of integrated societies, which marked the transformation from the Hobbesian world to the "social contract" world, have been the primacy of societal over individual interests and, consequently, the obligation of the authorities to impose the rules and norms of the whole on the deviants. Social control over dissidents is justified to keep the delicate unity of society from harm. Whether it is exercised by socialization or coercion, the purpose is unequivocal: "whoever refuses to obey the *general will* shall be constrained to do so by the whole body" (Rousseau 1968, 64, emphasis added). But what if the needs of the individual depart from the "general will"? Can the wants and aspirations of the individual be subordinated to societal expediencies without the repercussions such impositions might cause? Can the institutions of the system accommodate the frustration of the deviants, and if not, what are the consequences?

The assertion is that human beings possess inherent needs that must be satisfied. The idiosyncracy of mankind foils the accomplishment of these needs in an integrated framework. Hence, since the formation of human society, an incipient conflict of interest emerged between society and the people who compose it. This dialectic tension provides the fuel that animates international politics. International relations are the reflection of individuals' quest for the satisfaction of their needs. In their search for enhancements they join groups that uphold similar demands. These identity groups pursue the individuals' needs with amplified force. They perceive the system's attempts to enforce the law regardless of the group's claims, as illegitimate. The larger the portion of the population that sees the government's policy as illegitimate, the harder it is to maintain social control. At some point, when the critical mass shifts toward the challengers, the authorities have either to accept the demands of the aggrieved groups or relinquish their power to a more legitimized regime.[1]

The concept of human needs is constructive in two ways. It supplies a convincing epistemological scenario of politics within and across borders. This concept places unfulfilled human needs at the center of the political drive, as a powerful independent variable to political behavior. Needs are uncontrollable. They cannot be co-opted by governmental benefits or harnessed to societal expectations. If they are not satisfied, people will rebel. People prefer to gratify their needs and forego societal norms. The same logic accounts for entering a group and defying the establishment. It is the relentless pursuit of needs that incites collective political action.

At the same time, the human needs approach promotes methodological efforts by coalescing the micro and the macro analyses. Individuals, through their participation in social networks and associations, influence decision making at the governmental level. Thus, the human needs approach circumvents a serious pitfall that has hampered the realist perspective on international and domestic politics: the overstatement of a single level of analysis. A human needs approach penetrates all levels of human activities, thereby attenuating the micro-macro gap to suggest a combination of levels of analysis to work with.

Needs satisfaction is the mainspring of social change. Order and change in the world hinge upon the extent to which human needs are met or not. Individuals can materialize their needs only in a societal context, not in isolation. They join social networks to fully implement their needs and to obtain some control over the environment, which might obstruct human plans. This emphasis on the individual impels the researcher to reverse the direction of social control and the manner in which societies achieve stability. Traditionally, national interests and the priorities of the rulers were considered to be the principles that ordered society, and the citizens were expected to align behind the state's goals. Any discrepancies were "ironed out" by socialization or coercion. This scheme seems highly pernicious because innate human needs surface and upset the imposed order.

The stress on law, order, and stability in many instances precludes justice because "there is an inherent tension between the order provided by the system and society of states, and the various aspirations for justice that arise in world politics" (Bull 1977, 86). Thus, human needs should be the criteria for social goals and should deiermine the policy agenda. The state's institutions must adjust to the needs of the people and not vice versa. Moreover, policies should be conceived of and carried out according to the interpretation of needs and not in regard to the ideologies or values implanted by the ruling elite. Human needs theorists claim that sociopolitical problems can be solved only if a needs perspective is adopted, that is, "global problems will be resolved only by identifying the changes that are required in institutions and policies so as to ensure the legitimation of authorities and the satisfaction of needs" (Coate and Rosati 1988, 13).

A lucid definition of human needs is provided by Bay (1988, 88): a need is "any requirement for a person's survival, health, or basic liberties; basic meaning that, to the extent that they are inadequately met, mental or physical health is impaired. Thus, 'need' refers to necessities for not only biological survival but also for the health and development (physical and mental growth) of persons as human beings."

Human needs are understood here as an impetus for growth and advancement. If needs are not satisfied, fighting for them will be justified. Such a linkage between human needs and human behavior has been probed before by scholars in various disciplines such as biology, anthropology, philosophy, and sociology. But it was the psychological literature that influenced the writing of Abraham Maslow the most. Relying on McDougall (1908) and Murray (1938), Maslow's "A Theory of Human Motivation" (1943) ushered human needs theory into political science.

Maslow discerns five ranked levels of needs: physical, safety, affectional, self-esteem, and self-actualization. Hunger and physical insecurity must be satisfied prior to social recognition and prestige. Davies (1988) adopts but slightly modifies Maslow's classification. He merges the five categories into four by combining physical and security needs. However, Davies distinguishes between substantive needs—"those pursued primarily because they are inherently gratifying"—and instrumental needs—"pursued in the process of satisfying a substantive need."[2] Thus, the author sets another criterion for the priority of needs. Like Maslow, Davies reiterates the importance of a needs hierarchy: the basic, physical needs must be fulfilled prior to psychological needs. A hungry man does not pay much attention to his dignity.

Another proponent of the needs priorities is Sites. But his scale underlines consequences of dissatisfaction rather than the degree of urgency to fulfill needs. Thus he offers a gamut of unattended needs that result in the annihilation of a group, the inability to perform some tasks and, the less crucial case, disturbances in performance (as mentioned by Galtung 1988, 155). Sites (1973, 44) rejects the priority of needs because "all of which require fulfillment and, therefore, none of which is necessarily more important than others."

Nudler (1980) differentiates between universal needs—identity and growth—and derived needs, such as the need to transcend or love and participate. Bay (1988) also advocates the hierarchy of needs and he connects them with policy preferences. He enumerates four needs categories: survival, health, community, and liberty, which correspond to human, political, and legal rights granted and protected by the state. Gurr (1970, 25), rephrasing both Maslow and Davies, suggests only three categories of needs: welfare (physical and safety), power (influence and recognition), and interpersonal (self-esteem and self-actualization). His intention is to emphasize general conditions for collective violence rather than particular volitions of individuals; hence, the broader definitions of categories.

Other scholars grapple with human needs in their respective areas of interest. Enloe (1973) stresses ethnicity and conformity as a major need among underdeveloped nations, while Rokeach (1960) elaborates on ideologies and beliefs as attracting identity and belonging of individuals. Klineberg (1980, 31), a former chairman of the World Federation for Mental Health, proposes six categories of needs akin to different criteria of mental health: self-awareness, growth, integration, independence, perception of reality, and adjustment. Their dissatisfaction entails the deterioration of mental health. Galtung (1979) writes about needs in the context of international development. He comes up with four categories: security, welfare, freedom, and identity. All should be cultivated against violence, misery, repression, and alienation respectively. According to Galtung, those who are deprived of such needs are the third world, or the periphery nations, and those who deny needs are the core Western nations. Consequently, the disaffected periphery might rebel if the status quo prevails.

Sites (1973, 43) similarly postulates human needs as a catalyst for order and change. He accentuates that needs are fulfilled only within social relationships. This is why individuals, whose needs are not met by the regular channels, will break the societal norms and hurt others rather than quit the system altogether. Sites submits eight specific needs: response, stimulation, security, recognition, justice, rationality, meaning, and control.[3] Burton embraces Sites' insights but distinguishes between the role of "inferiors," those who seek fulfillment of their needs, and the role of "superiors," the privileged elites and authorities. The superiors have achieved their needs, so what is their stimulation now? Thereupon they assume a new need: the urge to preserve the prerogatives they acquired when they were chal-lengers of power (Burton 1987). This "role defense" need fosters conflicts and explains the activities of groups such as the death squads in South America or the Protestant paramilitary units in Ulster, Northern Ireland. These violent perpetrators represent ruling elites and majorities who have already satisfied their human needs. Nonetheless they deviate from societal norms in their chase after their role defense need.

As demonstrated, human needs can be approached and understood from various directions. However, it is apparent that regardless of the schol-arly discipline or the different emphases used in each conceptualization of needs, there is a common appreciation of needs as crucial for the building of social theory. This assertion stems from the ability of explanations based on human needs to account for the evolution of dynamic social relations through legitimization and delegitimization processes. Human needs, in that context, are not merely physical instincts of survival but "certain needs which must be fulfilled that are social in character, and are at least as im-portant as the so-called 'basic' needs of food and water" (Burton as quoted in Coate and Rosati 1988, 7).

Two illustrative points emerge after discussing the meaning of human needs: the important distinction between needs, values, and interests, and whether needs are universal or culturally-bound. Most scholars of the clas-sic tradition do not distinguish between needs and values. They see it more like a continuum of needs qua physical, primordial instincts, such as food and shelter, and values, which emerge with the development of society, for example, political participation or social justice. As such, the concept of needs reinforces the linear stage progression theories of development and modernization (Apter 1965, Pye and Verba 1965, Huntington 1968). But to better comprehend what underpins protracted conflicts, it is imperative to distinguish between the two concepts: needs *always* exist no matter what stage of development. They are *universal* and transcend cultures, while val-ues are culture-bound. The former develop in humans *because they are hu-mans,* whereas the latter emerge in line with the intrinsic nature of the specific society. A quest for self-esteem and recognition, which are agreed human needs, can be expressed in a successful hunt, the publishing of a book, or the murdering of a police officer depending upon the pertinent *values* of the perpetrators. Thus, values grow out of needs, but they mani-fest themselves disparately.

The implication derived is most important: values are more easily sub-ordinated by society's institutions and laws because they are determined by them. Needs, on the other hand, awkwardly coexist with norms and regulations. Once they become incompatible they cannot be subdued by authorities. Mistaking needs for values is costly to the stability of any system: wrong policies are implemented as a result of misperceived problems. The United States misinterpreted genuine needs like identity and respect as subversive ideologies and global expansionism in Vietnam and in Lebanon, thereby crippling their international policy. This is the core of protracted international conflicts: the inability to separate needs from values and, accordingly, the futile attempts of policymakers to inappropriately curb basic human drives. Needs cannot be subdued by societal regulations; they are beyond any conventions.

Closely linked to the needs/values distinction is the universal versus local needs dilemma. Sites, Burton, and Galtung forcefully promote the idea of objective and universal human needs that can be a global yardstick for the satisfaction of desires; a measurement whereby all institutions and policies are assessed in their attention to human grievances. Sites (1973, 43) concludes that "basic needs do exist and that they are more universal and less specifically cultural, than some behavioral scientists would have us believe." Others reject this contention claiming that needs indeed exist in all humans but that they constantly interact with, and therefore are shaped by, indigenous values that change across borders. Lederer (1980, 4) identifies two schools of thought in this controversy: the "universal-objective" and the "historical-subjective." One represents needs as immanent and all-encompassing to men; the other sees needs as conditioned by historical circumstances. She cautiously submits that "the two conceptions of needs . . . do not necessarily exclude each other, rather, they differ in perspective and . . . both of them are indispensable in the study of needs."

This distinction highlights the intricacies of understanding human needs. Objective approaches might obscure typical characteristics and local nuances of needs and wants borne out of specific locales and habits. The ambition for brevity and equal judgment might generate inaccuracies and misperceptions. Determining what is the objective criterion also posits a problem. The imposition of Western conventions and practices was a mistake that impeded modernization policies in the third world. On the other hand, the subjective conception of needs sows confusion as to whose needs are more precious, thus rendering decisions and policies completely relative, precarious, and arbitrary. This attitude is epitomized by labeling some international actors as terrorists and crazy while praising others for the same deeds. This ambivalence can be avoided by a strict and unequivocal standard of human needs.

Protracted Conflicts: Who?
Identity Groups as a Level of Analysis

Current conflict theories underestimate the importance of the aggrieved identity group and its contribution to the study of conflict. The underrated theoretical value of identity groups is epitomized in two basic assumptions of political realism: the predominance and political unity of the state and the strict differentiation between domestic and international politics. A new understanding of protracted conflict must challenge these two pillars of conventional realist wisdom by accentuating the capacity of aggrieved identity groups to disturb sociopolitical realities; and also by highlighting the processes by which identity group-related conflicts might escalate and expand regardless of national borders to the extent that domestic and international conflicts become indistinguished.

In order to become a formidable factor capable of wreaking havoc in the sociopolitical arena, the aggrieved identity group has to mobilize and becomes politically effective. In Starr's (1978) terms, it is not only the willingness to act, which is assumed to exist in any aggrieved community inspired by charismatic leaders and ideology, but mainly the wisely used structure of opportunities that determines the success or failure of the group and the extent of its defiance. Linking the motivation to act with the ability to seize opportunities is the organization of the group, which Tilly (1978, 53) defines as "the extent of common identity and underlying structure among individuals in a population."

What makes the identity group even more powerful is its communal-based organization. Oberschall's sociological typology of mobilization (1973) distinguishes between community ties and associational ties by their origin and scope: the former are traditional, primordial, and narrow whereas the latter are modern and broad. Other scholars have pursued this distinction and linked communal groups with sects and associational groups with movements (cf. Wolfsfeld 1988). Oberschall (1973, 119) concludes, though, that both kind of ties create a "sentiment of solidarity that can be activated for the pursuit of collective goals," and that such a task is especially feasible in segmented societies where "social control over the collectivity from outside weakens and shared sentiments of collective oppression increase" (1973, 121). The proposition put forth here is that identity groups are both sects and movements. They combine the attributes of the sect—the exclusiveness, the commonality of religion, geography, norms of behavior, and even dress code with the properties of a movement—the rational organizational structure, the long-term commitment to activism, and the wide, grass-roots appeal.

These characteristics make the identity group a potent actor in the sociopolitical arena. The inherent incompatibility between the state and the group is likely to turn the group into a conflictual actor. The incongruent orientations of order and unity of the state versus the sense of victimization and uniqueness of the organic group yield a bitter conflict that increasingly changes the profile of modern politics. An incentive to escalate into protractedness is mutually created by the government in its endeavors to quell the agitators before they amass enough power to become a major threat, and also by the identity group. As Nieburg (1969, 15) has pointed out: "the incidence of group violence increases as groups assume semi-sovereign functions as a challenge to, or substitute for the weakened legitimacy of the state." Therefore, in support of Azar, we see that identity group-related conflicts tend to be long, recurrent, violent, and hard to solve.

The study of conflict has been heavily biased toward one type of conflict: between nation-states. In this predominantly formal-legalistic perspective, political entities are governments that maintain full sovereignty over their territories and populace, and they alone are able to wage wars and move the wheels of history. Occasionally, evidence of another type of conflict came up. Historical recollections of clashes between movements, whole peoples and ethnic groups, have fascinated some observers (Cohn 1957, Hobsbawm 1963). Ultimately, however, these accounts were all shelved as anecdotal and theoretically inconsequential. Nonstate conflicts were conveniently termed "abnormal" and were not granted an ample amount of research.

Political realism, which advocated the predominance of the state in world politics, has been sanctified and funded by governments and bureaucracies. The theory was sought after as a safeguard and justification for the legal-rational political order that the modern nation-state embodied. It also made perfect sense: clear, parsimonious, and rigorous, political realism instilled order in a complex and multifarious reality. But reality, as seen in work on integration, transnational relations, and globalization, has fissured the conventional thought. The "abnormalities" of yesterday have repeatedly surfaced in the present. The term "nation-state" has become a misnomer, for most countries in the contemporary world host several *ethnies*, or identity groups, which defy the ruling ethnie or the state—the structure that tries to mold the idiosyncratic entities into a whole. The state as a cohesive unit of analysis requires a more profound, closer scanning in order to trace the roots of today's global turbulence. These are different dynamics and contentions from what we used to know. Rosenau (1990, 381), as one of the leading theorists of global change, draws a profile of modern, group-based conflict: "Taken together, the subgroupism of citizens, their expanded analytical skills, their greater cathectic abilities, and their redirected legitimacy sentiments constitute a powerful drive for questioning, if not challenging, authority. And once authority is challenged, compliance is no longer assured."

The focus on the growing influence of ethnic or religious identity groups can be called a return to community power. Such an orientation at the expense of formal authority has been fostered in the last three decades by several factors: a reaction of the primordial unit, the ethnie, against the pressure of the state and modern life; the spread of knowledge and the rise of an intelligentsia among deprived populations; the ideology of nationalism, which has emphasized shared historical heritage and common myths of descent, and thus amplified the innate solidarity built around ethnicity and religion; and finally, an intransigent international system of nation-states that refuses to acknowledge the needs and rights of nonstate actors on the global scene.

Understandably, this situation is not conducive to the regular conduct of interstate relations. Ignoring or trivializing the emerging problems of identity groups and their desire for recognition as being "nonstatal" and therefore irrelevant is perilous to global stability. The inability of the contemporary international system to incorporate and accommodate identity groups and, even worse, the reluctance of governments and state bureaucracies to take heed of collective needs as opposed to individual citizens' needs, are the core of modernity's most rapidly expanding type of conflict: the deep-rooted, protracted one. These conflicts will grow and spread as the state's instinct for survival confronts the identity group's vitality and resistance (see Rosenau 1990 for such arguments). Neither side seems to waver. In a state-biased world, violence "from above," for example, state terrorism and governmental repression, are condoned in the name of stability and order. Such violence is bound to breed violence and terrorism "from below" in the name of freedom and justice, and so the cycle of atrocities and cruelty endures.

Group identity formation and protracted conflicts are inextricably connected. Religion, ethnicity, and nationalism as well, reveal bonds between people of similar beliefs, customs, and life perspectives. Such shared viewpoints cut across issues and values and reflect immutable characteristics that cannot be discarded. They leave, as Azar notes, "an indelible mark of identity on each of its heirs. By universalizing a set of distinct social interactions for its members, [the identity group] becomes an expression of uniqueness vis-à-vis others" (1984, 90). In most cases individuals seek renewal of cultural and communal ties when they are insecure and in awe of a changing reality. The socialization process within the group creates dynamics of cohesion and unity by challenging frustration toward other groups and imputing suspicious behavior to outsiders. If prior incompatibilities exist between the group and the environment, they are reinforced and deepened by the psychological encouragement the identity group bestows on its members. The identity group perspective enables us to "peek" into the future of global politics in which the role of such groups will steadily increase. There is an urgent need, therefore, to build and accumulate data and knowledge of identity groups, their needs, ambitions, and actions.

Protracted Conflicts: How?
Ethnicity and Religion as Sources of Strife

The saliency of human needs in the enhancement and escalation of protracted conflicts is emphasized by their identity-driven nature. In the heart of ethnic and religious conflicts, the most prone to become protracted, lie permanent and irreconcillable differences between parties that demand full compliance, ultimate commitment, and readiness to sacrifice from their respective followers. Loyalty is contrived by dehumanizing and demonizing the rival and consolidating an "us-versus-them" perspective. Group identity is forged and encouraged by denying rights and needs of the other by underscoring the exclusiveness and preeminence of the self. The "chosen-people syndrome" (Peleg 1997) works overtime in such overwrought and impetuous contentions. In an age of declining ideological strife and diminishing socioeconomic quarrels, the ethnoreligious conflicts, which feed upon psychologically potent needs for group identity and group worth (Crighton and MacIver 1991, 138), occupy center stage.

Needs also intensify group building processes and dynamics of solidarity and cohesion. One of the most popular trends in organization and group theories is the interdependence concept, which stipulates the crystallization of a group by its members being positively interdependent in some way. Moreover, interdependence is considered by some theorists to be the underlying and most crucial process of group formation (Zander 1979). One of the bases upon which such interdependence is woven is the satisfaction of human needs. People join groups in order to better achieve personal goals and desires that they cannot sustain alone. Furthermore, "it is assumed that people have individual needs (motives,goals,drives,desires,etc.) that at least some of and probably most of these needs are satisfied directly or indirectly by other people" (Turner 1987). In this perception, human needs are given; they are individual properties that instigate collective action and expedite camaraderie and esprit de corps. In other words, unsatisfied human needs not only draw the battles lines but also shape and prepare the battling forces.

Another reason why ethnic and religious conflicts have a predisposition to protractedness and a proclivity to become intractable is their ascriptive nature and their highly charged symbolic content. Interethnic and interreligious rivalries and disagreements usually concern collective and indivisible goods. Contentions of this nature lack the objective criteria necessary to assess the legitimacy of demands or claims and calmly negotiate a compromise. Since disadvantage and feared loss are gauged in feelings, beliefs, and norms these conflicts acquire an intensity and vehemence unmeasured by disputes over divisible goods. While the latter are approached by considerations of give and take, bargaining and conciliation, the former are grounded in the elusive and irresolvable realm of justice and fairness.

The subjective essence of grievance and frustration render them impossible to grade or scale. Grievances are normative protests perceived and felt only by those who complain (Williams 1994). However, they create a formidable driving force that may affect mobilization and violence more than objective resources such as size, concentration, and coherence (Gurr 1993, 179). In his vast study, *Minorities at Risk,* Gurr (1993, 92) identifies indigenous rights as one of the major orientations of protracted conflicts in the last 50 years, whereby "grievances about discrimination and threats to group identity . . . motivated hundreds of protest movements" and resulted in "protracted communal wars spanning at least three successive five-year periods" (1993, 98).

Ethnic and religious conflicts are more likely to become protracted owing to the psychological and spiritual reassurance ethnic and religious groupings bestow on their followers. Needs and anxieties unanswered by secularism and modern life are attended to by the exclusive tradition and solidarity of ethnicity and by the devoutness and mysticism of religion. Shultz (1995, 79) identifies common features of ethnic and religious conflicts: they are marked by being part of severely divided societies, by permanent and irreconcillable differences between factions, by patronistic "us-versus-them" attitudes, and by readiness to violence.

Ethnic and religious grievances have spawned a number of protracted conflicts in recent years. Indeed they have become the most frequent generators of strife in an age of diminishing conventional wars and declining global rivalries. Ethnic-based protracted conflicts were heavily launched in, among other places, Somalia (Shultz 1995), Angola (Knudsen and Zartman 1995) and Ethiopia (Assefa 1990), while religiously motivated protracted conflicts are rampant in the Middle East and Asia (Bar Siman-Tov 1994, Euben 1995, Pipes 1996). However, this kind of protracted conflict is not limited to a certain area or periphery.

The specific case of religiously motivated protracted conflict demands special attention due to its wake and popularity in the advent of the new millennium. Protracted conflicts of this nature have occurred concurrently with the growth of *fundamentalism* in all three monotheistic religions and with an upsurge of worldwide religious revitalization. The phenomena of religion and revitalization are in many respects intertwined. They both imply a transformation of the human condition from dissatisfaction to fulfillment, or at least an attempt to bring about such a transformation. Wallace (1956) suggests that the historical origin of most religious movements has actually been in revitalization movements torn or split from their parent religion after failing to invigorate it from within. Thus, religion is a very appropriate backdrop for introducing revitalized and aggrieved identity groups. In Wallace's (1956, 28) formulation, all religions are "relics of old revitalization movements, surviving in routinized forms in stabilized cultures, and that religious phenomena per se originated in the revitalization process, such as in visions of a new way of life by individuals under extreme stress."

The cyclical connection between religion and revitalization is probed by Emile Durkheim from a different angle. In his famous distinction between the sacred and the profane, the modern capitalistic-individualistic world belongs to the latter (see Parsons 1968, 301). Religion plays a pivotal role in the modern world: it should control the material wants of individuals and promote social solidarity in an age of abating affinity. In short, religion is perceived as supplying the resource for the revitalization of society as a whole.

The entire transformation a person undergoes from an inactive observer of politics to an ardent participant is more cogently appreciated within a religious explanatory framework. Isaacs (1975, 143) asserts that religion "provides the means by which the religious person satisfies some otherwise unappeasable needs," but once these needs are threatened, adamant conflict and even violence are to be expected because of the unmitigated loyalty and emotional involvement. The most foreboding threat to religion at the twentieth century's end emits from modernity and the challenge it presents to the familiar truths of religion. Instead of grappling with a radically new and unpredictable present, many prefer to retreat to the comfortable refuge of faith. Furthermore, this self-reassurance is performed with great intensity: creeds are impassionedly reasserted and reinterpreted in letter and in spirit. This is how religious fundamentalism, the return to the bedrock of faith, is nurtured.

The crisis modernity has caused for religion is signified by secularism or heresy, but more extremely by pluralism. Plurality of thought undermines the monistic authority of orthodoxy and challenges the validity of its mores. Under these dire circumstances there are three options for the guardians of faith: reaffirmation of tradition in defiance of change; secularization of religion in admittance of change, or careful and prudent adjustment of tradition to meet the challenges of the times.

Berger (1979, 95–127) strongly supports the third option, which he calls "the inductive possibility," as the best way to combat the "heretical imperative" of modernity. This alternative is described as inductive because the justifications and explanations for being religious are "aggregated" and argued from experience, by reinspecting basic questions. The trial and error procedure reconciles the abiding precepts of faith with the inconstant social environment. It takes prudent and discerning spiritual leaders to forego some of their basic convictions for the expedience of their people. In the same vein, Pipes (1983) introduces the term "medieval synthesis" to denote the policy compromise Muslim leaders had formulated between the religious Shari'a law and changing human realities. This blend has come to be known as traditionalist Islam, as opposed to strict and ruthless fundamentalism. The synthesis worked well as "an immensely stable and attractive combination of ideal goals and pragmatic actions which held in several continents and over many centuries" (1983, 57).

Unfortunately, it is the first alternative—the reaffirmation of tradition, or "the deductive possibility" in Berger's terms—that revitalized religious groups adopt. Changes of a lesser magnitude may yield compromises and incremental acclimation but the acute and excruciating peril of modernity does not permit such a propitiatory response from the defenders of faith. Hence, the deductive option means that believers "reassert the authority of a religious tradition in the face of modern secularity. The tradition thus having been restored to the status of datum, of something given a priori, it is then possible to deduce religious affirmations from it at least more or less as was the norm in premodern times" (Berger 1979, 61). This means that militant religious groups exert themselves with a vengeance: the historical interval in which tradition was not certified, but taken for granted, must be smothered. Such earnestness and zeal provide a sure recipe for an enduring and steadfast struggle.

As Azar suggests in his seventh proposition, the most useful unit of analysis to comprehend protracted conflict is the identity group. Here, the most appropriate and efficient milieu in which to categorically combat the pluralist threat is the religious identity group. A complete set of alternative values must be cultivated in an insulated and protected ambience. The believers must be disconnected from a confusing reality and from contending versions of the truth. The leaders of the identity group try to "interpose a fact-proof screen" between their followers and the actual world (Hoffer 1951, 60). They do that by imbuing their adherents with strong in-group feelings and by reinforcing a spirit of cohesion and solidarity. Religion becomes the bond that secures the attachment of the followers to a framework that rearranges and realigns their thoughts, attitudes, and beliefs. The confirmation of faith is achieved by emphasizing the righteousness of fellow members. Appropriately Coleman (1957, 53) describes the religious identity group as "a mutual admiration society." In sum, the religious identity group is a zone of retreat for individuals in need of solace, a sanctuary for those who are threatened by uncertainty and who desire reassurance in an era of tumult. Isaacs (1975, 166) convincingly portrays this mood: "Life cannot be lived on earth by man standing on his own two feet alone. Confused enough, fearful enough, threatened enough, every man, even the most Enlightened, will find his way back to his knees and to his god."

But as much as defensive religion unifies its own members, it divides society as a whole. Thus, as argued by sociologists such as Coser, it has a dual nature: a focus of integration and loyalty and a source of societal cleavage and implacable opposition. The encouragement of in-group feelings coincidently fosters distinctions and cleavages *among* groups. This separateness is augmented because traditionally meaningful symbols develop within historically designated communities of believers. Hence, shared values are localized in particular affiliation groups, which render the religious experience and commitment of each group unique and exclusive.

This fragile pluralism is marred by perpetual suspicion and tensions. The tone of self-assurance of religious identity groups establishes an us-versus-them mentality and the conviction that the ideology of one's group is the only route to redemption. The leaders of the religious identity group implant in their disciples the feeling of being superior to others. Such a vision inherently excludes any alternative scenarios of salvation. The sense of superiority is profoundly entrenched. The more firmly these notions are held, the greater the animosity toward different religious views. Here is where an extremist state of mind converges upon the character of the religious identity group (Lipset and Raab 1970): the arbitrariness of thought, the intolerance of compromise and dissidence and the denigration of alternative identity groups. This dogmatism coupled with a staunch ideology and constantly fed by grievances and fear ultimately leads to collective action (Oberschall 1995). But must the collective action in the name of faith be violent?

Not necessarily, but frequently it is. The spirit and rhetoric of religion is fierce. It emphatically differentiates the believers from the infidels, the chosen from the unchosen, the saved from the damned. Hence, "the need, the duty, indeed the divine command to slay the Amalekites, to stone the sinner, to put heretics to the torch, nonbelievers to the sword. From these passions, from the wounds of these severances, great streams of blood have flowed" (Isaacs 1975, 153). Action motivated by unfulfilled needs in the religious context, and specifically violent action, operates as a unifying agent. The stress, the sense of common kismet and the confidence that you are right help release moral inhibitions about conflict and violence. As Hoffer (1951, 113) recognizes, "these are admirable qualifications for resolute and ruthless action in any field." Under such circumstances of determination, anguish, and defiance, protracted conflict becomes the norm rather than the aberration.

Protracted Conflicts: The End?
Changing Patterns of Negotiations

Ignoring human needs as the center of protracted social conflicts can severely debilitate attempts to negotiate and drastically hamper resolution. Azar warns in his ninth proposition that no compromises are possible when needs are at stake and that there is an urgent requirement for "non-power models." The conventional power politics modalities of international bargaining and negotiation rely on economic and territorial interests of the state. The realist assumption of scarcity and endemic competition for resources among actors constructs conflict management in terms of factual and zero-sum game perspectives. Human needs such as identity, recognition, and sense of security are not manageable in such terms. No wonder that conflicts motivated by needs escalate and turn protracted: leaders and negotiators bogged down in old routines and procedures of conflict resolution never really tend to the sources of discontent. There cannot be winners and losers in needs-based conflict. Unfulfilled needs must be satisfied on each side of the equation through a win-win solution lest disagreement prevails.

The human needs approach to protracted conflicts undermines some of the basic propositions of power politics negotiations. Fisher and Ury's (1981) seminal *Getting to Yes* suggests distinguishing between positions and interests when trying to resolve a dispute. Rigid positions stifle the ability to maneuver and decrease the flexibility necessary for reaching common ground; interests are pliable and more amenable to mutual understanding. Many times positions are merely a facade to deter others from making claims, whereas interests reflect one's volitions more accurately. Both terms are deficient, however, when needs-based conflicts are concerned. Positions stagnate talks; yet, interests are also highly problematic, as they disregard the delicacy and sensibility of needs and desires. States have interests; people have needs. Late-twentieth-century strife is less and less between states employing conventional armies; it is between substate groups that are composed of people propelled by genuine needs. To ameliorate these groups, a new framework of analysis and approach to conflict resolution are imperative.

Similarly, Fisher and Ury's proposition of separating the people from the problem is inadequate. Their conventional attitude leads them to assume that personal animosities and antagonism would interfere with the "cold-headed," professional interactions of problem solving. Not paying attention to the people on both sides and the grievances that motivate them is the main pitfall in relaxing tension. A human needs perspective ensures "due consideration to people and their relationships—they often are the problem" (Rothman 1989, 266). The competitive attitude must be supplanted by a cooperative one. Integrative, rather than distributive, solutions should be sought and encouraged. A collaboration between former rivals must be pursued interactively to create a positive-sum outcome destined to placate unfulfilled needs of all parties. Fights, games, and debates should usher in concerts: not winning or outweighing opponents but understanding mutual fears and deprivations may be the anecedents of peace in the next century.

Notes

1. A similar approach to the study of conflict is advanced by the resource mobilization school. The general model of this approach describes a domination structure versus contending groups vying for ascendancy. The incumbents and the challengers compete for resources and influence. Mobilization refers to the processes and dynamics in which actors on both sides engage to increase their resources: recruits, money, weaponry, or pur-

veyance. Resource mobilization theory is based on the utilitarian rational-choice model of joining or avoiding a conflict according to a cost benefit calculation. In such a design, elements such as group consciousness, ideology, and solidarity become less crucial. This is where needs theory, which underscores "non-rational" factors, departs from mobilization theory.

2. Analytically there are several attempts to "solve" the needs/values dilemma. Bay (1988, 88) differentiates between needs, which are analytic concepts that cannot be observed, and wants—"the measurable and detectable desires of people." He wrestles with Marcuse's dichotomy of "true" versus "false" needs, the latter being the manipulated needs implanted by the system in the minds of men to regard the elite's volitions as their own (1967, 245). While accepting the possibility of acquiring, or learning, needs, Bay shuns definite terms like "true" and "false."

3. Sites distinguishes here between the first four needs—those which cannot be fulfilled instantly—and the second four needs, which arise from the pulling and hauling processes of trying to achieve the other four needs. He intermitently refers to the last four needs as "desires."

References

Apter, D. 1965. *The Politics of Modernization.* Chicago: University of Chicago Press.

Assefa, H. 1990. "Conflict Resolution Perspectives on Civil Wars in the Horn of Africa." *Negotiation Journal* 6 (April): 173–183.

Azar, Edward. 1979. "Peace Amidst Development: A Conceptual Agenda for Conflict and Peace Research." *International Interactions* 6 (2).

———. 1984. "The Theory of Protracted Social Conflict and the Challenge of Transforming Conflict." In *Conflict Processes and the Breakdown of International Systems,* ed. Dina A. Zinnes. Monograph Series on World Affairs. Denver, CO: Graduate School of International Studies, University of Denver, pp. 81–99.

———. 1986. "Protracted International Conflicts: Ten Propositions." In *International Conflict Resolution: Theory and Practice,* eds. Edward Azar and John Burton. Essex, UK: Wheatsheaf, pp. 28–39.

Bar Siman-Tov, Y. 1994. "The Arab-Israeli Conflict: Learning Conflict Resolution." *Journal of Peace Research* 31 (1): 75–89.

Bay, C. 1988. "Human Needs as Human Rights." In *The Power of Human Needs in World Society,* eds. Roger Coate and Jerel Rosati. Boulder, CO: Lynne Rienner, pp. 77–98.

Berger, P. 1979. *The Heretical Imperative.* New York: Anchor Press.

Bull, H. 1977. *The Anarchical Society.* London: Macmillan.

Burton, John. 1968. *Systems, States, Diplomacy and Rules.* Cambridge: Cambridge University Press.

———. 1987. *Resolving Deep-Rooted Conflict: A Handbook.* Lanham, MD: University Press of America.

Coate, R., and J. Rosati, eds. 1988. *The Power of Human Needs in World Society.* Boulder, CO: Lynne Rienner.

Cohn, N. 1957. *The Pursuit of the Millennium.* New York: Harper Torchbooks.

Coleman, J. 1957. *Community Conflict.* Glencoe, IL: Free Press.

Coser, L. 1956. *The Functions of Social Conflicts.* New York: Free Press.

Crighton, E., and M. MacIver. 1991. "The Evolution of Protracted Ethnic Conflict." *Comparative Politics* 23 (2): 127–42.

Davies, J. C. 1988. "The Existence of Human Needs." In *The Power of Human Needs in World Society,* eds. R. Coate and J. Rosati. Boulder, CO: Lynne Rienner, pp. 23–33.

Deutsch, Morton. 1969. "Productive and Destructive Conflict." *Journal of Social Issues* 25 (1): 7–42.

Enloe, C. 1973. *Ethnic Conflict and Political Development.* Boston: Little, Brown and Company.

Euben, Roxanne. 1995. "When Worldviews Collide: Conflicting Assumptions About Human Behavior Held by Rational Actor Theory and Islamic Fundamentalism." *Political Psychology* 16 (1): 157–78.

Fisher, R., and W. Ury. 1981. *Getting to Yes: Negotiations Agreement Without Giving In.* Boston: Houghton Mifflin.

Galtung, Johan. 1979. *The True Worlds: A Transnational Perspective.* New York: The Free Press.

———. 1988. "International Development in Human Perspective." In *The Power of Human Needs in World Society,* ed. R. Coate and J. Rosati. Boulder, CO: Lynne Rienner, pp. 128–59.

Gurr, Ted R. 1970. *Why Men Rebel.* Princeton, NJ: Princeton University Press.

———. 1993. *Minorities at Risk: A Global View of Ethnopolitical Conflict.* Washington, D.C.: United States Institute of Peace Press.

———. 1994. "People against States: Ethnopolitical Conflict and the Changing World System." *International Studies Quarterly* 38 (September): 347–77.

Hewitt, C. 1977. "Majorities and Minorities: A Comparative Survey of Ethnic Violence." *Annals of the American Academy of Political and Social Science* 433 (September): 150–60.

Hobsbawm, E. 1963. *Primitive Rebels.* New York: W. W. Norton and Company.

Hoffer, E. 1951. *The True Believer.* New York: Harper and Row.

Horowitz, Donald. 1985. *Ethnic Groups in Conflict.* Berkeley: University of California Press.

Huntington, Samuel. 1968. *Political Order in Changing Societies.* New Haven, CT: Yale University Press.

Isaacs, H. 1975. *Idols of the Tribe.* New York: Harper and Row.

Keohane, Robert O., and Joseph S. Nye. 1977. *Power and Interdependence.* Boston: Little and Brown.

Klineberg, O. 1980 "Human Needs: A Social Psychological Approach." In *Human Needs: A Contribution to the Current Debate,* ed. K. Lederer. Oslo: Oesgelschlager, Gunn, pp. 19–35.

Knudsen, K., and W. Zartman. 1995. "The Large Small War in Angola." *Annals of the American Academy of Political and Social Science* 541 (September): 130–43.

Lederer K., ed. 1980. *Human Needs: A Contribution to the Current Debate.* Oslo: Oesgelschlager, Gunn.

Lipset, S., and E. Raab. 1970. *The Politics of Unreason.* New York: Harper and Row.

McDougall, W. 1908. *An Introduction to Social Psychology.* Boston: John Luce.

Maslow, A. 1943. "A Theory of Human Motivation." *Psychological Review* 50 (July): 370–96.

Marcuse, Herbert. 1967. *One Dimensional Man.* Boston: Beacon.

Murray, H. 1938. *Explorations in Personality.* New York: Oxford University Press.

Nudler, O. 1980. "Human Needs: A Sophisticated Human Approach." In *Human Needs: A Contribution to the Current Debate,* ed. K. Lederer. Oslo: Oesgelschlager, Gunn, pp. 131–50.

Nieburg, H. L. 1969. *Political Violence: The Behavioral Process.* New York: St. Martin's Press.

Oberschall, A. 1973. *Social Conflict and Social Movements.* Englewood Cliffs, NJ: Prentice Hall.

———. 1995. *Social Movements: Ideologies, Interest and Identities.* New Brunswick, NJ: Transaction Books.

Parsons, T. 1968. *The Structure of Social Action,* 2nd ed. New York: The Free Press.

Peleg, Samuel. 1996. "A Group Dynamic Model for Political Success: The Case of Israeli Extra-Parliamentarism." *International Journal of Group Tensions* 26 (2): 123–44.

———. 1997. "They Shoot Prime Ministers Too, Don't They? Religious Violence in Israel: Premises, Dynamics, and Prospects." *Studies in Conflict and Terrorism* 20: 227–47.

Pipes, D. 1983. *In the Path of God: Islam and Political Power.* New York: Basic Books.

———. 1996. "Muslim Exceptionalism." Presented at the annual meeting of the American Political Science Association, San Francisco.

Pye, L., and S. Verba, eds. 1965. *Political Culture and Political Development.* Princeton, NJ: Princeton University Press, Studies in Political Development 5.

Rokeach, Milton. 1960. *The Open and Closed Mind.* New York: Basic Books.

Rosenau, J. 1990. *Turbulence in World Politics: Theory of Change and Continuity.* Princeton, NJ: Princeton University Press.

Rothman, J. 1989. "Supplementing Tradition: A Theoretical and Practical Typology for International Conflict Management." *Negotiation Journal* 5 (July): 265–77.

Rousseau, J. J. 1968. *The Social Contract.* Translated by M. Cranston. New York: Penguin Books.

Shultz, R. 1995. "State Disintegration and Ethnic Conflict: A Framework for Analysis." *Annals of the American Academy of Political and Social Science* 541 (September): 75–88.

Sites, P. 1973. *Control: The Basis of Social Order.* London: Dunellen.

Starr, Harvey. 1978. "'Opportunity' and 'Willingness' As Ordering Concepts in the Study of War." *International Interactions* 4 (4): 363–87.

Tilly, Charles. 1978. *From Mobilization to Revolution*. Reading, MA: Addison-Wesley.

———. 1995. "State-Incited Violence 1900–1999." *Political Power and Social Theory* 9: 161–79.

Turner, J. 1987. *Rediscovering The Social Group: A Self-Categorization Theory*. New York: Blackwell.

Wallace, A. 1956. "Revitalization Movements." *American Anthropologist* 58: 264–81.

White, J. 1991. *Terrorism: An Introduction*. Pacific Grove, CA: Brooks/Cole.

Williams, R. 1994. "The Sociology of Ethnic Conflicts: Comparative International Perspectives." *Annual Review of Sociology* 20: 49–79.

Wolfsfeld, G. 1988. *The Politics of Provocation: Participation and Protest in Israel*. New York: State University of New York Press.

Zander, A. 1979. "The Psychology of Group Processes." *Annual Review of Psychology* 30: 417–51.

Part II

Empirical Investigation

CHAPTER SIX

Early Warning of Conflict in Southern Lebanon Using Hidden Markov Models[1]

Philip A. Schrodt

Introduction

The aphorism "history repeats itself" is a central theme in protracted conflict literature. Protracted conflicts, by definition, can involve the same territories, ethnic groups, issues, and even tactics over long periods of time. From the perspective of conflict *resolution,* this repetition is frustrating, as the parties to the conflict appear never to learn alternatives. From the perspective of conflict *management,* on the other hand, repetition simplifies the problem of recognizing an impending escalation of violence, so that steps can be taken either to prevent the escalation or alleviate the consequences.

This chapter will argue that protracted conflicts generate regularized sequences of events that are repeated—in a noisy fashion—over time. These sequences can be used to predict subsequent behavior in a manner similar to the cognitive processes used by many human political analysts and decision makers. I will demonstrate how a computational sequence-recognition method—the Hidden Markov Model—can be employed as a tool for systematic crisis monitoring and early warning efforts. The empirical analysis focuses on one of most conspicuous cases of protracted conflict in the contemporary international system, the tit-for-tat violence between Israeli and Arab military forces in southern Lebanon.

The problem of developing early warning indicators of political conflict has long been an important focus of quantitative international relations research. The pioneering arms race modeling work of Lewis Richardson, for example, was motivated in part by Richardson's assumption that unstable arms races were important precursors to war; Choucri and Robinson (1979), Singer and Wallace (1979), and Hopple, Andriole, and Freedy (1984) provide additional examples of early quantitative studies of this problem.

Azar's work on protracted conflict was continually informed by his parallel empirical development of the COPDAB (Conflict and Peace Data Bank) event data set (Azar 1980, 1984). But following a large and generally unsuccessful effort in the late 1970s to develop early warning indicators using event data (see Laurance 1990, Schrodt 1994), early warning research shifted in focus to other techniques. Most notable among these were the expected utility models of Bueno de Mesquita and his colleagues (Bueno de Mesquita 1981; Bueno de Mesquita, Newman, and Rabushka 1996); another substantial effort involved computational models derived from artificial intelligence methods (Cimbala 1987; Hudson 1991) and systems dynamics (Hughes 1984, Ward 1985).

Interest in event-based early warning began to revive about a decade ago, when the National Science Foundation's Data Development in International Relations project sponsored several new event data collections (Merritt, Muncaster, and Zinnes 1993). These efforts gained greater momentum in the policy community with the end of the Cold War, a transition that vastly complicated the monitoring tasks of governments and international organizations who were interested in conflict mediation. The earliest manifestation of this trend in the realm of event-based research were the efforts by Gurr, Harff, and others (Gurr and Harff 1996) to study the precursors and accelerators of ethnoconflict and state breakdown. By March 1997, a conference on early warning in Toronto attracted over a hundred representatives of academic, government, IGO, and NGO organizations interested in early warning.

Despite all this attention, early warning remains a difficult problem, whether it is studied with quantitative or qualitative methods. For example, notwithstanding billions of dollars of funding, access to a wide variety of information sources, and a clear focus on a single opponent, Western intelligence agencies failed to anticipate both the timing and characteristics of the collapse of the Warsaw Pact. Early warning is almost nonexistent in low-priority areas such as Somalia, Rwanda, and Sierra Leone.

In some of these cases, as I will argue below, early warning may be impossible for theoretical reasons. However, there are other cases where advances in communications and analytical techniques should make possible the development of indicators that would not have been feasible when quantitative early warning research began 30 years ago. Because they are regularized, protracted conflict situations are particularly good candidates for successful early warning efforts, which in turn could aid in the management of these conflicts.

Co-Adaptation and Sequence Recognition

The sequence analysis approach has a long history in political science. At the most fundamental level, it is simply a systematic rendition of the "case study" or "lessons of history" technique that has been used by decision makers since time immemorial (see May 1973, Mefford 1985, Neustadt and May 1986, Vertzberger 1990, Khong 1992). History is considered relevant to decision makers because they assume that if a particular set of events and circumstances observed in the past is repeated, the resulting events will also be repeated, or at least approximated.

This simple observation is both reinforced and attenuated by the fact that it is reflexive—the methods that decision makers use to interpret the past have an impact on how they create the future. If decision makers act consistently on the "lessons of history," then history will in fact have lessons. By itself, however, belief in the importance of historical examples is insufficient to create empirical regularities because of "Van Crevald's Law":

> War consists in large part of an interplay of double-crosses [and] is, therefore, not linear but paradoxical. The same action will not always lead to the same result. The opposite, indeed, is closer to the truth. Given an opponent who is capable of learning, a very real danger exists that an action will not succeed twice *because* it has succeeded once. (Van Creveld 1991, 316)

A conspicuously successful strategic innovation is unlikely to succeed a second time precisely because it was successful the first time. More generally, the work of the Santa Fe Institute on the "El Farol Problem" (Casti 1997) has demonstrated that social systems consisting of adaptive utility maximizers generally do not exhibit regularized behavior *because* the decision makers look at history. In computer simulations, these systems exhibit quasi-chaotic behavior that is *not* predictable. If the political world consists solely of rational adaptive agents, there is little point in trying to make predictions based on past behaviors.[2] There are undoubtedly some forms of international behavior (for example, changes in international exchange rates) for which this is true.

However, it is not true in all cases, and protracted conflicts are one such exception. Situations of international conflict usually involve organizational behavior rather than individual behavior, and for a variety of theoretical and practical reasons, organizations are substantially less likely to engage in rapidly adaptive behavior than individuals. Mature organizations are more likely to rely on rule-based standard operating procedures (SOPs) that are intended to insure that a specific set of stimuli will invoke a specific response (Cyert and March 1963, Allison 1971). A classical Weberian bureaucracy, unlike the adaptive maximizer of complexity theory, is designed to ensure the success of a sequence analysis approach.

The SOPs are themselves adaptive, they are designed to solve problems effectively and are often acquired inductively through historical experience. In a situation of protracted interaction, the SOPs of two antagonistic organizations are *co-adaptive*: each responds in part to the environment created by the other.[3] In most circumstances, this eventually brings the SOPs into a Nash equilibrium within the space of possible SOPs and neither can change strategies unilaterally without a loss of utility.

Co-adaptation to a Nash equilibrium is most likely to occur when the same organizations have been interacting over a long period of time, and when the payoff environment has been relatively stable. This is exactly the situation found in protracted conflicts and enduring rivalries. These are also characterized by the SOP "lock-in"—antagonists fight, on repeated occasions, over the same issues, often over the same territory, and without resolution.

Hidden Markov Models

The techniques for comparing two sequences of discrete events are poorly developed compared to the huge literature involving the study of interval-coded time series.[4] Nonetheless, several methods are available, and the problem has received considerable attention in the past two decades because it is important in the study of genetic sequences and computerized speech recognition. Both of these problems have potentially large economic payoffs, which tends to correlate with the expenditure of research efforts. Until fairly recently, one of the most common techniques was the Levenshtein metric (see Kruskal 1983; Sankoff and Kruskall 1983); Schrodt (1991) uses this in a study of the BCOW (Behavioral Correlates of War) crises (Leng 1987). Other nonlinear methods such as neural networks, genetic algorithms, and locating common subsets within the sequences (Bennett and Schrodt 1987, Schrodt 1990) have also been used. The sequence analysis approach is quite different from the statistical methods typically used to analyze event data. Statistical approaches generally require a regular, interval-level, time series that is generated by aggregating the data at fixed intervals (typically a month or a year) using a scaled value assigned to each category—for example, Goldstein's, (1992) recent WEIS (World Event-Interaction Survey) scale, or the earlier Azar-Sloan (1975) scale for the COPDAB data set. The advantage of this approach is that a wide variety of interval-level time series methods are readily available. The disadvantage is that the process of scaling behavior into a single conflict-cooperation dimension results in the loss of a great deal of information and introduces a large number of free parameters. For example, in principle (although almost never in practice), a month characterized by a large amount of conflict in the first two weeks (negative numbers on most scales), followed by a large amount of reconciliation in the last two weeks (positive numbers) could aggregate to a value close to zero, the same value as would occur in a month when nothing happened.

A second, more subtle problem occurs with aggregation: it removes the analysis away from the cognitive and organizational processes that are generating the events. While decision makers may do some aggregation—one of the most commonly used metaphors in political analysis is indicating whether a situation is "heating up" or "cooling down"—detailed political responses are usually triggered by specific sets or sequences of events, not by the crossing of some numerical threshold.

In political activity, unlike economic activity, both the stimuli and responses are likely to be discrete, not continuous. Prices of stocks or the levels of interest rates, for example, move in predictable adjustments and when they fail to move continuously across that range (as in an investigation of NASDAQ trading a couple years ago), suspicions are triggered. Furthermore, small changes in the price will almost always result in proportionally small changes of supply and demand. Political events, in contrast, move in jumps that are predicated on the prior state of the system. The fall of a single missile following a period of peace will trigger a major response, whereas the fall of a single missile during a period of war usually will go unnoticed. A model that can maintain the event data in its disaggregated form is, *ceteris paribus,* more likely to be successful in predicting actual behavior.

Hidden Markov Models (HMM) are a recently developed technique now widely used in the classification of noisy sequences into a set of discrete categories (or, equivalently, computing the probability that a given sequence was generated by a known model). While the most common applications of HMMs are found in speech recognition and comparing protein sequences, a recent search of the World Wide Web found applications in fields as divergent as modeling the control of cellular phone networks, computer recognition of American Sign Language, and (inevitably) the timing of trading in financial markets. The standard reference on HMMs is Rabiner (1989), which contains a thorough discussion of the estimation techniques used with the models, as well as setting forth a standard notation that is used in virtually all contemporary articles on the subject.

An HMM is a variation on the well-known Markov chain model, one of the most widely studied stochastic models of discrete events (Bartholomew 1971). As with a conventional Markov chain, a HMM consists of a set of N discrete states and a matrix $\mathbf{A} = \{a_{ij}\}$ of *transition probabilities* for going between those states. In addition, however, every state has a vector of M *observed symbol probabilities*, $\mathbf{B} = \{b_j(k)\}$ that corresponds to the probability that the system will produce a symbol of type k when it is in state j The states of the HMM cannot be directly observed and can only be inferred from the observed symbols, hence the adjective "hidden."[5]

While the theory of HMM allows any type of transition matrix, the model that I will be testing allows transitions only to the previous state and the next state (as well as remaining in the current state). This is an extension of the unidirectional "left-right" (LR) model that is widely used in speech recognition and analyzed in Schrodt (1998). The transition matrix A is therefore of the form:

$$
\begin{matrix}
a_{11} & 1\text{-}a_{11} & 0 & 0 & \cdots & 0 \\
a_{21} & a_{22} & a_{23} & 0 & \cdots & 0 \\
0 & a_{32} & a_{33} & a_{34} & \cdots & 0 \\
0 & 0 & 0 & 0 & \cdots & a_{n-1,n} \\
0 & 0 & 0 & 0 & \cdots & a_{nn}
\end{matrix}
$$

The individual elements of the model look like those in figure 6.1. I will refer to this as a "left-right-left" (LRL) model. A series of these individual elements form an HMM such as the six-state model illustrated in figure 6.2. Because I am using these models to study escalation behavior—conflict episodes that have a clear "beginning"—sequences are assumed to start in State A.

Figure 6.1   An Element of a Left–Right–Left Hidden Markov Model

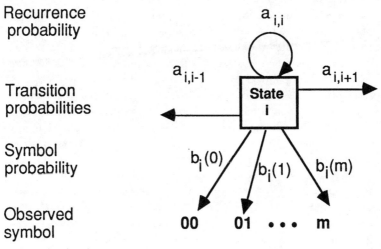

Recurrence
probability

Transition
probabilities

Symbol
probability

Observed
symbol

Source: Schrodt, July 1998, 36.

Figure 6.2   A Left–Right–Left (LRL) Hidden Markov Model

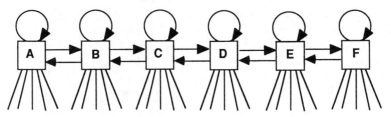

Source: Schrodt, July 1998, 37.

In empirical applications, the transition matrix and symbol probabilities of an HMM are estimated using an iterative maximum likelihood technique called the Baum-Welch algorithm. This procedure takes a set of observed sequences (for example, the word "seven" as pronounced by 20 different speakers) and finds values for the matrices A and B that locally maximize the probability of observing those sequences. The Baum-Welch algorithm is a nonlinear numerical technique and Rabiner (1989, 265) notes "the algorithm leads to a local maxima only and, in most problems of interest, the optimization surface is very complex and has many local maxima."

Once a set of models has been estimated, it can be used to classify an unknown sequence by computing the maximum probability that each of the models generated the observed sequence. This is done using an algorithm that requires on the order of N^2T calculations, where N is the number of states in the model and T is the length of the sequence. Once the probability of the sequence matching each of the models is known, the model with the highest probability is chosen as that which best represents the sequence. A technique called the "Viterbi algorithm" can be used to estimate the most likely set of hidden states that the system was in at each point in time.

Matching a lengthy sequence of symbols such as those found in event data coded with the 22-category WEIS scheme (McClelland 1976) generates probabilities on the order of $10^{-(T+1)}$. This probability is *extremely* small, even if the sequence was in fact generated by one of the models.[6] Usually, the important comparison is the *relative* fit of the various models. The measure of fit usually reported is the log of the likelihood; this statistic is labeled α (alpha).

For example, in a speech recognition application such as the recognition of bank account numbers, a system would have HMMs for the numerals "zero" through "nine." When a speaker pronounces a single digit, the system converts this into a set of discrete sound categories, then computes the probability of that sequence being generated by each of ten HMMs corresponding to the ten spoken numbers. The HMM that has the highest likelihood—for example the HMM corresponding to the numeral "three"—gives best estimate of the number that was spoken. If none of the probabilities are higher than some threshold, the system could decide that the number was unrecognizable and request that the speaker repeat the digit or transfer the call to a human operator.

The application of an HMM to the problem of generalizing international event sequences is straightforward. The symbol set consists of the event codes taken from an event data set such as WEIS or COPDAB. The states of the model are unobserved, but have a close theoretical analog in the concept of crisis "phase" that has been explicitly coded in data sets such as the Butterworth international dispute resolution data set (Butterworth 1976), CASCON (Bloomfield and Moulton 1989, 1997) and SHERFACS (Sherman and Neack 1993), and in work on preventive diplomacy such as Lund (1996).[7]

For example, Lund (1996, 38–39) outlines a series of crisis phases ranging from "durable peace" to "war" and emphasizes the importance of an "unstable peace" phase. In the HMM, these different phases would be distinguished by different distributions of observed WEIS events. A "stable peace" would have a preponderance of cooperative events in the WEIS **01–10** range; the escalation phase of the crisis would be characterized by events in the **11–17** range (accusations, protests, denials, and threats); and a phase of active hostilities would show events in the **18–22** range. The length of time that a crisis spends in a particular phase would be proportional to the magnitude of the recurrence probability a_{ii}.

The HMM has several advantages over alternative models for sequence comparison, such as the Levenshtein metric or neural networks. First, if $M \gg N$, the structure of the model is relatively simple. For example an LRL model with N states and M symbols has $2(N-1) + N(M+1)$ parameters compared to the $M(M+2)$ parameters of a Levenshtein metric. HMMs can be estimated very quickly, in contrast to neural networks and genetic algorithms. While the resulting matrices are only a local solution—there is no guarantee that a matrix computed from a different random starting point might not be quite different—local maximization is also true of most other techniques for analyzing sequences, and the computational efficiency of the Baum-Welch algorithm allows estimates to be made from a number of different starting points to increase the likelihood of finding a global maximum. The HMM model, being stochastic rather than deterministic, is specifically designed to deal with noisy input and with indeterminate time; both of these are present in international event sequences.

An important additional advantage of the HMM is that it can be *trained by example*. This contrasts with scaled aggregative methods that assign weights to individual events in isolation and make no distinction, for example, between an accusation that follows a violent event and an accusation during a meeting. The HMM requires no scaling or temporal aggregation and models the relationship between events by using different symbol observation probabilities in different states. This is particularly important for early warning problems, where critical periods in the development of a crisis may occur over a week or even a day. Finally, indeterminate time means that the HMM is relatively insensitive to the delineation of the start of a sequence. HMMs estimated from international event data tend to contain one or two "background" states that correspond closely to the distribution of events generated by a particular source (such as, Reuters/WEIS) when no crisis is occurring. A model can simply cycle in this state until something important happens and the chain moves into later states characteristic of crisis behavior.

Data and Early Warning Criteria

The event data used in this chapter were machine-coded to the WEIS (McClelland 1976) system from Reuters new reports lead sentences obtained from the NEXIS data service for the period April 1979 through May 1997 using the Kansas Event Data System (KEDS) program (Gerner et al. 1994; Schrodt, Davis, and Weddle 1994).[8] KEDS does some simple linguistic parsing of the news reports—for instance, it identifies the political actors, recognizes compound nouns and compound verb phrases, and determines the references of pronouns—and then employs a large set of verb patterns to determine the appropriate event code. Schrodt and Gerner (1994) and Huxtable and Pevehouse (1996) discuss extensively the reliability and validity of event data generated using Reuters and KEDS. A 00 nonevent was added for each day during which no events were recorded in either direction in the dyad. Some days contained multiple events.

The focus of the early warning analysis is tit-for-tat (TFT) military conflict between Israel and various Arab military organizations in southern Lebanon. Prior to 1982, this usually involved Palestine Liberation Organization (PLO) military forces; after 1985, it usually involved the Amal or Hizballah militias based among the Shi'a Moslem population in southern Lebanon.

The siutation in southern Lebanon is a quintessential protracted conflict. The area has seen substantial military contention from almost the beginning of the Zionist presence in Mandatory Palestine—for example, the frequently targeted northern Israeli town of Kiryat Shimona is named in memory of eight Jewish settlers who died in one such clash in 1920. There is also ample reason to believe that organizational SOPs govern behavior on both sides: Israel, the PLO, and the Shi'a militias all have extensive political and command infrastructures. With one major exception—the transition of anti-Israel forces in southern Lebanon from Palestinian to Shi'a—the actors have remained the same and, consequently, organizational co-adaptation is likely to have occurred over time. The analysis of the protracted conflict skips over the 1982–1985 period during which the military opposition shifted from the PLO to the Shi'a forces and the SOP co-adaptation had not stabilized between Israel and its new opposition in the region.

Two different predictive targets will be analyzed: the number of TFT incidents, and the Goldstein-scaled score of the ISR>LEB conflict.[9] A TFT conflict is defined as a use of force (WEIS 22) by one party (either Israel or Lebanon) followed by a reciprocal use of force by the other within two days. Figure 6.3 shows the time series for these two sets of data aggregated by month.

The success of the prediction will be assessed with cross-correlation— the correlation of W_{t-k} with X, where W is the warning indicator and X_t is the behavior to be predicted.[10] Most of the assessment will be done with cross-correlograms such as Figure 6.5 (see p. 144): high correlations at negative values of the lag imply that X correlates with *earlier* values of W (thus, W is an early warning indicator); high correlations at positive values of the lag imply that X correlates with *later* values. (Positive "lags" are not early warning, but frequently are useful for diagnostic purposes.) A custom program is used to compute the cross-correlations appropriately, despite the splice in the data set. The resulting sample size is around 160 and the critical values of r for a two-tailed significance test are:

$$p=0.10: \quad r > 0.131 \qquad p=0.05: \quad r > 0.155 \qquad p=0.01: \quad r > 0.203$$

Figure 6.3   Times Series of the TFT and Goldstein Scores

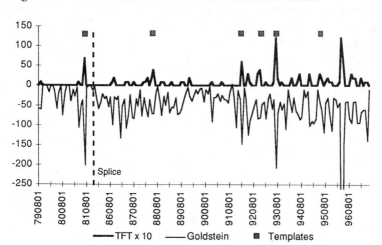

Source: Schrodt, July 1998, 38.

Note that the empirical analysis employed here violates virtually all the assumptions of the standard significance test for correlation, so these critical values should be considered illustrative only.

Estimation Algorithm

The HMM parameters were estimated by extensively modifying the source code written by Myers and Whitson (1995). Their C++ code implements an LR Hidden Markov Model and the corresponding Baum-Welch maximum likelihood training algorithm. I translated this code from the Solaris C++ environment to a Macintosh CodeWarrior ANSI C environment, in the process combining Meyers and Whitson's separate driver programs for training and testing into a single program, and modifying the input format to handle the WEIS sequences. The source code for this program is available at the KEDS web site: http://www.ukans.edu/~keds. I also extended the code to handle the LRL model, and implemented the Viterbi algorithm described in Rabiner (1989) in order to estimate the most likely state sequence.[11]

The resulting program is very fast—estimation of the HMM matrices using six 100-event sequences with a 45-symbol set and 64 Monte-Carlo iterations of the initial matrix took about 45 seconds on a Power Macintosh 7100/80—and the computation of the probability of a sequence being generated by a particular HMM is nearly instantaneous. The program requires about 1 Mb of memory for a system using 45 codes, 6 states, and 100-event sequences. The largest arrays required by the program are proportional to $(M+T)*N$, where M is the number of possible event codes, T is the maximum sequence length, and N is the number of states. Consistent with the CASCON and SHERFACS approaches, the models I estimated used six states.

Results

To determine whether the HMMs could be used to develop an early warning model by using analogies, I first identified six months in the ISR-LEB (Israel-Lebanon) data series that involved TFT conflict. These are the "templates" for the behaviors I am trying to identify and predict. The template months are

| July 1981 | [7]May 1988 | [6]February 1992 [6] |
| October 1992 | [7]July 1993 | [12]May 1995 [5] |

where [n] gives the number of TFT events in the following two months. These choices of templates are deliberately somewhat arbitrary, as the objective of this exercise is "learning by example." In addition to the template model, I also computed a "background" HMM that consisted of the 100 events prior to each of the ten randomly chosen dates. The background model is likely to be necessary because the fit of the HMM is very sensitive to the number of nonevents (see Schrodt 1998) and only the *difference* between the fit of the template and background HMMs was likely to give meaningful results.

In order to identify TFT behavior, the activities of both parts of the dyad were included in the model. This was done by recoding the LEB>ISR events with codes **23** through **44,** corresponding to the original WEIS codes **01** to **22.** If no event occurred with either dyad, the **00** nonevent was assigned to the day. The resulting model contains 45 event codes (2*22 + 1).

The early warning sequence for each template consisted of the 100 events *prior* to the first day of the template month.[12] This is again a bit arbitrary, as the actual outbreak of TFT violence does not necessarily occur early in the month. However, because the objective of this exercise is early warning, I am trying to model the period *leading up to* the initiation of TFT violence, not the violence itself. The alpha series for the fit of each month in the time series is generated by taking the 100 events prior to the end of the month and calculating the probability that this sequence was generated by the model. According to the underlying theory of HMMs, we should see a correlation between the fit of the template HMM—or the difference between this fit and the fit of the background model—and the TFT series. Figure 6.4 shows an example of the difference of the two series and, for comparison, the Goldstein-scaled series.

Figure 6.5 shows the cross-correlation of the three measures—background alpha, template alpha, and difference—with the TFT measure; the cross-correlation with the Goldstein score shows a similar pattern, except with the signs reversed.[13] At first glance, these cross-correlations appear to provide strong support for using HMMs as early warning indicators: There is the expected high correlation at +1 and +2 months (when the 100-event sequence is likely to coincide closely with an actual TFT sequence) and a tantalizing early warning cross-correlation centered at about −4 months. However, these impressive cross-correlation patterns have the *wrong sign!* If the theory is correct, one should see *positive* correlations with the TFT measure and *negative* correlations with the Goldstein scale. Yet, the opposite, quite conspicuously, occurs.

Figures 6.4 Time Series of Difference between Template and Background Alphas with Goldstein Scores

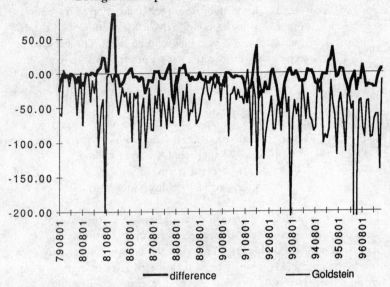

Source: Schrodt, July 1998, 39.

Figure 6.5 Cross-Correlation of TFT with Background and Template Model Alphas

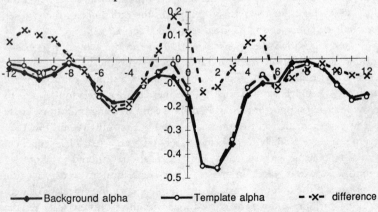

Source: Schrodt, July 1998, 40.

The reason for these anomalous results is that the length of each monthly sequence in *days* (as distinct from events) is cross-correlated with both measures. This pattern is very similar to the cross-correlation curves in figure 6.5, and accounts for both the sign of those curves and the fact that they coincide. In general, the alphas for both models decrease as the number of true events increases (and hence the length of the sequence in days decreases). The high negative values of the Goldstein score, and the high positive values of the TFT score coincide with periods of high activity, hence the direction of the correlation. The number of events versus nonevents almost completely dominates the calculation of the alphas in this data set.

One redeeming feature comes out of this calculation: In figure 6.5 the *difference* between the background and template alphas shows a relatively high correlation—in the correct direction—with the TFT series. This peaks at a lag of −1 month, which is to be expected because several of the TFT sequences extend across two or more months. Whereas, the templates are based on sequences that terminate at the end of the month before the TFT sequence.

Figure 6.6 shows the alpha-difference (Δ) and TFT series. Using a threshold of Δ>2.0 and a lag time of zero to two months for the TFT events, only one false positive occurs—just prior to the 1982 splice—and generally months where the alpha-difference is greater than 2.0 occur contemporaneously with TFT months. All the templates are identified correctly. There are, however, a large number of false negatives: Only about half of the TFT points are associated with Δ>2.0 points, and interestingly the model misses the major incidence of TFT violence involving Hizballah rocket attacks and the Israeli "Operation Grapes of Wrath" in the spring of 1996.

Figure 6.6 suggests that while the difference between the background and template alphas cannot be used for early warning, it can be used for *monitoring* an event data stream for a specific type of behavior that has been defined by a set of analogies. Thus, for example, if a human analyst identified a certain pattern of behavior that she thought was a good early warning indicator, an HMM-based system could monitor a set of event sequences (such as, those produced by a machine-coding system using the Reuters newsfeed) and alert the analyst when that sequence was observed. Similarly, if an analyst wanted to evaluate whether a specific type of event sequence could be used as an early warning indicator, it would be easy to search a set of event data to determine other instances of the sequence.

Figure 6.6 Time Series of Difference between Template and Background Alphas with the TFT Scores

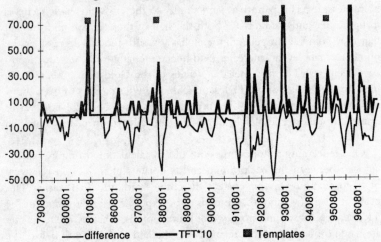

Source: Schrodt, July 1998, 41.

Early Warning Using Hidden States

An additional indicator derived from the HMM might be useful for early warning: the hidden state of the system. As noted earlier, the Viterbi algorithm allows one to compute the sequence of hidden states that has the maximum likelihood for a given model and sequence of observations. If the theory underlying the use of the HMM is correct, we should see a system spending more time in the early states of the template model as it begins to approach a TFT event. The proportion of time spent in those early states could then be used as an early warning indicator.

I used a two-stage process to estimate such models:

1. Estimate a series of HMMs using Monte-Carlo methods that randomly varied the initial **A** and **B** matrices (64 experiments).
2. Repeat the first stage a large number of times (for example, 128 or 256) and select the HMM that maximizes the total cross-correlation at lags -2, -3, and -4 between the TFT measure and QBC, that is, the proportion of time the system spends in states B and C.

In other words, this technique searches across a large number of estimated models to find one with the desired early warning behavior. The search phase in the second stage is necessary for two reasons: First, there are a large number of local maxima in the estimation even when Monte-Carlo experiments are used. Second, even if some state or states of the model can serve as a leading indicator, there is no guarantee in an LRL model that these will be states B and C. Consequently the system needs to systematically search for those models where states B and C serve an early warning function.

Figure 6.7 shows the cross-correlations for two such models, Q52 and Q61 (labeled according to their total cross-correlation r's at lags −2, −3, and −4) and the QBC statistic. These two models provide the sought after early warning indicator, although curiously the cross-correlation of Q52 peaks at a lag of −5 even though it was selected for the shorter lags. The alpha curve, on the other hand, looks identical to that in figure 6.5—even after selecting the model for the cross-correlation of QBC, alpha responds only to the number of nonevents in the sequence.

It is important to note that the cross-correlation patterns seen in figure 6.7 are *not* typical; only a very small number of models show this behavior, and most estimated models have QBC cross-correlations near zero. The obvious question arises as to whether these estimates are sensitive to

Figure 6.7 Cross-Correlation of TFT with for Q_{BC} and Alpha Models for Q52 and Q61

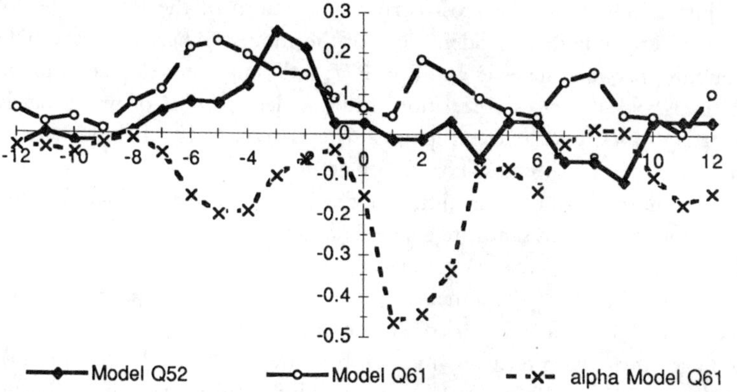

Source: Schrodt, July 1998, 42.

political characteristics found in the event data, or are merely a computer-assisted exercise of "beat the significance test." For starters, I would note that models with high QBC cross-correlations emerge quite consistently from this technique. In other words, I am presenting typical results of a search across 128 or 256 models, not the best results that I achieved over months of supercomputer computation. The successful early warning models are rare, but not very rare.

To provide a stronger test, I estimated some models using a split sample design. The data set was divided in half at July 1990, then I searched for an HMM that maximized the QBC × TFT cross-correlation for the data prior to July 1990. I then calculated the cross-correlations for only the second half of the data (t ≥ July 1990). In the split sample, the sample size is around 70 so the illustrative critical values of r are:

$$p = 0.10 \quad r > 0.198 \quad p = 0.05 \quad r > 0.235 \quad p = 0.01 \quad r > 0.306$$

Most of the same templates were used as before,[14] so the estimated model includes information from the second half of the data set, but the selection criteria on the model do not.

The results of this exercise are shown in figure 6.8 for one such model, labeled P77. Consistent with the search algorithm finding true characteristics of political behavior, the early warning cross-correlation found in the first half of the data set is also found in the second half. In addition, the cross-correlations at leading time points are quite random. The model also provides some early warning for the Goldstein scale, again consistent with theoretical expectations.

Figure 6.9 shows the cross-correlation pattern of the P77 model for each of the individual hidden states of the model. (There is a very tight coupling between states D and E in P77, and hence these are combined.) As expected, the cross-correlations show a clear pattern of progressively later lag times, with two exceptions: state B actually lags behind state A, and state F shows no cross-correlation at all.

Examining event probabilities in the B matrix, the high-probability events in the various states are generally consistent with theoretical expectations. State A has broad range of cooperative and conflictual observation probabilities that may be a measure of an escalation phase before the outbreak of TFT conflict. The state D/E combination seems to involve a lot of negotiation, with relatively high probabilities in the WEIS 03 (consult), 06 (promise), and 12 (accuse) categories. High probabilities in the B and C vectors are concentrated in the verbal conflict categories (WEIS 11 to

Figure 6.8   Q$_{BC}$ Cross-Correlation for the P77 Model

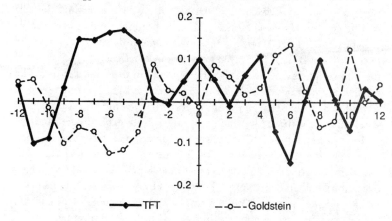

Source: Schrodt, July 1998, 43.

Figure 6.9   Cross-Correlation with TFT by States in the P77 Model

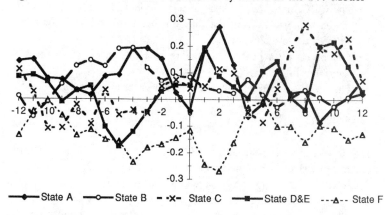

Source: Schrodt, July 1998, 44.

14) without any compensating consultations and promises, which may be why those states function as early warning indicators.

I repeated these split sample tests on a random set of data that have a similar marginal distribution of events but no auto-correlation. The search algorithm was able to find models that produced high cross-correlations at lags −2, −3, and −4 between the first half of the TFT series and the QBC statistic computed on the models generated from the random data, albeit at a slightly lower level (0.60 to 0.65 in the random data versus 0.72 to 0.77 in the ISR-LEB data). However, none of the other characteristics found in the split sample tests on the real data are found in the simulated data. These models do not produce high cross-correlations at lags −2, −3, and −4 in the second half of the data, and there is no pattern to the correlations of the states other than those for which the models were explicitly selected.

In summary, is the QBC early warning indicator sensitive to actual political events or is the observed cross-correlation pattern just luck? Supporting the chance interpretation is the fact that models producing early warning are exceptional rather than typical. However, HMM parameter estimates are highly underdetermined, both in terms of the large number of local maxima in the estimation procedure, and in the structure of the parameters. Therefore, estimated models will always exhibit a variety of behaviors. Supporting the reality of the model is the fact that several characteristics of the P77 estimates are consistent with the underlying theoretical model:

- The QBC indicator works in a split sample test;
- The cross-correlation of the different states are consistent with their order in the model;
- The observation probabilities of the various states are distinct and plausible; and
- These characteristics do not occur in a set of random data.

Conclusion

This study of HMMs as models of TFT behavior in the protracted conflict in southern Lebanon has produced tantalizing, but hardly conclusive, results. In this concluding section, I will address three issues. First, to what extent are HMMs likely to be effective as a general early warning method? Second, how could the estimation procedure be improved and how does it compare to conventional linear methods? Finally, what theoretical insights does this exercise provide about protracted conflict processes?

Generality

My theoretical justification focused on the use of sequence analysis methods in predicting protracted conflicts that are characterized by co-adapted

SOPs. From the practical standpoint of designing systems for early warning, the amount of conflict generated by protracted conflicts is not inconsequential—southern Lebanon is just one of many cases—and merely being able to anticipate these cases would be a substantial improvement over the status quo.[15]

However, Lebow (1981), Leng (1993), and others have suggested a number of common patterns in conflict escalation and, if these can be systematically characterized by event data sequences, they could be used as early warning indicators. Therefore, my sense is that this ability of HMMs to classify sequences of behavior will make them useful in other forms of early warning beyond the case of protracted conflict. HMM models might also be made more robust if they were predicated on the values of other variables—for example, the presence of ethnolinguistic divisions, income inequality, or the level of industrial development in an area—that may not be apparent from the events alone.

At the same time, the co-adaptation argument suggests that there are a couple of categories of conflict where sequence analysis will *not* work for early warning. One category involves situations where the conflict involves new organizations confronting each other for the first time. For example, I would be surprised if sequence analysis (or any other dynamic model) could predict the initial phases of the American-Iranian hostage crisis, the initial phases of the Soviet intervention in Afghanistan, or the United Nations intervention in Somalia. Sequence analysis will also be less effective in dealing with situations where there has been significant strategic innovation, such as the 1967 and 1973 Middle East wars.[16] These situations are extremely difficult for humans to anticipate—that's the whole idea!—and may be formally chaotic in the sense of systems dynamics. All these propositions could be tested if the appropriate event data were available.

A remaining problem in the development of a practical monitoring or early warning system involves the trade-off of Type I and Type II errors. At the Toronto early warning conference, I heard both of the following sentiments expressed (by different individuals in different organizations):

- "If the system gives me any false alarms, it will have no credibility" (low tolerance for Type I errors);
- "I don't care how many false alarms the system gives; just make sure it gets the real crises" (low tolerance for Type II errors).

Clearly a single system cannot satisfy both audiences, but it should be possible to create distinct systems with differing levels of sensitivity. A system that provides a simple "heads up" alert can afford to generate more false alarms than a system that provides a "start shipping $30 million of emergency food aid" alert, to say nothing of a "send the Marines" alert.

From the perspective of developing a global early warning system, the problem is not just developing one or two indicators or models but rather developing a number of them. We are unlikely to be able to develop, with physics-like reductionism, a single theory of human conflict behavior because of the very substantial information processing capabilities of humans. Humans can be motivated to kill each other—and are so motivated on a regular basis—for quite a wide variety of reasons. The protracted conflict in southern Lebanon is somewhat similar, but hardly identical, to that involving Israel and the Palestinians—many of the same actors are involved, although not the same issues—but both are quite different from the protracted ethnic conflict in Rwanda and Burundi. Yet they are all protracted. This suggests that as an initial step, one would want to develop a number of contextually specific models based on archetypal sequences.

Estimation

From the standpoint of estimation, the most troublesome aspect of the HMM approach is the high variance of the parameter estimates. This is apparently an inescapable characteristic of the technique: Baum-Welch estimation is a nonlinear method and there are no conditions that one can impose to identify the parameters.

That said, there are obviously more systematic ways to search for a global maximum (or at least a set of high local maxima) than the Monte-Carlo method employed here: the structure of the problem is almost begging for the use of a genetic algorithm (GA).[17] In addition, Rabiner (1989, 273–274) indicates that in speech recognition problems, the maximization is particularly sensitive to the initial values of the symbol observation probabilities in the **B** matrix, although not the transition probabilities in the **A** matrix. In an LRL model, however, the **A** matrix may also be sensitive to the initial parameter estimates—for example, it would be helpful to force state A to be the background state.

Even with these modifications, it seems likely that a practical early warning model will require a certain amount of fine-tuning. For example, the six-state model appears to be roughly the correct size and it is consistent with earlier theoretical formulations of crisis phase, but increasing or decreasing the number of states might improve the fit. Another arbitrary parameter that could be modified is the 100-event sequence length—why not 64 events or 128 events? Such tweaking apparently is quite common in the development of speech recognition software, and would be recommended in the development of any early warning system.

A recent paper by Hinich (1997) makes some interesting observations about the limited utility of standard linear forecasting models—for example the Box-Jenkins paradigm—in dealing with political behavior. Hinich observes that the stochastic linear model provides very poor predictions (particularly in the long term) if the system is highly autoregressive and, in a later discussion, noted that linear estimates are predicated on the stochastic disturbance terms of the process being independent. In the tightly interlinked and historically sensitive systems that characterize protracted conflicts, behavior is autoregressive but the errors are not independent, and consequently the utility of linear models is severely compromised.

Using the Levant as an example, regional political behavior is autoregressive in the sense that the effects of disturbances such as the Lebanese civil war, Israel's invasion of Lebanon, the outbreak of the Palestinian *intifada,* or the assassination of Israel's prime minister Yitzhak Rabin, will be apparent in the event data series for a period of years. Or, to get into a *really* autoregressive series, it is not coincidental that some of the territory involved in the current Israeli-Arab conflict is dotted with fortifications remaining from the Crusades—a millennium in the past—or that the border between Maronite and Druze control in the Lebanese civil war is just a few kilometers south of the famous Nahr al-Kalb, a canyon containing inscriptions from passing armies dating back to the Babylonians and the Egyptian pharaoh Ramses II.

Meanwhile, organizational SOPs will cause error disturbances to be correlated. Any random outbreak of violence in the Arab-Israeli conflict sets off a ritualized set of accusations and protests by the antagonists, and attempts at mediation and appeals for restraint by regional and international actors: the pattern depends only on who initiated the violence. In fact, if one removes the proper names, much of the Reuters record for this period is difficult to classify by date: Many a traveler in the region has had the unsettling experience of reading a newspaper for several pages only to notice, after finally encountering some glaring anachronism,[18] that the newspaper is three weeks, three months, or even three years out of date.

Because of these characteristics, the linear modeling approach is not going to work very well. Those same characteristics, however, improve the likelihood that a sequence comparison approach will work. Additional prima facie evidence of this is found in the failure of the earlier DARPA (Defense Advanced Research Projects Agency) efforts. Linear prediction techniques (unlike nonlinear methods) were well-developed at the time of the DARPA work, and the computer power available at the time was sufficient for estimating these models. If event prediction could have been solved using linear methods, this probably would have been discovered a quarter century ago.

Theory

On the theoretical level, the first thing that we gain from this approach is a reproducible method of evaluating whether sequence based precursors exist in protracted conflicts. In particular, the HMM does not involve the human hindsight bias that plagues the evaluation of early warning indicators using qualitative historical comparison. If one takes the WEIS machine coding dictionaries and the quantitative definition of a TFT event as a given, only four free parameters separate the early warning indicator from the Reuters text: the choice of training examples, the sub-sequence length, the number of hidden states in the HMM, and the number of Monte-Carlo experiments used in the estimation. All other parameters are determined from the data. The fact that machine coding removes the effects of human hindsight bias from the event coding further increases the possibility that the early warning indicators are real rather than determined by idiosyncratic coding and scaling decisions.

This in turn may also allow us to successfully distinguish *actual* protracted conflicts—conflicts resulting from co-adaptive SOPs—from conflicts that are merely repetitive and result from the tails of the Poisson distribution. Protracted conflicts have precursors; Poisson conflicts do not. Again, the sequence analysis approach—the indeterminacy of the HMMs notwithstanding—has the advantages of transparency and reproducibility. The estimated HMM parameters should also provide some insight into what is important in a precursor and what is not.

Once a number of contextually specific models have been developed and verified, then the next stage of theory development would be finding common characteristics of those models. The extant theoretical literature provides plenty of guidance on this issue. In addition, some of the contextual differences might be linked to exogenous static variables that could classify which models apply in which circumstances. But one needs first to demonstrate that these conflicts are predictable in a contextually-specific sense before trying to generalize the models. Generalizations can be made from studying apples and oranges, but fewer can be made from studying apples and bowling balls, or apples, Apple Records, and Apple Computers.

The status of statistical early warning is often similar to that of the apocryphal talking dog who can't get the punch line of a story right ("Damn dog never could tell a joke"). If we expect perfection, we miss the fact that the dog can talk at all. For example, the summary of the State Failures Project (Esty et al. 1995, iii) notes that the statistical model works in "only" two-thirds of the cases, and concludes that human experts must continue to be used in assessing risks of state failure. It does not, however, present any evidence that human experts have a higher accuracy rate.

In the present state of our knowledge, it is not clear whether statistical forecasting—using this or some other method—will be superior to human forecasting. My guess is that human forecasting will be better for some types of conflicts (for example, those that are linked to relatively obvious ideological or economic changes and that do not manifest themselves in discrete events), and worse in others (such as situations that can be predicted only by monitoring a fairly diffuse set of indicators consistently over a long period of time). The development of statistical early warning methods might proceed more rapidly by using a "bottom-up" approach of solving the cases that look easy first—and relegating these to low-level monitoring—and classifying some other cases as unsolvable with the existing theory and technology.

In an era of modern communications, with its accompanying increase in both the information available to human analysts and the analysts' understanding of each other's cultures, human political forecasting has scored some impressive victories, most notably the 40-year balancing of the military standoff of the Cold War. But at the same time, the list of major changes over the past 20 years that were not anticipated in sufficient time for the international community to respond is significant:

- the stability of the Islamic Republic of Iran,
- the Soviet invasion of Afghanistan and the subsequent failure of that effort,
- the collapse of the Warsaw Pact,
- the economic disintegration of the Soviet Union (although the *pattern* of dissolution was anticipated correctly),
- the civil war in Yugoslavia,
- the civil war in the Great Lakes,
- the structure of political power in Somalia,
- Iraq's invasion of Kuwait, and of course,
- the Palestinian *intifada*,

which was anticipated neither by the Israeli occupation forces nor by the leadership of the PLO. There is plenty of room for improvement here.

Note that many of these crises do not fall into the category of protracted conflicts (although the Great Lakes and the *intifada* clearly do, Somalia might, and Yugoslavia and the Soviet Union probably do on a longer time scale) and I am not suggesting that a single event based model would take care of all of these. However, a set of models with different theoretical basis and in all likelihood distinctly different coding systems (that are simple to implement with machine coding), but having in common the use of inexpensive, open-source material such as Reuters and analytical methods designed to deal with nominal irregular time series might be able to predict a large class of these behaviors.

Notes

1. The WEIS-coded Middle East event data set and the estimation programs used in this analysis, as well as additional supporting charts, can be downloaded from the Kansas Event Data System web site: http://www.ukans.edu/~keds. My thanks to Larry Bartels, Scott Bennett, Deborah Gerner, Joshua Goldstein, Walter Mebane, Mohan Penubarti, and Jas Sekhon for helpful comments on earlier presentations of the hidden Markov approach.

2. Predictions might be made on the basis of other characteristics of the system, such as the effects that economic or technological changes have on the utility functions of the actors. If the system exhibits chaotic attractors, predictions could also be made about the *range* of strategic outcomes. But, in the absence of a completely specified model and complete information, one cannot make point predictions about the behavior of a chaotic system.

3. A detailed discussion of the concept of co-adaptation is beyond the scope of this chapter, but general discussions from a natural science perspective can be found in Maynard-Smith (1982) and Kauffman (1993); Anderson, Arrow, and Pines (1988) discuss a number of social science applications, and Schrodt (1993) applies the concept to the issue of international regimes.

4. This section is taken from Schrodt (1998) with minor modifications.

5. This is in contrast to most applications of Markov models in international politics where the states correspond directly to observable behaviors (see Schrodt 1985 for a review).

6. Assume that each state has ten associated WEIS categories that are equally probable: $b_i(k)=0.10$. Leaving aside the transition probabilities, each additional symbol will reduce the probability of the complete sequence by a factor of 10^{-1}. The transition probabilities, and the fact that the WEIS codes are not equiprobable, further reduce this probability.

An insurmountable disadvantage of this computation is that one cannot meaningfully compare the fit of two sequences to a single HMM unless the sequences are equal in length. In other words, it is possible to compare a sequence to a series of models, but one cannot compare the fit of several arbitrary sequences to a single model.

7. Sherman and Neack (1993) provide a review of the evolution of these data sets. Schrodt and Gerner (1997) demonstrate that distinct political phases—defined statistically using clusters of behavior—are found in event data sets covering the Middle East.

8. The NEXIS search command used to locate stories to be coded was: (ISRAEL! OR PLO OR PALEST! OR LEBAN! OR JORDAN! OR SYRIA! OR EGYPT!) AND NOT (SOCCER! OR SPORT! OR OLYMPIC! OR TENNIS OR BASKETBALL!)

Only the lead sentences were coded and a sentence was not coded if it contained six or more verbs or no actor was found prior to the verb (sentences meeting these criteria have a greater-than-average likelihood of being incorrectly coded by KEDS). This produced a total of 3,497 ISR>LEB and LEB>ISR events for the entire April 1979 to June 1997 period.

While KEDS is capable of distinguishing between different actors who are likely to engage in the use of force in Lebanon—for example Amal versus Hizballah—I did not do so in this study. Forces allied with Israel—notably Israel's client militia, the "South Lebanon Army"—are coded as Israeli rather than Lebanese. The coding probably underestimates activity prior to 1982, when some uses of force in southern Lebanon were coded as Palestinian rather than Lebanese.

9. The Goldstein scores for ISR>LEB and LEB>ISR are highly correlated, with r = 0.82 (N = 171), so only one of these dyads is analyzed.

10. The calculation of the cross-correlation does not include 1982–1985, although the sequences fitted to the HMM include information from this period when that is necessary to complete a 100-event sequence (for example, the January 1986 to March 1986 subsequences include some events from 1985).

If the 1982–1985 period is included in the assessment of predictive power, the results are considerably weaker. Although, to the extent that I looked at them, they are generally consistent with the results of the spliced model. While the focus of military conflict is southern Lebanon, some of the Israeli retaliation occurs well outside of this area—air attacks on militia camps near Beirut are fairly common and are included as TFT events. Attacks by the Arab forces operating from Lebanon, whose air power has been confined to the occasional motorized hang glider, are exclusively on Israeli and South Lebanon Army forces operating in southern Lebanon and attacks into the Hula valley and western Galilee (notably Kiryat Shimona and environs).

11. The Meyers and Whitson code is clean, well-documented, and survived my translation to run correctly the first time. I would assume that either my C code or their C++ code would port easily to a DOS/Windows or OS/2 environment for those so inclined. In the process of extending the model to the LRL form, I rewrote the estimation equations to correspond exactly to those in Rabiner. The Meyers and Whitson implementation differed slightly from Rabiner's equations, presumably because their models estimate a separate vector for "transition symbols."

   The source code used in this analysis of the LRL model has not been posted on the KEDS web site because it contains a rat's nest of poorly documented #if . . . #endif blocks to allow all various different analyses to be done within a single program. With that caveat, the code is available on request.

12. Why 100? The length of the warning sequence is a free parameter and other values might work better, depending on the application. I did some experiments early in the research with sequences of 50 and 200 events in addition to the 100 event length; the results were roughly comparable but 100 appeared to produce somewhat better cross-correlations. Given the vagaries of timing in this region—for example the effects of de facto unilateral cease-fires during various religious holidays—it is unlikely that the model will be very sensitive to the length of the sequence.

13. A more technical version of this analysis, with additional figures, is available in the "papers" section of the KEDS web site.

14. Due to a minor bug in the program, the first template (July 1981) was replaced by the 100-event sequence ending in May 1997. Because May 1997 precedes TFT behavior in June 1997, it is still a legitimate template.

15. Of course, if timely early warning resulted in effective action to head off the violence, it would eventually invalidate the model. The likelihood of encountering this "problem" seems remote.

16. The innovation occurred on the part of Israel in 1967 and Egypt and Syria in 1973. These are examples of strategic military innovations but the same arguments apply to diplomatic innovations such as Camp David and Oslo.

17. My thanks to Walter Mebane and Jas Sekhon for this suggestion.

18. The glaring anachronism is frequently an item of popular culture, which is less static in this region than political conflict.

References

Allison, Graham T. 1971. *The Essence of Decision.* Boston: Little, Brown.

Anderson, Philip W., Kenneth J. Arrow, and David Pines, eds. 1988. *The Economy as an Evolving Complex System.* New York: Addison Wesley.

Azar, Edward E. 1980. "The Conflict and Peace Data Bank (COPDAB) Project." *Journal of Conflict Resolution* 24 (March): 143–52.

————. 1984. "The Theory of Protracted Social Conflict and the Challenge of Transforming Conflict Situations." In *Conflict Processes and the Breakdown of International Systems*, ed. Dina A. Zinnes. Denver: University of Denver Graduate School of International Studies, pp. 81–99.

———— and Thomas Sloan. 1975. *Dimensions of Interaction*. Pittsburgh, PA: University Center for International Studies, University of Pittsburgh.

Bartholomew, D. J. 1971. *Stochastic Models for Social Processes*. New York: John Wiley & Sons.

Bennett, D. Scott, and Philip A. Schrodt. 1987. "Linear Event Patterns in WEIS Data." Presented at the annual meeting of the American Political Science Association, Chicago.

Bloomfield, Lincoln P., and Allen Moulton. 1989. *CASCON III: Computer-Aided System for Analysis of Local Conflicts*. Cambridge: MIT Center for International Studies.

———— and Allen Moulton. 1997. *Managing International Conflict*. New York: St. Martin's Press.

Bueno de Mesquita, Bruce. 1981. *The War Trap*. New Haven, CT: Yale University Press.

————, Bruce, David Newman, and Alvin Rabushka. 1996. *Red Flag over Hong Kong*. Chatham, NJ: Chatham House Publishers.

Butterworth, Robert L. 1976. *Managing Interstate Conflict, 1945–74: Data with Synopses*. Pittsburgh, PA: University of Pittsburgh University Center for International Studies.

Casti, John L. 1997. *Would-Be Worlds*. New York: John Wiley & Sons.

Choucri, Nazli, and Thomas W. Robinson, eds. 1979. *Forecasting in International Relations: Theory, Methods, Problems, Prospects*. San Francisco: W.H. Freeman.

Cimbala, Stephen J. 1987. *Artificial Intelligence and National Security*. Lexington, MA: Lexington Books.

Cyert, Richard M., and James G. March. 1963. *A Behavioral Theory of the Firm*. Englewood Cliffs, NJ: Prentice-Hall.

Esty, Daniel C., Jack A. Goldstone, Ted Robert Gurr, Pamela T. Surko and Alan N. Unger. 1995. "Working Papers: State Failure Task Force Report." November 30, 1995. McLean, VA: Science Applications International Corporation.

Gerner, Deborah J., Philip A. Schrodt, Ronald A. Francisco, and Judith L. Weddle. 1994. "The Machine Coding of Events from Regional and International Sources." *International Studies Quarterly* 38 (March): 91–119.

Gurr, Ted R., and Barbara Harff. 1996. *Early Warning of Communal Conflict and Humanitarian Crisis*. Tokyo: United Nations University Press, Monograph Series on Governance and Conflict Resolution.

Goldstein, Joshua S. 1992. "A Conflict-Cooperation Scale for WEIS Events Data." *Journal of Conflict Resolution* 36 (June): 369–85.

Hopple, Gerald W., Stephen J. Andriole, and Amos Freedy, eds. 1984. *National Security Crisis Forecasting and Management*. Boulder, CO: Westview.

Hinich, Melvin. 1997. "Forecasting Time Series." Presented at the 14th Summer Conference on Political Methodology, Columbus, Ohio.

Hudson, Valerie, ed. 1991. *Artificial Intelligence and International Politics.* Boulder, CO: Westview.

Hughes, Barry B. 1984. *World Futures: A Critical Analysis of Alternatives.* Baltimore, MD: Johns Hopkins.

Huxtable, Phillip A., and John C. Pevehouse. 1996. "Potential Validity Problems in Events Data Collection." *International Studies Notes* 21 (Spring): 8–19.

Kauffman, Stuart A. 1993. *The Origins of Order.* Oxford, UK: Oxford University Press.

Khong, Yuen F. 1992. *Analogies at War.* Princeton, NJ: Princeton University Press.

Kruskal, Joseph B. 1983. "An Overview of Sequence Comparison." In *Time Warps, String Edits and Macromolecules,* eds. David Sankoff and Joseph B. Kruskal. New York: Addison-Wesley, pp. 1–44.

Laurance, Edward J. 1990. "Events Data and Policy Analysis." *Policy Sciences* 23 (May): 111–32.

Lebow, Richard N. 1981. *Between Peace and War: The Nature of International Crises.* Baltimore, MD: Johns Hopkins.

Leng, Russell J. 1987. *Behavioral Correlates of War, 1816–1975.* (ICPSR 8606). Ann Arbor, MI: Inter-University Consortium for Political and Social Research.

———. 1993. *Interstate Crisis Behavior, 1816–1980.* New York: Cambridge University Press.

Lund, Michael S. 1996. *Preventing Violent Conflicts: A Strategy for Preventive Diplomacy.* Washington, DC: United States Institute for Peace.

May, Ernest. 1973. *"Lessons" of the Past: The Use and Misuse of History in American Foreign Policy.* New York: Oxford University Press.

Maynard-Smith, John. 1982. *Evolution and the Theory of Games.* Cambridge, UK: Cambridge University Press.

McClelland, Charles A. 1976. *World Event/Interaction Survey Codebook.* (ICPSR 5211). Ann Arbor, MI: Inter-University Consortium for Political and Social Research.

Mefford, Dwain. 1985. "Formulating Foreign Policy on the Basis of Historical Programming." In *Dynamic Models of International Conflict,* eds. Urs Luterbacher and Michael D. Ward. Boulder, CO: Lynne Rienner Publishing, pp. 401–25.

Merritt, Richard. L., Robert. G. Muncaster, and Dina. A. Zinnes. 1993. *International Event-Data Developments: DDIR Phase II.* Ann Arbor, MI: University of Michigan Press.

Myers, R. and J. Whitson. 1995. *Hidden Markov Model* for automatic speech recognition (C++ source code). <<http://www.itl.atr.co.jp/comp.speech/Section6/Recognition/myers.hmm.html>>.

Neustadt, Richard E., and Ernst R. May. 1986. *Thinking in Time: The Uses of History for Decision Makers.* New York: The Free Press.

Rabiner, L. R. 1989. "A Tutorial on Hidden Markov Models and Selected Applications in Speech Recognition." *Proceedings of the IEEE* 77 (2): 257–86.

Sankoff, David, and Joseph B. Kruskal, eds. 1983. *Time Warps, String Edits, and Macromolecules: The Theory and Practice of Sequence Comparison.* New York: Addison-Wesley.

Schrodt, Philip A. 1985. "The Role of Stochastic Models in International Relations Research." In *Theories, Models, and Simulation in International Relations,* ed. Michael D. Ward. Boulder, CO: Westview, pp. 199–222.

————. 1990. "Parallel Event Sequences in International Crises, 1835–1940." *Political Behavior* 12: 97–123.

————. 1991. "Pattern Recognition in International Event Sequences: A Machine Learning Approach." In *Artificial Intelligence and International Politics,* ed. Valerie Hudson. Boulder, CO: Westview, pp. 169–93.

————. 1993. "Rules and Co-Adaptation in Foreign Policy Behavior." Presented at the annual meeting of the International Studies Association, Acapulco, Mexico.

————. 1994. "Event Data in Foreign Policy Analysis." In *Foreign Policy Analysis: Continuity and Change.* eds. Laura J. Neack, Jeanne A. K. Hey, and Patrick J. Haney. New York: Prentice-Hall, pp. 145–66.

————. 1998. "Pattern Recognition of International Crises Using Hidden Markov Models." In *Non-Linear Models and Methods in Political Science.* ed., Diana Richards. Ann Arbor, MI: University of Michigan Press.

————, Shannon G. Davis, and Judith L. Weddle. 1994. "Political Science: KEDS—A Program for the Machine Coding of Event Data." *Social Science Computer Review* 12 (Winter): 561–88.

———— and Deborah J. Gerner. 1994. "Validity Assessment of a Machine-Coded Event Data Set for the Middle East, 1982–1992." *American Journal of Political Science* 38 (August): 825–54.

———— and Deborah J. Gerner. 1997. "Empirical Indicators of Crisis Phase in the Middle East, 1982–1995." *Journal of Conflict Resolution* 41 (August): 529–52.

Sherman, Frank L., and Laura J. Neack. 1993. "Imagining the Possibilities: The Prospects of Isolating the Genome of International Conflict from the SHERFACS Dataset." In *International Event-Data Developments: DDIR Phase II.* eds. Richard L. Merritt, Robert G. Muncaster, and Dina A. Zinnes. Ann Arbor, MI: University of Michigan Press, pp. 87–112.

Singer, J. David, and Michael D. Wallace. 1979. *To Augur Well: Early Warning Indicators in World Politics.* Beverly Hills, CA: Sage.

Van Creveld, Martin. 1991. *Technology and War.* New York: Free Press.

Vertzberger, Yaacov Y. I. 1990. *The World in Their Minds: Information Processing, Cognition, and Perception in Foreign Policy Decision Making.* Stanford, CA: Stanford University Press.

Ward, Michael D., ed. 1985. *Theories, Models, and Simulations in International Relations.* Boulder, CO: Westview Press.

CHAPTER SEVEN

Protracted Conflict, Intervention, and Revolution: Case Studies of Nicaragua and the Philippines

Marc V. Simon

Introduction

S talemated domestic conflicts take many forms; Azar's work on protracted social conflict presents an important one. When stalemates endure for a long period of time, and especially when they become "protracted" in Azar's sense, the costs of the conflict, both physical and psychological, become intense. Furthermore, because protracted conflicts often involve ethnic or communal groups who do not live neatly within one state, they are prone to spillover into other states and to attract intervention from other states. Empirically, intervention tends to intensify domestic conflicts and increase their duration (Gurr and Duvall 1973; Pearson 1974; Rasler 1983), making it all the more imperative that we understand them. The study of stalemated domestic conflicts begins with some obvious questions. What causes stalemates? Are all stalemates the same? What causes stalemates to change, escalate, or de-escalate over time? What leads one side or the other to gain advantage in such conflicts? What factors promote or discourage intervention in these conflicts? What causes stalemates to endure or to end?

Our goal should be to understand the processes that lead to stalemates in general, so that we can begin to identify particular conflict patterns of stalemates—some of which might fit well with the concept of protracted social conflict. The processes that lead to stalemate must be linked to micro-level causes of government and opposition behavior. This will allow us to understand why and how the patterns change, to identify situations where change is likely (such as crises, as discussed in the chapter by G. Dale Thomas), and to identify particularly unstable situations when the conflict pattern is sensitive to small changes in these causal factors.

Strategies for capturing these underlying conflict processes can take several forms. One could apply a conflict resolution perspective and use the human needs approach (such as, Burton 1990), which fits protracted social conflict theory (see the chapter by Gil Friedman). This would provide an understanding of the incompatibilities between the actors in conflict and, of the extent to which grievances are linked to structural issues, and help determine whether the incompatibilities are "constant-sum," which makes solutions difficult to find. The conflict resolution approach is well grounded in the "microfoundations" of the conflict and it explains the difficulties in resolving the conflict, but is less useful for understanding the various causes of escalation and de-escalation during the stalemate. An alternative approach, which I adopt here, is to construct a formal model, grounded in the dominant social movement theories of collective action (Lichbach 1995) and political opportunity structure (McAdam et al. 1996), to explain the escalation pattern of domestic conflict.

In previous work (Simon 1994) I developed a formal, action-reaction, differential equation model of domestic conflict. I describe a version of the model in this chapter, and explain how it yields four fundamental underlying "dynamics" of domestic conflict—each of which can lead to a stalemate. I argue that the four dynamics are relatively stable, and that the actors in conflict can intuitively understand the nature of each dynamic. I analyze each dynamic to show the incentives it poses for the government and opposition in conflict, as well as for any interveners. The chapter concludes with two short case studies, on Nicaragua and the Philippines, which illustrate the explanatory force of the model and lead to more hypotheses that can be tested in further research.

The Formal Model's Structure
and Relation to Other Works

In this section I will describe the model of escalation of domestic conflicts developed in Simon (1994). The appendix to this chapter contains the mathematical description and algebraic analysis, for those few readers interested in these aspects of the model. The model's structure is related to other models in the literature on protest and social movements, and some of these models will be discussed to highlight the modeling choices I have made.

The model is a two-equation, nonlinear, action-reaction model—one equation for the government and the other for the opposition. Its dependent variables are the "hostility" levels pursued by the government and opposition in conflict. By hostility level I mean the level of opposition resistance or government repression.[1] The model is based on assumptions, taken from the literatures on social movements about the forces that cause actors in domestic conflicts to escalate or de-escalate. Before I elaborate on those, I want to emphasize that its structure is based on some assumptions about how participants in domestic conflict understand their opponent's behavior.

The nonlinear structure of the model implies that the government and opposition have a "rate of change" in their hostility level that is applied to the current level of hostility:

dY/dt = rate × Y, where Y is government
repression level, and rate = f (X, Y) (1)

dX/dt = rate × X, where X is opposition
resistance level, and rate = f (X, Y) (2)

It is reasonable to assume that each actor thinks about the other in the following terms. The leaders of the government ask, "how much resistance is there now?" (X), as well as "are the rebels growing stronger or weaker?" (rate). From this information they arrive at an estimate of the direction and overall rate of change of the hostility level of their opponent (dX/dt).

The nonlinear mathematics of the model, together with the possibility that the rates for each actor can be positive or negative, produces four fundamental patterns of conflict or "dynamics" that I describe later. For these dynamics to be meaningful, and for the actors to make strategic choices based on these dynamics, they must be at least intuitively apparent to the actors. In the model, the dynamics are described by the sign and slope of an isocline for each equation. To understand the isocline, the government, for example, must be able to perceive whether and to what extent the opposition is generally weakened or strengthened by increases in government hostility. This is the sort of "reactiveness" captured in the models of Kowaleski and Hoover (1995). Their survey of the literature on domestic conflict revealed a predominance among governments and oppositions of what they call "sensitivity" and what I call "predatory"—a situation where actors are deterred by increases in opponent's hostility, and provoked by decreases (Hoover and Kowaleski 1992). I argue that by observing their opponent's reaction over time (using some sort of Bayesian decision process), actors in domestic conflicts can make reasonable estimates of the "reactivity" of their opponent—thus they can know the underlying conflict dynamic and can observe change in that dynamic.

My effort to model the underlying conflict dynamic is somewhat related to the effort to find a "curve of revolution" (Francisco 1995, 278)— or more specifically, to understand the relationship between state repression and societal protest. Earlier works have hypothesized and tested the simple inverted-U curve relationship between repression and protest (such as, Hibbs 1973, DeNardo 1985, Muller and Weede 1990, and Opp 1994). Francisco's work (1996, 1995) has shown that, empirically, the inverted-U curve does not account for protest across time. That is, protest is not highest at moderate levels of repression, and lowest under very high and very low repression. Francisco (1995) tested the inverted-U hypothesis within the structure of two common action-reaction model structures, the predator-prey model (Tsebelis and Sprague 1989) and Lotka-Volterra models, on data from East Germany, Czechoslovakia, and the *intifada*. He found only moderate support for the inverted-U pattern in Czechoslovakia, and none elsewhere. His work shows that in the context of these two model structures, there is no simple pattern of conflict that applies in even a small number of conflicts across time.

Francisco's work is important in that it tests two general model structures of domestic conflict that exist in the literature as well as the most important component, which must be built into any model structure, the interaction between repression and protest. My conclusion from his findings is that the best model structure and the interaction relationship are likely to be context dependent—that is, they probably vary in different types of conflicts. Thus a more general model with the flexibility to represent many general contexts is an appropriate place to look for answers in the study of stalemated domestic conflicts.

The model presented in this chapter allows the relationship between repression and protest to take several forms based on changes in the sign and magnitude of various parameters. In particular, the interactive terms in the model allow for the relationship between repression and protest to be either deterrence or escalation (Lichbach 1987), or, in Kowaleski and

Hoover's (1995) terms, sensitive (+), opportunistic (-), or imperturbable (0). Others are working more specifically on modeling this interaction (see especially Moore 1997, 1998), and their work may yet provide the empirical foundation for building better models.

Despite Francisco's finding that nonlinear models did not fit his cases (1995, 275), I continue to use a nonlinear model for three reasons. First, as noted above, the nonlinear structure is consonant with the intuitive questions that leaders ask about their opponents in domestic conflicts. Second, the nonlinear model does not necessarily produce oscillation, but generates four different conflict dynamics, each of which can generate a stalemate (nonlinear models do have stable equilibria). Third, this model is a more general form of a class of population growth models (Maynard-Smith 1974) from which the predator-prey model is derived: The assumptions that these models imply about growth in general are appropriate for the growth of hostility.[2]

My choice of an action-reaction, differential equation model over a rational choice, game theory, or expected utility model also involves some compromises. The latter tend to stress power relationships and strategic components of escalation; the former emphasize interactive components of escalation. Smoke (1977), building on Schelling (1966), conceptualizes two components of escalation—the rational, bargaining component and the interactive, action-reaction, "phenomenal" component, which can produce uncontrolled escalation. Action-reaction models capture the latter well. To strengthen the ability of my action-reaction model to capture the rational, strategic elements of escalation, I have applied some insights from the "collective action research program" (CARP) (Lichbach 1995) in developing the parameters of the model, especially the opposition equation. These are supplemented by insights from the resource mobilization tradition (McCarthy and Zald 1977, Tilly 1978) and the more recent "political opportunity structure" (POS) line of inquiry (see McAdam et al. 1997, Reising 1998).

It is to those parameters of the model that we now turn.

Describing the Parameters of the Model

This discussion will focus on the factors that determine the rates in each equation; the factors that determine whether each side is growing weaker or stronger in its ability to change its hostility level. I begin with the government equation (4), presented in table 7.1.

Table 7.1   Changing Levels of Repression and Resistance in Civil Conflict

$$dX/dt = \{p[R + rY] - X] + c[C - Y]\} \times X \quad (3)$$
$$dY/dt = \{a[H + hX] - Y] + b[B - X]\} \times Y \quad (4)$$

Table 7.2   An Overview of Symbol Definitions

Hostility

X,Y	Current levels of hostility pursued by opposition X and government Y
dX/dt, dY/dt	Escalation or deescalation: the change in hostility level over time

Hostility Thresholds for Loss of Support/Resources

C	Government coercion above this deters opposition resistance, reduces resources; below this it encourages resistance
B	Legitimacy threshold: government repression above B risks a legitimacy crisis in the general population, thus inhibiting repression; below B repression is encouraged

Variable Hostility Thresholds

H + hX	Level of government repression at which elite supporters begin to desert the state
R + rY	Level of opposition resistance which further escalation brings a decline in resources

Parameters for Variable Thresholds

H	Hostility levels supported by the government in the absence of unrest
h	The degree to which the government supports higher levels of repression as opposition resistance increases
R	Resistance level with the most support within the opposition
r	The degree to which the opposition supports higher levels of resistance as government repression increases

Relative Magnitude of Factors which Influence Hostility Level

Government	a	Capability to move toward preferred repression level
	b	Concern about a legitmacy crisis/breakdown
Opposition	c	Impact of state coercion
	p	Capability to move toward preferred resistance level

Constraints
All lower-case parameters lie between 0 and 1

Government Repression Model:
Capabilities, Willingness, and Breakdown

The government is represented as a unitary rational actor that responds to threats to its security by using some degree of repression.[3] The baseline level of repression that is supported within the government is H. This level increases with resistance by the opposition: in general, the more resistance that is encountered, the more repression is desired. The h parameter represents the "reactiveness" of the government to changes in the opposition's resistance. Governments can be highly reactive or more consistent in their policy.[4] Too much or too little repression may lead to alienation of elites in the polity, which Lichbach (1995, 69–70) and Goldstone (1991), among others, identify as increasing the chance of revolution. Thus the government will react to differences between the current level of repression and the amount preferred by policy elites.

The capability of government to move toward this preferred level of repression (H) is represented by the (a) parameter. Weakened or divided governments may not possess the resources to effectively repress revolts; such governments often turn to interveners who can increase the government's capabilities with the provision of aid.

The other major factor affecting government hostility is the potential for a breakdown of the state, as discussed by Skocpol (1979). Her analysis of revolutions indicates that states in major civil conflicts risk alienating the general population (and especially the dominant groups in society) because of the policies they pursue in the conflict. The resource strain of domestic resistance and international pressures may push a state near the point of a "breakdown of state structures," which, as Skocpol argues, paves the way for revolutionary outcomes. A loss of *legitimacy* in the eyes of dominant societal groups is an indication of potential breakdown (Skocpol 1979, 15), a theme in literature on revolutions (see Starr 1994).

The model assumes that policymakers are aware of such situations and do react to them, apart from the earlier issue of capabilities. Thinking in terms of the conflict process, the state's worries about breakdown are really worries about uncontrolled (opposition) escalation, which would exacerbate resource strain. A breakdown threshold (B) is defined as the level of resistance (often an indicator of low legitimacy) at which policymakers sense that a breakdown is imminent. When unrest is well below breakdown levels, governments tend to increase hostility toward protesters (perhaps due to bureaucratic norms). When the breakdown threshold (B) is surpassed, the government reduces repression, making concessions in order to prevent revolution. This behavior fits the pattern of revolutions that authors from Brinton (1952) to Goldstone (1982) have described, where states offer concessions immediately preceding revolutions in a vain attempt to survive. The influence of potential breakdown on the government hostility level, denoted by the b parameter, varies widely depending on the type of government and the civil conflict. Skocpol (1979) argues that the effectiveness of coercive organizations, their position within the state, and their links to society are likely to determine the government's vulnerability to breakdown.

Opposition Resistance Model: Resources and Repression

Lichbach's (1995, 257) work on collective action argues that domestic conflicts can be conceived of as a struggle of both governments and oppositions to solve their own collective-action/free-rider problems and to exacerbate those of their foe. This framework accounts for and is compatible with many of the insights of the resource mobilization (RM) theories on which the Simon (1994) model was originally based. The RM perspective argues that control over resources is a main way in which governments and oppositions overcome the collective action problem.

Still, there is no magic formula for mobilization that is easily modeled. Groups must develop *strategies* for obtaining resources and solving collective-action problems. Since these strategies are subject to vigorous debate, can we model an opposition as a rational, "resource maximizer" and unitary actor?

I attempt to do so. Often we see a variety of rebel groups opposing a government but using different strategies—terrorism, urban violence, rural organization, nonviolence, and so on. Yet oppositions are concerned foremost with conserving membership; if strategies are not effective, members can "exit," weakening the original group. However, those who exit often form or join other opposition groups with different strategies but similar goals. Indeed, Tilly (1984, 31) argues that opposition groups in social movements consciously "attempt to create a coherent actor, or at least its appearance," in spite of their differences regarding strategy or other issues.

Equation (3), presented in table 7.1, considers sets of rebel groups that have broadly similar goals in opposing the current regime as one "opposition." Within that opposition, a variety of strategies (modeled as levels of resistance) are pursued by individual rebel groups. I assume that each group wants to maximize its resources, and will pursue a level of resistance that achieves this aim. Further, I assume that strategies that are most effective in countering the state will bring in the most resources. People and resources flow to a group that is effective in opposing the state and away from a group that is ineffective (DeNardo 1985).

The first term of equation (3) captures these dynamics. I assume that resources are flowing into and out of protest groups due to various causes (recruitment, defections, gain/loss of resources during protest, and so on). The threshold R is conceptually defined as the optimal level of resistance for the whole opposition. Empirically, one can think of this parameter, which is similar to H in the regime equation, as the resistance level or "strategy" of the factions or groups within the opposition that have the most resources and therefore dominate the movement. The existence of many factions means that varied strategies will compete for resources, and so those that emerge as strongest can be thought of as "optimal" within the constraints imposed by the particular geographic, political, and cultural conditions. Thus the model's treatment of the opposition as a unitary actor does not omit internal debate within an opposition nor the reality that oppositions contain many groups.[5]

When the composite level of opposition resistance (X) is below R, less aggressive factions will realize that more resources can be gained than lost by escalating resistance; when resistance is above R, more resources are lost than gained by escalating resistance. As a whole, the opposition behaves rationally, like Gilpin's (1981, 50) hegemonic challenger, by maximizing its resources and therefore its chance of success by seeking the optimal level of resistance.[6]

The model recognizes that the opposition may move toward this optimal strategy at varying rates, depending on the number of factions, their organizational resources, and the effectiveness of their strategies. The p parameter represents the rate at which the opposition as a whole adjusts to its optimal level of resistance. Empirically, we can think of p as the strength of the opposition (coalition) organization, since more unified oppositions will have more resources and therefore more quickly approach the optimal level of protest R.

To summarize, R is the optimal (not actual) level of resistance, given existing and expected resource flows and the desires of group members. Like the government's H threshold, R is also affected by the actions of the enemy. The effects of regime repression on the level of rebel unrest are discussed in the following section.

Coercion by the State

As noted earlier, the effect of coercion on dissent is a major puzzle within conflict studies: under some conditions coercion deters unrest, and under others protest escalates unrest (Lichbach 1987, 268–71). In general, however, the literature identifies three fundamental processes of interaction between levels of coercion and protest, and each is incorporated in the model. High levels of coercion by the state should have a strong deterrent effect (Muller and Weede, 1990). Yet sometimes coercion, particularly if perceived as excessive or illegitimate, stimulates more unrest (Gurr 1970, 238; Gupta et al. 1993; Rasler 1996). Finally, low levels of coercion can embolden protesters, facilitating (Tilly 1978, 100) increased collective action and resistance, either nonviolent (Muller and Weede, 1990) or in general (Tsebelis and Sprague 1989, 551; Salert and Sprague 1980; Jackson et al. 1978).

In equation (3), repression (Y) is assumed to reduce unrest, as long as it is above some expected coercion threshold C. If repression is below C, the state's weak attempt to stifle protest stimulates more rebel resistance. The degree to which the rebels' hostility level is influenced by repression is denoted by c.

The third process whereby repression increases protest is modeled as a direct effect on the optimal level of resistance R. I assume that as the government becomes more repressive, a more forceful level of resistance is legitimized, and so protesters will desire to increase resistance in return. Rebel groups must show that they have the resources to effectively resist a repressive regime if they are to attract more support (see Lichbach 1995, 62–78) I assume that, in general, as repression increases, resource inflows to protest groups will increase only if the group increases its level resistance. Thus, R increases linearly at a rate r with increases in repression (Y), reflecting the reactiveness and mobilization potential of the opposition.

By separating the various effects of repression on the level of resistance, the model simultaneously accounts for processes that can work in opposite directions. When repression is high, it may be effective in deterring unrest, yet it also increases R, the optimal level of resistance. Low regime coercion, while it may initially stimulate more unrest, also keeps R from growing. Thus different government strategies have different implications for rebel unrest, and the model helps us sort out the *processes* that explain these outcomes.[7]

As a whole the model above describes a general view of the conflict process between governments and oppositions. The model synthesizes insights from the major works in the field, and creates a framework that is adaptable to civil conflicts in many cultural and political contexts. In table 7.3 below I supplement the more process oriented definitions discussed

Table 7.3 **Empirical Indicators of Parameters that Determine Conflict Dynamic**

Parameter	Process Definition	General Empirical Indicators	Theoretical Frameworks Emphasized*
p	ability to move resistance toward R + rY	Capabilities, organizational strength	CARP, RM
r	belligerent reactiveness to increases in Y	Ideology, norms, culture	Framing
c	deterrent or provocative effect of repression	Capabilities, vulnerability, ideology	RM, CARP, Framing
a	ability to move repressive toward H + hX	Capabilities, organizational strength, political unity or division	POS, CARP
h	belligerent reactiveness to increases in X	Ideology, norms culture	Framing
b	influence of legitimacy on Y	Type of regime, bureaucratic norms, ideology	POS, CARP, Framing

Note: *CARP = collective action research program (Lichbach 1995); RM = resource mobilization (e.g., McCarthy and Zald 1977; Tilly 1978); POS = political opportunity structure (e.g., Tarrow 1989, 1994); Framing (see McAdam et al. 1996)

above with some general empirical indicators for some of the key model parameters to give the reader a sense of how these might apply in different contexts and over time. Furthermore, table 7.3 shows that the model consciously integrates processes and explanations emphasized in all the major theoretical approaches in contentious politics—the type of synthesis called for in McAdam et al. (1997). The next section describes the four underlying conflict dynamics produced by the model.

Characteristics of the Model: Conflict Dynamics

Algebraic analysis of the model (see appendix A) produces the four conflict dynamics described below. The basic technique is to set the rates to zero and then determine the conflict patterns that can emerge. The inequalities that determine the sign and slope of the zero-change line or

Table 7.4   Inequalities to Determine whether Actor Is Predatory

	Inequality	Sign of Slope	Predatory?
Opposition	pr > c	+	yes
	pr < c	−	no
Government	ah > b	+	yes
	ah < b	−	no

isocline, and thus the predatory disposition of each actor, are given in table 7.4.

A positive slope means that the actor tends to increase hostility in response to increases by the other side; I label this situation "predatory," using terminology from predator-prey models. Since each actor can be either predatory or nonpredatory, this table yields four basic escalation dynamics and ten basic conflict patterns that are illustrated in figures 7.1 through 7.4 and briefly discussed below.

Each conflict dynamic can produce at least two patterns, one of which is stalemate. State predation describes the common situation where the government is advantaged in a low level conflict with an opposition; it often wins (figure 7.1a), but frequently the opposition maintains itself and something like a protracted conflict (figure 7.1b) develops; this is elaborated below.[8] In rebel predation, we might see a government that may be holding onto a stalemate though it is near collapse (figure 7.2a; Zaire 1992–1996 may be an example); alternatively, figure 7.2b illustrates the last phase in cases of successful revolution (Nicaragua 1979, Iran 1978).

Commensalism describes a situation where both sides have a capacity for significant escalation, and each increases its capabilities after confrontations with the opponent. Commensalism often occurs when rebels become strengthened after a long period of state predation; in this case we would see a protracted conflict escalate quickly, perhaps to a new, higher-level stalemate (figure 7.3a; Nicaragua in early 1978 is an example). The potential for unbounded escalation (figure 7.3b) should make stalemates in this dynamic more volatile and perhaps short-lived than others. Competition (figures 7.4a–d) is probably rarer and also likely to be short lived. Each actor is weakened by confrontations with the opponent—each is non-predatory. The side with greater resources tends to have the upper hand, though either can win or lose. The volatility of competition is seen in figure 7.4a, which shows an unstable equilibrium where either side can win merely by a quick escalation. An example of competition discussed later in

Figure 7.1a   State Predation—State Wins

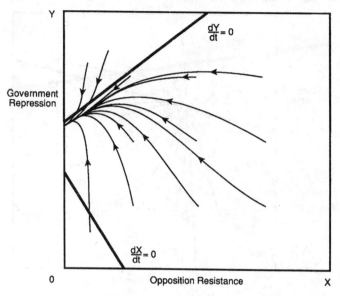

Note: For figures 7.1–7.4 the curved lines represent the path of the conflict from various starting points; the bold lines represent the isoclines.

Figure 7.1b   State Predation—Stalemate

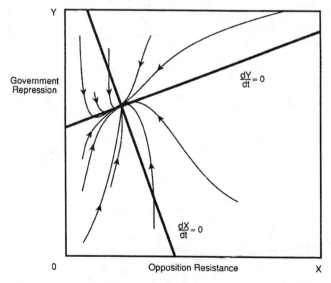

Figure 7.2a Commensalism—Stalemate

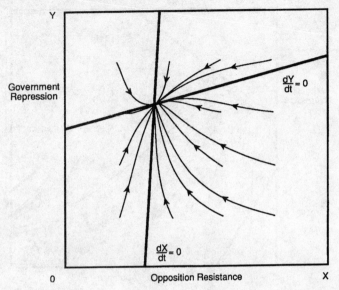

Figure 7.2b Commensalism—Unbounded Escalation

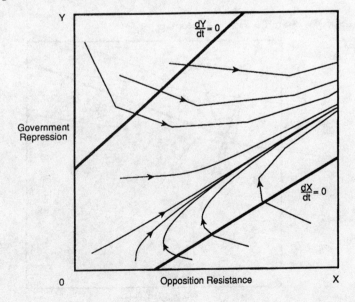

Figure 7.3a   Competition—Unstable Equilibrium with Threshold

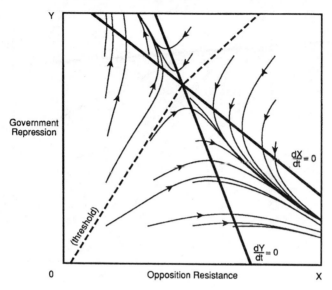

Figure 7.3b   Competition—Stalemate

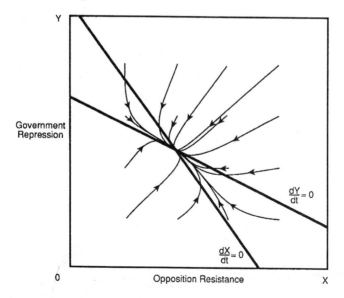

Figure 7.3c   Competition—State Wins

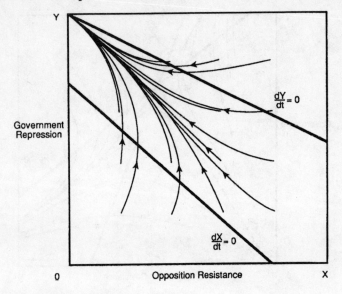

Figure 7.3d   Competition—Rebels Win

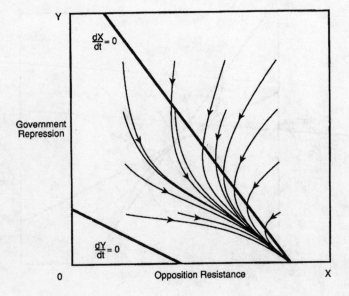

Figure 7.4a   Rebel Predation—Stalemate

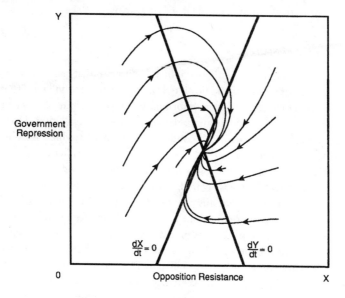

Figure 7.4b   Rebel Predation—Rebels Win

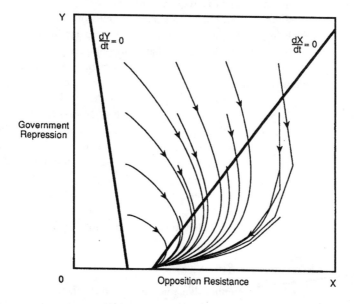

the Philippines case is late-1985-early–1986 when Marcos' call for an election split both the opposition and his own army.

The Nature of Stalemates

A striking characteristic of these conflict dynamics is that each one can generate a stalemate—that is, the hostility level of the conflict will tend to move toward, or return to, a stable equilibrium. The model tells us that stalemates can favor either the government, the opposition, or escalation. However, when we observe a stalemated conflict, the manner in which hostility returns to some equilibrium level does not reveal the conflict dynamic—we must investigate the underlying parameters ($p, r, c, a, h,$ and b; see table 7.3) to understand which side is favored. In many real world protracted conflicts, it often seems as if one side (usually the government) is "winning" and the other side (usually the opposition) is "losing," though the conflict endures. Most of these situations fit state predation, a dynamic where the stalemate favors the government. As examples, consider the Israel-Palestine conflict, or conflicts in developing countries like the Philippines (1972–1982; 1987–), Guatemala (1954–), or Indonesia (East Timor, 1974–). As Lichbach (1995) points out, the government has many advantages compared to the opposition in solving its collective-action problem, so we should expect that, even in stalemate, the government is frequently in a superior position.

The figures also indicate that actors that are predatory do not lose; this implies that during a stalemate, each actor strives to attain or maintain predatory posture while undermining that of its opponent. However, predation is not sufficient for victory; in the three dynamics from which victory is possible (see figure 7.5 below), one side wins by increasing its hostility level not its reactiveness (that is, raising the level of its isocline rather than making it more sloped, see Simon 1994). Moreover, the level of hostility in the stalemate is not determined by the dynamic—all of them can produce a high- or low- level stalemate. The parameters most responsible for the level of conflict are the government's baseline hostility level (H) and the opposition's optimal resistance level (R) (see appendix A). Even a nonpredatory opposition can keep a stalemate going for a long time if R is high enough. To understand stalemates, then, we must examine the predatory posture of the actors as well as their preferred hostility levels.[9]

Paths of Repression and Revolution

If we assume that the conflict dynamics are relatively stable, in the sense that they change less frequently than the hostility levels of the conflict, then the model yields another interesting implication. Empirically, I assume that situations that change the predatory posture of either actor—from predatory to nonpredatory or vice-versa—tend to be fairly discrete and usually dramatic. Therefore the conflict dynamic, which only changes when one actor changes its predatory posture, will change visibly and abruptly, as opposed to the more continuous, smooth changes in hostility levels. Given this, a change in conflict dynamic is an important event in a civil conflict that generates all sorts of new incentives for the actors involved, particularly interveners.

This conceptualization of a change in the conflict dynamic is similar to concepts in other frameworks that trigger changes in actors' behavior. The change in dynamic presents a new "opportunity structure" (McAdam et al. 1996), a period of uncertainty about escalation (Rosenau 1964), or even (to use a policy model) a crisis or focusing event (Kingdon 1984).

If it is unlikely that both actors can change their predatory disposition at the same time, then the dynamics are logically linked to each other, creating paths that lead to government or opposition victory. These paths are illustrated in figure 7.5 below.

Figure 7.5   Paths of Civil Conflict

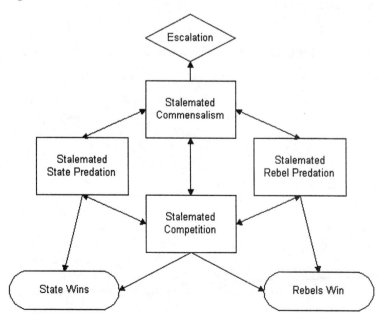

Figure 7.5 shows the set of constraints faced by all participants as they maneuver toward desired outcomes in the conflict. It offers a map of how to get from the current dynamic to a preferred outcome. Understanding the map and the conflict dynamics leads to hypotheses about the strategies that actors will pursue in the conflict, outlined below.

Hypotheses Related to the Conflict Dynamics

Table 7.5 summarizes some hypothesized characteristics of the four escalation dynamics generated by the model. Most conflicts will pass through several of these dynamics over time. Understanding the conflict dynamic also helps to explain the incentives it poses for governments, oppositions, and interveners to pursue particular strategies in the conflict. Some of these are contained in table 7.5 as well.

The case studies that follow are a preliminary attempt to examine the plausibility of these hypotheses and the other implications of the model discussed above. I will first summarize the events of the cases and argue that particular periods of the conflicts fit particular dynamics. In the course of that discussion I will identify the causes that led the dynamics to change at particular times. Finally, I will examine whether the interveners, government, and opposition acted as if they understood the incentives posed by the dynamics, as shown in figure 7.5 and table 7.5 above.

Case Studies: Nicaragua and the Philippines

Nicaragua, 1961–1979: Event Summary and Conflict Dynamics

Analysis begins in 1961 with the formation of the principle opposition group, the Sandinistas (FSLN).[10] Though they began with about 20 poorly-trained and -equipped guerrillas, and little to moderate support from the populace, by 1979 the Sandinistas led a coalition that overthrew the governing regime. The model focuses analysis on the growth of the opposition's organizational strength, the mobilization potential in the population, and the extent and effectiveness of the regime's coercion to explain shifts in the rebel isocline. Like most oppositions, the Sandinistas began as weak, nonpredatory resisters who throughout most of the 1960s barely avoided total defeat. After repeated cycles of confrontation, defeat, retreats, and regrouping, by the early 1970s, they achieved an enduring but low-level resistance (Booth 1985, 138–141). The guerrilla core of the group was well organized, and it learned to become integrated with the peasant com-

Table 7.5 Hypothesized Characteristics of the Four Conflict Dynamics

	State Predation	Commensalism	Competition	Rebel Predation
Frequency[1]	most common	less common	least common	rare
Duration[2]	longest	varied	varied	short
Stability[3]	most stable	low	least stable	low
Likely forms of intervention	military and/or economic aid	troop intervention; peace enforcing	troop intervention; peacekeeping	troop intervention for government; military and/or economic aid for rebels
Likely intervener response time[4]	slow	moderate	most rapid	slow for rebels; rapid to aid state
Possible intervener motives	support government or maintain rebellion	prevent spillover or humanitarian disaster	preempt other interveners; prevent spillover	forestall rebel victory; win favor with likely rebel victors, or a final try to save government

Notes: [1]Frequency refers to the likelihood that any civil conflict will experience this dynamic.

[2]Duration refers to the time that a single civil conflict is likely to spend in a given dynamic relative to the entire length of that conflict.

[3]Stability refers to the relative ease with which a conflict can be changed from this dynamic to another dynamic.

[4]Response time is the time it takes interveners to change their behavior measured from the point when the conflict changes into the given dynamic.

munities in the countryside for support. Yet the Sandinistas were not very effective in mobilizing the masses, who resented Somoza's rule, until after the 1972 earthquake in Managua. The general consensus among analysts of this post-earthquake period of the Nicaraguan conflict is that the naked greed shown by Somoza and the National Guard in the aftermath of the earthquake cost Somoza's regime the support of middle- and upper-sector business elites that had been the core of Somoza's internal legitimacy (Booth 1985, 81–85; Crawley 1984, 150; Diederich 1981; Pastor 1988; Walker 1986, 32; Lake 1989, 19–20). In addition, increasing repression, resulting from the imposition of martial law, split the Sandinista organization while stimulating more mobilization among the masses. For a brief time after the earthquake, then, the conflict fits the competition dynamic where both sides are nonpredatory. Due to some helpful intervention by the United States and the Somoza regime's inclination toward repression, the government recovered its predatory status shortly afterward, returning the conflict to state predation.

Increased repression, martial law, and ideological disputes eventually split the Sandinistas into three factions; they were not predatory, but were able to increase their preferred level of resistance over previous levels, and increased their overall organization and support in society in spite of the split.

The most significant turning point in the conflict was the January 1978 assassination of the prominent international and domestic symbol of moderate resistance to the Somoza regime, the editor of *La Prensa*, Pedro Joachim Chamorro. This provoked massive demonstrations and spontaneous popular uprisings all over the country. This stimulated the Sandinistas to reunite, strengthened moderates, and helped forge stronger links between moderate and radical groups. This period marks the beginning of predation for the opposition, turning the conflict dynamic into commensalism. Interestingly, the Sandinista's growth was essentially led by increases in popular mobilization, which caused leaders to strengthen their organization, rather than the other way around. The Sandinistas benefitted from the earthquake, the assassination, and Somoza's excessive repression, which caused popular resentment to become high enough for the rebellion to eventually succeed.

After the earthquake the Somoza regime imposed martial law, and maintained it, with the exception of a few months, until September 1977 (Diederich 1981, 106, 144). Martial law represented an increase in hostility, but also an increase in reactiveness as Somoza redoubled his efforts to wipe out the Sandinistas. However, the government began losing support among the middle class and eventually the elites due to Somoza's mishandling and abuse during the reconstruction period. The government was not significantly influenced by this loss of legitimacy until the Chamorro assassination, which further alienated the elite, who now feared that no one was safe from repression. Once the conflict moved to a new, higher-level stalemate in the commensalism dynamic, regime resources became more taxed, as capital flight, the loss of elite support, and even some U.S. political pressure on human rights issues stressed the government's capacity to the point where the possibility of breakdown due to resource strains and loss of legitimacy had become important. As the conflict escalated to civil war levels, treasury resources dwindled, new draft calls failed, and the size of the National Guard shrank as the rebels began their "final" offensive in May 1979. At this point, the government had lost enough capacity that rebel predation began. The strategy of the rebels to continue escalating the confrontation pushed the regime to defeat by mid-July 1979.

In summary, the Nicaraguan conflict exhibited all four conflict dynamics: competition during the December 1972-February 1973 earthquake interlude; commensalism from January 1978 to May 1979; rebel predation during June-July 1979; and state predation at other times.

The Philippines, 1968–1989:
Event Summary and Conflict Dynamics

The starting date again coincides with the founding of the principle rebel group—the New People's Army (NPA)—in opposition to the regimes of Ferdinand Marcos and later Corazon Aquino.[11] The analysis ends in 1989 for convenience, though the conflict endures in state predation today. During the 1968–1983 period the conflict exhibits state predation; after this, I conclude that the dynamic changes to commensalism following the assassination of Benigno Aquino, who like Chamorro of Nicaragua was an internationally prominent, moderate opponent. An unlikely turn of events changes the conflict to competition during early 1986, as Marcos calls a snap election in order to maintain power. Following Marcos' fall in February 1986, the rise of Corazon Aquino restores state predation.

Organized mainly by José Maria Sison on Mao Tse-tung's 75th birthday (December 26, 1968), the 35-member NPA began a slow development that by the end of 1983 makes it a group of (approximately) 20,000 guerrillas, 100,000 supporters, and 1,000,000 sympathizers with control over 20 percent of Filipino villages (Chapman 1987, 14, 130; Kessler 1989, 56). The NPA was Maoist in orientation and pursued an internal growth strategy that focused on building the organization and shunning nearly all intervener aid.

The NPA was very weak until the early 1970s, and moderate opponents were almost invisible until Marcos imposed martial law in 1972. This decree allowed Marcos to stifle unrest, but more importantly permitted him to retain power and destroy the Philippines' democratic institutions. The regime became completely dominated by Marcos and the Armed Forces of the Philippines (AFP), which increased in size from around 50,000 troops in 1972 to 100,000 by 1975 and at least 200,000 by the early 1980s (Kessler 1989, 108). The large size of the army, plus technology supplied by the United States, supplemented by the major U.S. military presence at its Clark and Subic bases made the NPA's job immeasurably more difficult than that of the Sandinistas, who faced a National Guard only a tenth as big as the AFP.

The rebel isocline was negative sloping, though moving closer to a predatory posture through 1983. After being nearly destroyed following martial law, the NPA grew in the countryside, mobilizing and building support in the barrios. While their existing organization was strong, they did not broaden their base by making significant ties to urban and other moderate opponents until after the Aquino assassination. As Tilly (1975) argues, a national opposition is fundamentally stronger than a communal or localized one. The Aquino assassination, which was blamed on Marcos, was an event that stimulated massive protest by moderates and radicals, increased mobilization potential, and most importantly increased ties between moderates and radicals. This reduced the vulnerability of the opposition to AFP repression, which made the opposition predatory. By 1984, it was clear even to the United States that Marcos was in trouble from the growing rebellion (Committee on Foreign Affairs 1984). To cope with commensalism, Marcos pursued strategies to change the dynamic.

In November 1985, Marcos called for a snap election to demonstrate popular support for his rule. The plan was designed to split the opposition, and in one way it was successful: the NPA boycotted the election, but moderates and many NPA rank and file united around the candidacy of Corazon Aquino, Benigno's widow. By splitting the moderates and radicals, the snap election weakened rebel organization and thus their isocline ceased to be predatory. But the snap election had an unintended consequence; it provided an opportunity for reform-minded officers in the AFP to pursue a coup. Essentially, the regime faced a split that reduced Marcos' capacity to repress the rebels and threatened to produce breakdown. Thus the regime's isocline turns negative as well, and the conflict dynamic changed from commensalism to competition.

After the rigged election, Marcos was unable to stem the domestic and international tide of protest that sought his ouster. Finally, the reform segment of the AFP mutinied in support of Aquino. The mutiny was supported by thousands of moderate, mainly urban, protesters in the streets; this can be interpreted as a massive loss of legitimacy that made the government isocline slope more and more negative, creating unstable competition, where the opposition's "people power" escalation succeeded in removing Marcos' ability to use repression. The mutiny succeeded, and Marcos accepted exile in Hawaii when the United States asked him to leave the Philippines at the last moment (Karnow 1989, Chapman 1987).

Aquino assumed power, pursued some reforms, and enjoyed massive popular support. The reunified government and military returned to predation, while the NPA was weakened by the loss of moderate supporters and organization. Still, the NPA retained much of its resources in rural areas; it regrouped and refocused its efforts on regaining lost organization and membership. A new stalemated conflict in a state predation dynamic continued through the end of the period of analysis in 1989 and into the 1990s.

Conflict Dynamics and Their Effect on Intervention in Nicaragua and the Philippines

In this section I will examine two core hypotheses: (1) that intervener behavior is likely to vary based on the model configuration that describes the dynamics of the civil conflict, and (2) that a change in model configuration, which reflects a major change in the civil conflict pattern, signals the likely time when significant changes in intervention are likely to occur. Because an intervener may choose among several substitutable policy alternatives (Most and Starr 1989), we do not expect a perfect correspondence between intervener behavior and the incentives posed by conflict dynamics. I argue that the conflict dynamics present opportunities, and that changes in the conflict dynamic produce strong signals that are likely to be heard in intervener bureaucracies and make action more probable. However, intervener decision making is not in the model, so we cannot expect the intervener to behave in accord with the incentives posed by the target conflict. There are at least two levels of games (Putnam 1988) going on in the intervener, and I have left one (bureaucratic politics in the intervener) out. Still, the following discussion shows that the hypotheses in table 7.5 are at least as relevant as other hypotheses connecting conditions in the target conflict to intervener behavior, notably that behavior changes due to increased uncertainty (Rosenau 1964) or escalation (Rasler 1983) in the conflict.

State Predation

State predation in the cases of Nicaragua and the Philippines is the longest lasting and most stable dynamic, as we would expect from table 7.5. The government can, by escalating repression, limit dissent, leaving the rebels to struggle to maintain their organization and avoid defeat. The forms of intervention during the periods discussed also fit our expectations: military aid, training, and economic aid continued to both countries, mainly from the United States, throughout the bulk of state predation. The one exception is the period of state predation in the Philippines under the Aquino government.

The levels of aid proposed and received were much higher than during the state predation period under Marcos. This might be explained as a reward for Aquino's professed commitment to national reconciliation, her implementation of a dovish strategy against the insurgents, and a commitment to fewer human rights violations. However, unlike the Marcos period, the Aquino government faced significant internal dissent, with hawk and dove factions vying for support. The main vulnerability for Aquino's government was internal, not external, strife (the a parameter instead of the b parameter in the model).

Thus, during the six coup attempts against Aquino in the first three years of her rule, it makes sense that the United States reacted with increasing intensity to stave off the coup and stabilize the government. The internal instability of the Aquino government called out for more aid than the relatively secure Marcos regime of the 1970s. Given the state predation dynamic, we still expect U.S. intervention to be the minimum needed for the maintenance of a predatory regime. Thus, even during the most threatening coup attempt, the United States ordered only that airplanes stationed on its bases provide a show of force in support of the Aquino faction of the military—direct intervention in the conflict was not necessary. Had the opposition been predatory (creating commensalism), or had the coup attempts threatened to create a breakdown of the regime (creating competition), the model indicates that the United States would have had incentive to act much more forcefully to avoid an unstable situation which may even have brought rebel predation.

As for intervener aid to the opposition in state predation, in general we expect minimal aid, weapons, and sanctuary to be provided to the rebels by interveners to help them maintain the insurgency in the face of a predatory state. The Philippine case is particularly interesting in that the NPA had essentially no intervener support for at least ten years preceding Aquino's rise. We would expect that the change from commensalism to state predation would tend to reduce any support that the NPA had received, since their movement, which had come so close to victory, appeared highly weakened after Aquino's rise.

We would also expect such nearly defeated rebel groups to seek out new aid to avoid total defeat, and this did occur with the NPA in spite of their previous ideological commitment to self-sufficiency. As Chapman (1987, 21–22) notes, after the rise of Aquino, some leading NDF, CPP, and NPA members became open to aid from the Soviet Union or other sources, as long as no strings were attached. Unfortunately for the rebels, the Gorbachev era and the end of the cold war meant that such aid was not likely to be sent.

Competition

In competition we expect a short lived, perhaps unstable dynamic where interveners have incentive for fast and forceful action to save their allies and preempt their opponents. In Nicaragua, for six to eight weeks following the 1972 Managua earthquake, the Somoza regime was vulnerable to breakdown and its capacity to resist coup attempts or rebel attacks was severely weakened. For three days after the earthquake anarchy reigned, and the National Guard disbanded and went home to their families or to loot. The United States responded to this situation by sending troops and aid to protect Somoza and help him restore order. Nations aiding the rebels did not respond dramatically, reflecting the minimal external support that the rebels had developed as well as the brief timeframe where a response might have been effective (Booth 1985). The quick and forceful U.S. response may have preempted any advantage that external supporters of the rebels would have achieved by an increase in aid.

The Philippine example of competition demonstrates some similar intervener behavior. After the snap election announcement, the United States encouraged both the Aquino faction of the opposition and the reform (RAM) segment of the military with verbal support and some indirect aid (Chapman 1987). In the end, the U.S. offer of sanctuary to Marcos (with its implicit demand that he step down) made the Aquino victory possible and restored state predation (Karnow 1989, Chapman 1987). The response time of U.S. action was quite rapid, however it was obviously less forceful. This reflects the lack of potential counter-intervention to aid the NPA. The absence of other interveners, combined with the presence of favorable alternatives to Marcos (no strong moderate force existed in Nicaragua in 1972), gave the United States more time to act and more instruments to use.

Rasler's escalation hypothesis does not account for U.S. actions in these cases, since the competition dynamic was associated with a deescalation in the conflicts. Examining only escalations in hostility would lead us to expect changes in intervention at several other times in Nicaragua and the Philippines where it did not occur. For example, in Nicaragua the 1974 Sandinista Christmas party raid and subsequent martial law era represents a significant escalation that produced little change in intervener behavior (Booth 1985). In the Philippines, the imposition of martial law in 1972, resulted in a significant increase in the level of conflict in the Philippines, but no major change in the pattern of U.S. support of the Marcos regime (Bonner 1987, Kessler 1989). In this latter example, one could argue that since the opposition was becoming weaker as a result of martial law, this escalation did not threaten U.S. interests since its side was "winning." The model supports the cynical view (for those who might have hoped for intervention to save Philippine democracy) that since the underlying conflict dynamic of state predation had not changed, this escalation was not a significant signal to the United States that policy needed to be altered.

While the escalation hypothesis does not work for the competition dynamic, Rosenau's uncertainty hypothesis does apply to both the Nicaraguan earthquake and the Philippine snap election periods. The model supplements this hypothesis by providing a tool to formalize the conditions under which uncertainty about conflict outcomes is likely to be high. There were other points in the Nicaraguan conflict during which uncertainty was high but when no major changes in intervention resulted: for example, the period of Somoza's heart attack and recovery in 1977 (Booth 1985). While the possibility of a coup or succession crisis loomed high, the actual pattern of the civil conflict did not depart from state predation. Therefore, using the model, we expect no major change in intervener behavior, although some might have judged that uncertainty about the outcome was high.

In the Philippines, the other points of uncertainty generally matched changes in the conflict dynamic. For instance, the 1983 Aquino assassination marked both a point of uncertainty and a change from state predation to commensalism. Yet examining uncertainty alone tells us nothing of the timing and nature of changes in intervention, while the model does give us clues. U.S. actions after the Aquino assassination and during the final fall of the Marcos regime were quite different, reflecting the different opportunities posed by each conflict dynamic. In general, we would expect more decisive, rapid intervention in the more unstable dynamic of competition than in commensalism. As discussed in the next section, that is what occurred.

Commensalism

Commensalism, essentially, describes a condition where rebel and regime hostilities feed off each other and can produce a lasting cycle of escalation. Compared with state predation, the rebels may now seem to be "winning" in the sense that their mobilization and hostility levels tend to *rise* as a result of confrontations with the regime in contrast to the defeat and rebuilding cycles of state predation. (See Booth 1985, 145, and Chapman 1987, 239, for descriptions of rebel growth after confrontation in this period.) Stalemates in commensalism produce more uncertainty, since unbounded escalation is a possibility; thus, this makes commensalism an important component for models of both enduring rivalries as well as protracted conflicts. We expect interveners to react forcefully in ways that might prevent unbounded escalation, limit the damage that any escalation does to their ally, and in some cases to prevent the conflict from spilling over into other countries.

During the commensalism period in Nicaragua from January 1978 to June 1979, we see changes in the actions of backers of both Somoza and the rebels (Booth 1985, 131–34). The United States significantly stepped up its human rights sanctions on Somoza, going from verbal denunciations to canceling its 1979 military assistance loan. Later we see the greatest change in the United States' behavior, when the United States and the Organization of American States (OAS) staged a concerted effort to mediate the conflict and negotiate a removal of Somoza while keeping elements of the National Guard intact.[12]

Supporters of the FSLN also increased their efforts to topple the regime throughout 1978. Costa Rica's new president, Carazo, reversed his opposition to the Sandinistas due to popular pressure and allowed increases in sanctuary, freedom of movement, and recruitment by the FSLN in Costa Rica. Diplomatically, Costa Rica, Panama, and Venezuela began an offensive against Somoza in 1978. Costa Rica broke relations with Somoza in October; using the OAS, these nations put pressure on Somoza and opposed other central American nations such as Honduras, Guatemala, and

El Salvador who wished to send Somoza aid. Finally, Panama, after giving asylum to the guerrillas who raided the Nicaraguan National Palace, began to transfer arms shipments to the rebels. Arms from Latin American sources, including a few from Cuba, entered Panama and were shipped through Costa Rica to the FSLN (Pastor 1988; Booth 1985, 133; Christian 1985, chapter 8).

In the Philippines, the commensalism period from 1984 to December 1985 produced a gradual but significant increase in economic and military aid from the United States. From a baseline average of about $150 million in economic and military aid in fiscal years 1981–1983, there was a doubling of aid to nearly $300 million in 1984, and over $400 million in 1985 (Agency for International Development 1986, Congressional Quarterly Almanac 1983–1986, Committee on Foreign Relations 1985, 7). No significant diplomatic or military actions were taken by the U.S. government to demonstrate its support for Marcos in addition to these aid increases. However, a large increase in Congressional testimony demonstrates growing U.S. concerns about a rebellion that had been previously ignored (Committee on Foreign Affairs 1984, Committee on Foreign Relations 1985). The signal sent by the change in the conflict dynamic was received; the U.S. response was perhaps more limited than expected because of the unique situation in which the opposition had no intervener support. Thus, the stalemate in commensalism was not as threatening as it might have been.

The commensalism dynamic produced a major escalation in both conflicts and raised uncertainty about whether Somoza and Marcos would retain power; thus, both of our alternative hypotheses apply. What the model adds here is to interpret this escalation as a fundamental change in the conflict rather than as some temporary fluctuation. It also identifies the main levers that actors can try to pull to try to make their opponent nonpredatory. Simply increasing repression will not work for a government, as it does in state predation. Marcos in particular seemed to understand this, and chose a strategy (the snap election) that split his opposition's organization (affecting p) and almost kept him in power.

Rebel Predation

Rebel predation occurred in Nicaragua during June and July 1979. In this dynamic we expect interveners to react quickly to either maintain the regime or push the opposition to victory. However, if it is low legitimacy that makes the state nonpredatory, this is difficult to reverse, and so interveners supporting the government may also work with factions of the government or opposition that might gain power if the rebellion succeeds. Stalemates should not endure as long in this dynamic as they do in state predation, because here we are only one step away from revolution, supporters of the government have reason to defect as the probability of victory diminishes (Lichbach 1995).

In Nicaragua, we find significant changes in intervener behavior. After the failure of mediation, the United States pulled back from the conflict and was hopeful that the apparent stalemate meant that Somoza could control the conflict and would not fall to the FSLN. By mid-June their perceptions adjusted to the realities of rebel predation. U.S. predictions about the likely length of Somoza's survival changed from two years to one week (Pastor 1988, 140); the U.S. national security advisor, Zbigniew Brzezinski, argued strongly for major troop intervention to prevent a communist takeover, but President Carter rejected this advice (Pastor 1988, 147; Lake 1989, 226). The United States chose to manage the conflict by again trying to negotiate some way to remove Somoza, preserve the National Guard, and keep the Sandinista's power diluted in a new government.

For the rebels, the May-June 1979 period brought a significant increase in arms shipments to aid their "final" offensive. This supplemented the weapons delivered in an earlier boost in supplies after FSLN unity was apparent in January 1979. In May, the arrival point of incoming arms was redirected to Costa Rica instead of Panama; this sped up supply and gave Panama's leader Torrijos the ability to deny their role in assisting the rebels and especially any collaboration with Cuba. Large amounts of Cuban arms were flown to the rebels from May through July (Christian 1985, 79–80, 96; Diederich 1981, 282–3). This was a departure from Fidel Castro's previous position that he could best help the rebels by "not . . . help[ing] at all" (Booth 1985, 134; Christian 1985, 91). The Cuban arms connection was aided by Costa Rica, who also denied that Cuba was involved to the United States, and spearheaded diplomatic efforts to help the guerrillas and hinder Somoza (Pastor 1988).

Thus the final shift of the Nicaraguan conflict from commensalism to rebel predation did produce shifts in intervener behavior. Interveners on behalf of the rebels did significantly increase aid in the hope that a final offensive would push Somoza from power. The United States, seeing their ally in serious danger of losing, did strongly consider a major troop intervention. However, the Carter administration chose to substitute diplomatic efforts in lieu of a full scale invasion; the domestic costs of intervention, the risk of "another Vietnam," and Carter's commitment to multilateral action made the cost of invasion prohibitive (see Lake 1989, Pastor 1988).

Conclusion

The evidence presented in these case studies demonstrates that by helping us think about civil conflicts in terms of underlying conflict dynamics, the model explains when and how intervener, government, and opposition behavior is likely to change. This can be especially important in the study of protracted conflict where we are concerned with sudden or sharp increases in violent conflict, and puzzled by the challenges of conflict management and resolution. Overall the model identifies the timing and nature of intervention-changes better than applying more general notions of escalation and uncertainty.

As I have shown in the analysis of the Nicaraguan and the Philippine struggles, major changes in a civil conflict do have an impact on intervention decisions. This longitudinal examination of two civil conflicts, aided by the theoretical framework of the model, helps us to understand that an escalation caused by, for example, a change from state predation to commensalism is more significant than an escalation that does not change the underlying conflict dynamic. We are also able to understand that de-escalations, which often create uncertainty, present vastly different incentives for interveners depending on whether they represent a shift into competition or into a state predation dynamic.

Finally, we can better understand the stalemates that occur in civil conflicts if we examine the underlying conditions that I argue create different conflict dynamics. A stalemate in state predation is fundamentally different than one in commensalism, even though the conflict pattern and hostility may not appear much different. Marcos' election strategy illustrates this point—the strategy would not make sense in state predation (when his choice was martial law) but is reasonable in commensalism where the opposition is now less vulnerable (c) to coercion and has a stronger, more unified organization (p). The same applies for U.S. attempts to limit Somoza's repression during commensalism, because in an escalated conflict it would be legitimacy (b) rather than resources constraints (a) that would make his government nonpredatory.

In future research, more rigorous tests of the model can be conducted by applying the growing amount of quantitative and event data on revolutions to test either the functional form of this model or some of its implications about intervener, government, and opposition behavior. My objective in modeling the processes of civil conflict is to formalize our intuitive understanding of such conflicts, and to improve our sense of why one side or the other is "winning" or advantaged in a stalemate. We should develop models that can tell a theoretically grounded story that explains why the conflict takes the path that it does and what sort of methods might be used to change that path. Normatively I hope that such knowledge could be used to reduce the violence and suffering in such conflicts and promote a just resolution.

Appendix 7.a   Equilibrium Isoclines (Zero-change lines)

Set $dX/dt = 0$ in equation (1) and solve for X^*; set $dY/dt = 0$ in equation (2) and solve for Y^*. These formula are given below. From these equations, we derive inequalities which determine the sign of the slope of X^* and Y^* and therefore the model configuration or conflict dynamic.

$$\text{Opposition: } dX/dt = 0 \qquad Y = \frac{pR + cC}{c - pr} + \frac{pX^*}{pr - c} \qquad (5)$$

$$\text{Government: } dY/dt = 0 \qquad Y^* = \frac{aH + bB}{a} + \frac{ah - bX}{a} \qquad (6)$$

The intercepts, which effect the overall hostility level of the conflict, are:

Government Y-intercept $= H + bB/a$;
Opposition X-intercept $= R + cC/p$.

Notes

1. The use of hostility level as the dependent variable implies that accommodation is represented as a reduction in hostility level. Other modelers (Lichbach 1987, Moore 1998) rightly attempt to represent hostility and accommodation as separate dimensions, noting that the particular mix of the two is very important in determining the reaction of the other actors. While I attempt to capture some of these processes in other parts of the model, I acknowledge this limitation of the action-reaction, differential equation structure.

2. The structure of both models (see equations 3 and 4 in table 7.1) simplifies to:

   $$dY/dt = aY + bXY - cY^2.$$

   Here, we get the result that the (b) coefficient describes the effect of interaction of X and Y (regime and rebel hostility, foxes and rabbits) on the growth rate of Y. This means that in the absence of interaction (b=0), Y grows logistically ($aY - cY^2$) rather than without bound. This makes substantive sense for both animal populations and hostility levels: food or resource scarcity eventually limits growth.

3. In Simon (1994) a distinction was made between hawkish and dovish factions within the government. Representing the government as a binary actor allowed for more discussion of strategy; however for my purposes here I can treat the government as a unitary actor without affecting the underlying conflict dynamics produced by the model.

4. This assumption that states determine an appropriate level of repression and then act to move the conflict toward this "ideal" is similar to assumptions in Jackson et al. (1978, 636). Model 1's "threshold" design captures this dynamic quite well.

5. The model can be applied to cases with many opposition factions, as long as those factions do not use a significant portion of their resources fighting each other. Lebanon in the 1980s or Angola in 1974 would not be good cases; however, conflicts in the Philippines, El Salvador, or Nicaragua are appropriate.

6. As an example, imagine three rebel factions: F1 with 1000 members, F2 and F3 with 100 members each. The dominant group pursues a strategy that scores 700 units of resistance per month (on some hypothetical scale). The resistance level pursued by F2 scores 10; F3 scores 5 units of resistance per month. Weighing the level of resistance by group size, the optimal level for the opposition is F1's strategy, 700/1000 or 0.7. The opposition as a whole is resisting at 715/1200 or 0.6. So, in this case, the opposition would gain resources if F2 and F3 increased resistance to the 0.7 level.

7. Gupta et al. (1993) notes that the relationship between repression and dissent varies with regime type; the thresholds of this model are flexible enough to accommodate such variation.

8. The labels given to the conflict patterns in figures 7.1–7.4 are simplifications, of course. A state "victory" means that, over time, opposition resistance goes to zero. It does not mean that rebels are forever defeated and barred from reorganization. Similarly, stalemate does not mean that there is no variation in conflict levels, it means that events that change the level of conflict will be temporary fluctuations, and that the conflict will tend to settle back to the old equilibrium level, other things being constant.

9. Though the model does not explicitly link the resource drain caused by escalation or a high-level stalemate back to the isocline parameters that determine the predatory posture, we know that this process occurs in real conflicts. This is the one area where the model misses an important arena for strategy—actors often use escalation in order to weaken their opponent's capabilities (a and p in the model). Whether this strategy can be successful varies greatly by context, therefore I could not represent it in this general model.

10. For more detail, see Booth (1985), Walker (1986), Diederich (1981), Crawley (1984), and Christian (1985). For U.S. policy during the Carter administration see Pastor (1988) and Lake (1989). These are the principle sources on which the discussion of Nicaragua is based.

11. The other significant rebellion in the Philippines is a conflict between the Muslim Moro peoples on the island of Mindanao who seek political autonomy and independence. Because the NPA and other rebel groups had limited ties to this rebellion, because NPA goals were not separatist, and because the regime regarded the two conflicts as separate, I do not include the Moro conflict in this analysis.

12. One exception to the model's high performance is the timing of the U.S. mediation effort in Nicaragua. While this change in U.S. behavior came during the period of commensalism, thus supporting the thesis that patterns of intervention will vary between configurations, the timing of mediation lagged months behind the Chamorro assassination. The U.S./OAS mediation effort coincided more directly with the escalation of the conflict after the National Palace raid and the September 1978 uprisings than it did with the January 1978 killing.

References

Agency for International Development. 1986. "Aid to the Philippines." National Security and International Affairs Division. Washington, DC: U.S.GAO/NSAID-87-24.

Bonner, Raymond 1987. *Waltzing with A Dictator: The Marcoses and the Making of American Policy.* New York: Times Books.

Booth, John A. 1985. *The End and the Beginning: The Nicaraguan Revolution,* 2nd ed. Boulder, CO: Westview Press.

Brinton, Crane. 1952. *The Anatomy of Revolution,* rev. ed. New York: Prentice-Hall.

Burton, John. 1990. *Conflict: Resolution and Prevention.* New York: St. Martin's Press.

Chapman, William 1987. *Inside the Philippine Revolution.* New York: W.W. Norton and Company.

Christian, Shirley. 1985. *Nicaragua: Revolution in the Family.* New York: Random House.

Committee on Foreign Relations, U.S. Senate. 1985. "Insurgency and Counterinsurgency in the Philippines." November. Washington, DC: U.S. Government Printing Office.

Committee on Foreign Affairs. 1984. "The Situation and Outlook in the Philippines." Testimony by Richard Armitage before U.S. House of Representatives, Foreign Affairs Committee, Subcommittee on Asian and Pacific Affairs, October 4.

Congressional Quarterly Almanac. 1986. Vol. 42, p. 169. Washington, DC: Congressional Quarterly.

————. 1985. Vol. 41, p. 375. Washington, DC: Congressional Quarterly.

————. 1984. Vol. 40, p. 397. Washington, DC: Congressional Quarterly.

————. 1983. Vol. 39, p. 514. Washington, DC: Congressional Quarterly.

Crawley, Eduardo. 1984. *Nicaragua in Perspective.* New York: St. Martin's.

DeNardo, James. 1985. *Power in Numbers.* Princeton, NJ: Princeton University Press.

Diederich, Bernard. 1981. *Somoza.* New York: E.P. Dutton.

Francisco, Ronald A. 1995. "The Relationship between Coercion and Protest: An Empirical Evaluation in Three Coercive States." *Journal of Conflict Resolution* 39 (June): 263–82.

————. 1996. "Coercion and Protest: An Empirical Test in Two Democratic States." *American Journal of Political Science* 40 (November): 1179–1204.

Gilpin, Robert. 1981. *War and Change in World Politics.* Cambridge, UK: Cambridge University Press.

Goldstone, Jack. 1982. "The Comparative and Historical Study of Revolutions." *Annual Review of Sociology* 8: 187–207.

————. 1991. "An Analytical Framework." In *Revolutions of the Late Twentieth Century.* eds. Jack Goldstone, T. Gurr, and F. Moshiri. Boulder, CO: Westview Press, pp. 37–51.

Gupta, D. K., H. Singh, and T. Sprague. 1993. "Government Coercion of Dissidents: Deterrence or Provocation?" *Journal of Conflict Resolution* 37 (June): 301–39.

Gurr, T. R. 1970. *Why Men Rebel.* Princeton, NJ: Princeton University Press.

———— and R. Duvall. 1973. "Civil Conflict in the 1960s: A Reciprocal Theoretical System with Parameter Estimates." *Comparative Political Studies* 6 (July): 135–70.

Hibbs, D. A. 1973. *Mass Political Violence: A Cross-National Causal Analysis.* New York: John Wiley.

Hoover, Dean and David Kowalewski 1992. "Dynamic Models of Dissent and Repression." *Journal of Conflict Resolution* 36 (March): 150–89.

Jackson, S. B. Russett, D. Snidal, and D. Sylvan. 1978. "Conflict and Coercion in Dependent States." *Journal of Conflict Resolution* 22 (December): 627–57.

Karnow, Stanley 1989. *In Our Image: America's Empire in the Philippines.* New York: Ballantine Books.

Kessler, Richard J. 1989. *Rebellion and Repression in the Philippines.* New Haven, CT: Yale University Press.

Kingdon, John. 1984. *Agendas, Alternatives, and Public Policies.* Boston: Little, Brown.

Kowalewski, David, and Dean Hoover. 1995. *Dynamic Models of Conflict and Pacification.* Westport, CT: Praeger Publishers.

Lake, Anthony. 1989. *Somoza Falling.* Boston: Houghton Mifflin.

Lichbach, Mark I. 1987. "Deterrence or Escalation? The Puzzle of Aggregate Studies of Repression and Dissent." *Journal of Conflict Resolution* 31 (June): 266–97.

————. 1995. *The Rebel's Dilemma.* Ann Arbor, MI: University of Michigan Press.

Maynard-Smith, J. 1974. *Models in Ecology.* Cambridge, UK: Cambridge University Press.

McAdam, Doug, John D. McCarthy, and Mayer Zald. 1996. "Opportunities, Mobilizing Structures, and Framing Processes—Toward a Synthetic, Comparative Perspective on Social Movements." In *Perspectives on Social Movements,* eds. Doug McAdam, John D. McCarthy, and Mayer Zald. Cambridge, UK: Cambridge University Press, pp. 1–20.

———, Sidney Tarrow, and Charles Tilly. 1997. "Toward an Integrated Perspective on Social Movements and Revolution." In *Comparative Politics: Rationality, Culture, and Structure,* eds. Mark Lichbach and Alan Zuckerman. Cambridge, UK: Cambridge University Press, pp. 143–73.

McCarthy, John D. and Mayer Zald. 1977. "Resource Mobilization and Social Movements: A Partial Theory." *American Journal of Sociology* 82: 1212–41.

Mitchell, C. R. 1970. "Civil Strife and the Involvement of External Parties." *International Studies Quarterly* 14 (June): 166–94.

Moore, Will H. 1997. "Dissent and Repression: A Comparative Time-Series Analysis." Paper presented at the Annual Meeting of the American Political Science Association, Washington, DC (August): 28–31.

———. 1998. "Repression and Dissent: Substitution, Context, and Timing." *American Journal of Political Science* 42 (July): 851–73.

Most, Benjamin and Harvey Starr. 1989. *Inquiry, Logic, and International Politics.* Columbia, SC: University of South Carolina Press.

Muller, E. N. and Erich Weede 1990. "Cross-National Variation in Political Violence: A Rational Action Approach." *Journal of Conflict Resolution* 34 (December): 624–51.

Opp, K. 1994. "Repression and Revolutionary Action: East Germany in 1989." *Rationality and Society* 6 (January): 101–38.

Pastor, Robert. 1988. *Condemned to Repetition: The United States and Nicaragua.* Princeton, NJ: Princeton University Press.

Pearson, Frederic. 1974. "Foreign Military Interventions and Domestic Disputes." *International Studies Quarterly* 18 (September): 259–90.

Putnam, Robert D. 1988. "Diplomacy and Domestic Politics: The Logic of Two-Level Games." *International Organization* 42 (3): 427–60.

Rasler, Karen 1983. "Internationalized Civil War: Dynamic Analysis of the Syrian Intervention in Lebanon." *Journal of Conflict Resolution* 27 (September): 412–56.

———. 1996. "Concessions, Repression, and Political Protest in the Iranian Revolution." *American Sociological Review* 61 (February): 131–52.

Reising, Uwe. 1998. "Domestic and Supranational Political Opportunities: European Protest in Selected Countries 1980–1995." Paper presented at the annual meeting of the Midwest Political Science Association, Chicago, IL (April): 23–25.

Rosenau, J. N. 1964. "The International Relations of Internal War." In *The International Aspects of Civil Strife,* ed. J. N. Rosenau. Princeton, NJ: Princeton University Press, pp. 45–91.

Salert, Barbara and John Sprague. 1980. *The Dynamics of Riots.* Ann Arbor, MI: Inter-University Consortium for Political and Social Research.

Schelling, Thomas. 1966. *Arms and Influence*. New Haven, CT: Yale University Press.

Skocpol, Theda. 1979. "State and Revolution: Old Regimes and Revolutionary Crises in France, Russia, and China." *Theory and Society* 7 (1): 7–95.

Simon, Marc. 1994. "Hawks, Doves, and Civil Conflict Dynamics: A 'Strategic' Action-Reaction Model." *International Interactions* 19 (3): 213–39.

Smoke, Richard. 1977. *War: Controlling Escalation*. Cambridge, MA: Harvard University Press.

Starr, Harvey. 1994. "Revolution and War: Rethinking the Linkage between Internal and External Conflict." *Political Research Quarterly* 47 (June): 481–507.

Tarrow, Sidney. 1989. *Democracy and Disorder: Social Conflict, Political Protest, and Democracy in Italy 1965–1975*. New York: Oxford University Press.

———. 1994. *Power in Movement*. Cambridge, UK: Cambridge University Press.

Tilly, Charles. 1984. *Big Structures, Large Processes, Huge Comparisons*. New York: Russell Sage.

———. 1975. "Revolutions and Collective Violence." In *Handbook of Political Science*, vol. 3., ed. F.I. Greenstein and N. Polsby. Reading, MA: Addison Wesley, pp. 483–555.

———. 1978. *From Mobilization to Revolution*. Reading, MA: Addision-Wesley.

Tsebelis, G., and J. Sprague 1989. "Coercion and Revolution: Variations on a Predator-Prey Model." *Mathematical and Computer Modelling* 12 (4–5): 547–59.

Walker, Thomas. 1986. *Nicaragua, the Land of Sandino*. Boulder, CO: Westview Press.

CHAPTER EIGHT

Yielding Ground:
Loss and Conflict Escalation in
Sri Lankan Protracted Social Conflict

Michael Kuchinsky

(We are here) to work for the attainment of freedom for the Tamil speaking people of Ceylon by the establishment of an autonomous Tamil state within the framework of a federal union of Ceylon. (Federal Party of Ceylon, 1956) (Kearney 1973, 9)

The Tamil people must accept the fact that the Sinhalese majority will no longer permit themselves to be cheated of their rights. (Mrs. Bandaranaika, May 2, 1967) (Kearney 1973, 163)

Democracy is finished in this country. You have to have peace and stability to have democracy and Ceylon has neither. (United National Party President, Junius Jayewardene, April 24, 1971) (Patin 1972, 308)

(We) charge the Sinhalese majority with having violated the rights of the Tamil community by means of a system of planned and state aided colonizations and recently encouraged encroachments calculated to make the Tamils a minority in their own homeland. (Vaddukodai Resolution, 1976) (Little 1994, 82)

If the Sinhala are the majority race, why can't they be the majority. (Cyril Matthew, Minister of Labor, Aug. 4, 1983) (Tambiah 1986, 32)

This time, the Tamil professional and entrepreneurial class has been destroyed. (Neelan Thiruchelvan, Tamil United Liberation Front, Aug. 31, 1983) (Tambiah 1986, 32)

Introduction

This collection of quotations representing Sinhalese and Tamil community and political party leaders over the course of three decades exemplifies the phrase used by David Little to describe the Sri

Lankan conflict—a "general symmetry of violence; two representations of history each challenging the other's basic claim of legitimacy (Little 1994, 106). The conflict seen in Sri Lanka shares a common "genus" with the Sudan, Cyprus, the Punjab, and the Balkan region; namely, it is a protracted social conflict.

Protracted social conflict (PSC) characterizes conditions of intrastate violence and war, linking together the competing material, cultural, and identity aspirations of two or more social groups. Concerns over communal identity, limited participation in governance, deprivation of security and basic needs, and grievances over distributive justice intertwine to create a network of multivariate hostility (Azar 1990, 2; and see Samuel Peleg's chapter in this volume).

PSCs are durable, identified by their cycles of escalation and de-escalation over time (see Gil Friedman and G. Dale Thomas' chapters in this volume). They move from conditions of unsteady peace, where warfare is replaced by suspicious tolerance and sporadic acts of violence, to escalating levels of violence and war (Boulding 1978, 43). Thus, PSCs combine an intractable triad of opportunity (an extended history), motive (the multivariate web of conditions producing social group hatred), and willingness as witnessed by the historical frequency and savagery of the participants.

The dual dangers of PSCs lie in their chronic capacity to inflict damage and death upon the participants, which incapacitates movements toward stability and resolution, while potentially inducing external interventions that destabilize their regions (see Marc V. Simon's chapter in this volume). The "outcome of such an extended process include deterioration of general security conditions for all communities, state institutional paralysis, a petrification of communal cleavages, psychological ossification based upon intercommunal mistrust and fear, and increased dependency on external sector assistance" (Azar 1990, 17).

PSCs frequently occur in underdeveloped states under conditions where social integration and nation-building have been incomplete. This condition makes the resolution of a PSC all the more difficult due to the simultaneous occurrence of both conflictual and cooperative behavior under extreme forms of conflict and violence, the shifting definitions of distributional justice, and an evolving set of demands and issues in and between times of escalation and de-escalation (Azar 1985, 60–69).

Since independence in 1948, Sri Lanka's historical profile coincides with the above characterization of PSCs. Tamils and Sinhalese, the primary ethnoreligious social groups, have shared territory and developed mutual mistrust and enmity. Their common history has been punctuated by cycles of escalating intercommunal social violence. Their rivalry extends and becomes self-justified through a tangled web of religious myth, legislated majority group self-promotion, economic and social underdevelopment and victimization, and communal persecution.

Sri Lankan violence is a form of structural escalation in which the cycles advance through the many inter-relationships held by the conflicted parties, as well as through the groups and their leaders' needs and perceptions of themselves and their enemies. Structural escalation is self-perpetuating, featuring mutual individual and group dehumanization and polarization, and a deterioration of relationships within perceived zero-sum games (Rubin, Pruitt, and Kim 1994, 82–116). With its focus on identity as a human need (see Peleg in this volume), to constrain or resolve a PSC and its escalation requires more than the standard methods of bargaining, coercion, or temporarily increasing one group's material assets. Having taken note of a PSC's profile leads to the question of whether their cyclical escalations signal a triggering mechanism in the decisions to resume increased levels of violence.

Herein lies this study's hypothesis. Because PSCs are anchored by threats to communal identity, distributional justice, and human needs (table 8.1), times preceding and during conflict escalation will be marked by the language of victimization and loss between social groups and their

Table 8.1 Human Needs Definitions

1. Identity—constitutes a recognizable set of attributes distinguishing groups; for ethnic groups, this is most readily apparent in issues concerning language, religion, and race.
2. Recognition—constitutes a condition of tolerance between identity groups, their respect of group differences, and in advanced settings, an affirmation of such differences.
3. Security—constitutes a condition of peaceful co-existence between identity groups unhindered by threats, coercion and violence.
4. Development—constitutes the processes leading towards socio-economic growth under conditions of relative justice, frequently characterized by levels of attainment in education, income, human rights or other quality of life indicators.
5. Control—constitutes a participation in society variable measuring the opportunity of involvement in political processes and institutions.

Source: From John Burton, *Conflict: Resolution and Prevention.* New York: St. Martin's Press, 1990.

leaders, and by the need to avoid further losses to communal identity and needs satisfaction. PSC escalation is this study's dependent variable, while perceived or real losses to communal identity and needs are the independent variables. Loss to communal identity is understood to be related to cultural issues of language, religion, history, and/or a traditional homeland. Needs based theories incorporate other losses for the communal group—such as, the ability to participate in and control issues of governance, and the human developmental needs of education, economic opportunity, and security. Escalation in protracted social conflict becomes symptomatic of perceived communal illegitimacy and the disempowerment of one group at the hands of the other. A formal presentation of the hypothesis is as follows:

> As communal identity groups and their leaders engaged in a protracted conflict perceive and express issues *framed by losses* to cultural identity, security or development needs, or participatory opportunities for governance, then the protracted social conflict will move into another phase of escalating conflict.

Theoretical Groundwork

The study's hypothesis presumes three preliminary questions. Why loss? How important are human needs? How vital is identity when shaping events? Theories that answer each question, ground the study's hypothesis.

Prospect theory suggests that the orientation during conflict escalation reflects a perception of a declining status quo or condition of parity between parties (see Levy 1992). Issues separating groups are framed so that their declining positions become evident. Using prospect theory when situations are framed as "loss" helps explain dynamics of both continuation and escalation of conflict. The theory posits that greater risk is taken by those who perceive their position as one of loss, in order to avoid such outcomes. Experiments done on individual risk acceptance/aversion patterns indicate a greater willingness to accept risk when faced with outcomes of additional loss rather than gain.

The duration of such conflicts extends in order to avoid further losses by one or both parties, exhibiting efforts of unusual perseverance. The period of time linking one status quo condition to another is the period of renormalization. As one who helped apply the theory to international politics, Jervis contends that loss looms as a larger consequence than the magnitude of violence, constricts the negotiation spaces between the conflicted parties, limits the utility of bargaining as concessions only imply further conditions of loss, increases the tensions brought on by simultaneous perceptions of weakening positions, and increases the risk of war as both parties perceive themselves to be defending the status quo in order to avoid loss and fear (Jervis 1992, 187–203).

Though it is criticized for having a narrow experimental history, a limited empirical research base, a theoretical gap regarding framing, and a difficulty establishing clear differences between loss aversion and utility gain (Levy 1992, 283–309), Stein and Pauly (1993) use prospect theory as a more adequate predictor for decision making. Using content analysis in cases such as the Israeli decision not to enter the Gulf War, and trade negotiations between Japan and the United States, the authors affirm the importance of domestic subnational units in directing foreign policy decisions, the place of emotion in decision making, the language of loss in confrontations, and the identified trade-offs of losses made by decision makers (Stein and Pauly 1993, 2–34).

Human need (or its frustration) is the ground from which protracted conflicts grow. John Burton, a close collaborator with Edward Azar in the study of PSC, underscores the universal nature of human needs, which presuppose a process for individual and social development. Though related to the interests and values of particular groups, needs are distinguished (according to Burton) by their permanence, the loss of which gains quickly in significance. Borrowing from Abraham Maslow's hierarchy of needs theory and Paul Site's taxonomy of needs, Burton (1990) identifies five basic needs (which are presented in table 8.1): identity (communal language, history, religion, and homeland); recognition (perceived attitudes of tolerance, acceptance, or encouragement within a society; also related to theories on multicultural appropriation); security (nonviolent and unthreatened coexistence); development (opportunities for economic, educational, and human rights growth); and control (participation in governance and political institutions). Burton's five concepts are operationalized in the parentheses as they appear in the Sri Lankan case. Conflict ensues with the repetitious frustration and denial of their attainment, usually under a pretext for social order, and continues even after material satisfactions have been met (Burton 1988).

Related to this process is the work of James Davies who sees a causal relationship between the frustrated expectations of one group once needs satisfaction began, and revolutionary behavior: "The crucial factor is the vague or specific fear that ground gained over a long period of time will be quickly *lost*. This fear does not generate if there is continual opportunity to satisfy continually emerging needs; it generates when the existing government suppresses or is blamed for suppressing such opportunity" (Davies 1971, 137). Davies' theory becomes an important corrective for helping explain the anomalous character of the 1971 case examined below.

Human needs satisfaction also relates to questions of legitimacy in governance within multicultural settings. Whereas legality of authority is based upon control and coercive ability, legitimacy profiles the reciprocity and distributive justice within relationships, the quality of authority over time and the dynamics of changing conditions between groups and is thus unachievable through means of coercion (Burton 1990, 124–127).

Of all the needs incorporated within the network of discontent that is protracted conflict, the one that looms largest—identity—also distinguishes the conflicted parties. Behind identity stands an "ethnie," or an identifier set of experiences providing a communal group with a mythic sense of origin, history, ontology, and destiny as it moves toward integration and nationalism. Ethnie provides core narratives to develop the vitality of communal identity, sustain the group's collective history, and support its claims (Smith 1991, 71–122). Identity in international politics is always a passionate process within a variegated world of groups (Connor 1994, 141) whose aims support the splintering tendencies of self-determination (Moynihan 1994, 143–174).

Communal identity is a strong theme in studies of conflict. Horowitz (1985) substantiates PSC's ironic condition in which cooperative behavior exists amidst highly conflicted times and issues, when describing parallel and hierarchial ordering of ranked and unranked social/identity groups. For Horowitz, there exist social structures in which ethnic groups cross class boundaries (parallel) but that are still ranked hierarchically, incurring structural dissatisfactions of status and participation in a belief of group entitlement by the more marginalized ethnic group (Horowitz 1985, 185–228). This irony, conflict and yet cooperation, suggests an unfinished integration process between groups who share proximity but not history in protracted conflict cycles. Gurr's *Minorities at Risk* project which provides data to distinguish types of ethnic goals while it establishes a link between communal identity and needs satisfaction, and Juergensmeyer's efforts to pit religious identity movements against Western secularization and modernization in *The New Cold War,* add to the evidence linking identity with conflict.

The idea that identity cyclically re-emerges in protracted conflict as a dynamic (as opposed to a static) concept is described in Esman's *Ethnic Politics* (1994). Political ethnic identities relate a politics of self-definition within a set of constructs and constraints (another group, government, and so on) external to the ethnic group in a set of two-level games within the group, between the groups, and with other external actors. Problems associated with essentialist constructions of identity are minimized by a now evolutionary and interactive process, where the grievances and aspirations that motivate ethnic politics change over time. Changes in an ethnic group's status (another form of loss) brought on by changes in legislation or regulation exemplify Esman's dynamic inter-relationship model for ethnic conflict.

Returning to the study's hypothesis, the variables representing losses to cultural identity, participatory ability, and specific economic and security needs congruent to the context are embedded in prospect theory and its language of loss aversion. Protracted conflicts like Sri Lanka provide ample environment for the consequences of loss to the human needs and identity of social groups.

Methodology

The study can be seen as a heuristic research model to test the applicability of prospect theory as a means of clarifying the enigma of recurring cycles of violence in PSC. If the model holds, then the time preceding and during escalation periods within cases of PSC will exhibit frames of victimization and loss to communal identity and needs as they are understood by the ethnic groups and their leaders. Loss acts as a triggering mechanism for renewed conflict. If this is the case, to observe issue framing in a language of loss would serve as a warning, prompting the need for earlier mediation and resolution.

The World Handbook of Political and Social Indicators provides indicators of domestic conflict escalation (Taylor and Jodice 1983). These include protest demonstrations, riots, armed attacks, deaths, political assassinations, and governmental sanctions imposed and removed. The data identify three years showing significant increases in domestic violence in Sri Lanka—1958, 1971, and 1977. These same indicators were used to establish 1983 as a fourth year for the study.

The study used a modified time-series design for the four periods of conflict escalation in Sri Lankan protracted conflict. Each case stands independently from the other with 25 years separating the first from the last. The data sources used precede periods of intense conflict by three to six months, and proceed through the time of conflict. In this way, the study represents a structured focused comparison of events across similar cases. The year of Independence, 1948, was used as a baseline of reference due to Ceylon's use of three official languages, namely English, Sinhalese, and Tamil. A similar series of cases approach was used on the data where identical coding questions and concepts of needs were asked of the data sources.

Content analysis was used to evaluate primary data sources. Articles from the four years of Ceylon/Sri Lanka coverage were collected and analyzed from the *Christian Science Monitor* and the *London Times*. Although these papers were chosen for their perceived journalistic excellence, international reputation and coverage, their content remains suspect due to each paper's inherent level of bias towards subjects and the editorial decisions of coverage space.[1]

The Taylor and Jodice survey used the *New York Times* for its data collection and analysis, two additional newspapers, and identical categories for coding internal violence and re-confirming the four years of escalation, which adds a layer of control and internal validity to the case study. As a result of Sri Lanka's historical relationship with Great Britain, and in order to increase international coverage, articles from *The Economist* and *The Statesman* were also analyzed in light of their coverage of the Sri Lankan situation during the four years of the study.

To ascertain whether there is violence is a relatively simple matter of counting using the Taylor and Jodice categories of protests, riots, governmental sanctions, and deaths. To measure whether loss and loss aversion operates within a period of escalating conflict is more difficult, demanding interpretation in light of case history knowledge. A series of questions similar to those used by Stein and Pauly's prospect theory studies were used to code news coverage and their relationship to issues of loss, loss aversion, and/or victimization of communal identity and basic human needs.

The set of Stein-Pauly questions is included in Appendix 1, while needs were operationalized using Burton's categories, as noted above. As an example, the recorded statements from a political party official decrying the loss of Tamil as an official Sri Lankan language would be coded as the "presence" of loss in cultural and historical identity. So too, would have been the use of Tamil or Sinhalese origins (frequently mythic) to justify or protest current perceived abuses. Presence or absence of both violence and the loss variables were coded with values of one or zero (see Appendix 2).

Secondary source data was used to help ascertain the climate for loss in Sri Lanka. Though most quality of life or socio-economic status data collected globally use national statistics, some more recent Sri Lankan studies breakdown information according to categories of Buddhist/Sinhalese or Hindu/Tamil. This type of information relates directly to two of Burton's need categories—development and control. Sources of this information are not independent agencies but Sri Lankan government ministries. Indicators appropriate to the Sri Lankan case include levels of education and in particular the accessibility to higher education, trends in ethnic population percentage changes within traditional Tamil regions due to government internal colonization policies, the ethnic extent of governmental patronage, and the extent of political participation afforded competing ethnically based political parties for governing Sri Lanka.

A Climate for Loss

How does Sri Lanka become a suitable study to use concepts of loss and risk assertiveness? Aspects of both pre- and post-independence history lend themselves to perceptions of loss for PSC cycles. Combining interpretations of mythic history (Smith 1991, Connor 1994) with the interactionist model for ethnic conflict (such as, Esman 1994, Horowitz 1985, Moynihan 1994) provides a descriptive layer of Sri Lankan conditions that complement the study's primary research.

Using data from the mid-1980s, Sri Lanka's roughly 15 million people are broken down as Sinhalese Buddhist (74 percent of the total population), Sri Lankan Tamils (12.6 percent), Indian Tamils (5.6 percent), Muslims (7.4 percent), and other (Christians, and so on 0.4 percent) (Committee for Rational Development 1984, 2). Tamils are conventionally distinguished to reflect differences in origin and location.

Though integrated throughout Sri Lanka, concentrations of population polarize Tamil and Sinhalese districts. Sri Lankan Tamils predominate in the northern and eastern regions including the urban centers of Jaffna, Trincomalee, and Batticola (all deep water ports), while Sinhalese dominate in the western, southern and central districts including the urban centers of Colombo, Kandy, and the largest Buddhist center in Anuradhapura. Muslim populations concentrate in the eastern districts.

Territorial polarization reflects traditional myths of origins espoused by Tamil and Sinhalese political parties and their leaders either to justify the ongoing conflict or to separate issues by parties. Sinhalese Buddhists use a C.E. fifth-century history and the Buddhist apologetic entitled the *Mahavamsa* to claim supremacy within the island. The document cites the Vijayan migration from Arayan North India in the fifth century B.C.E., its movement blessed by Gautama Buddha, to establish a permanent site of Buddhist purity. The document provides a "history" of Sinhalese conquests that unifyied the island and culminated in its defense with King

Dutthagamani's victory over the invading Dravidian Tamils from South India in what is now Jaffna (de Silva 1987, 20–29). The myth supports contentions that Sri Lanka was destined to be Sinhalese; that the Sinhalese identity is based upon a distinct biological nature, a common language, and a sacred history of inheritance; and that Theravedic Buddhism was the singular religion of the Sinhalese (Nissan and Stirrat 1990, 20–29).

Tamil myths promote territorial originality, and claim that the first Tamil people preceded the Sinhalese migration by a thousand years. They subscribe to a set of document fragments known as *Yalpanna Vaipava Malai,* which identify the Sri Lankan north as being given over by the Kingdom of Kandy in the c.e. thirteenth century (Hellman-Rajanayagam 1990, 107–122). These stories also affirm particular migrations, separate state histories, a closeness to India, the uniqueness of Jaffna and its environs, and racial, linguistic, and religious distinctions.

As suggested by one Sri Lankan historian (de Silva 1987), herein lie roots for the continuation of ethnoreligious animosity. The myth of Buddhist destiny competes with the Tamil myth of territorial originality and their legal claim to traditional lands.[2] The Sri Lankan colonial experience began under Portuguese and Dutch domination—excepting the regions of Jaffna (Tamil) and the Kingdom of Kandy (Sinhalese), which were later incorporated under British colonial rule. Britain increased the Tamil population with Indian immigrants in order to expand its agribusiness in tea. Trincomalee and Battacola became naval installations, while Colombo became the colonial capital. The British gradually shifted to indigenous rule, advancing Tamil leaders to positions of governance, in the bureaucracy, education, and business, due to their fear of Buddhist extremism and the various Sangha led Buddhist revivals of the late-nineteenth and twentieth centuries (Rogers 1990, 87–106).

These perceptions of mythic history became important to Sri Lankan leaders. President Jayewardene quoted liberally from the *Mahavamsa* in 1977 to support his constitutional changes (Kripes 1990), as did President Bandaranaika upon acieving independence and during the Sinhalese Only Language movement and Act of 1956 (Manogaran 1987, 11). As mythic histories are incorporated into Sri Lankan politics, they justify protracted cleavages over territorial autonomy versus a unitary state, language and religion, losses and gains to economic and educational opportunity, and the security brought by tolerated histories and identities (de Silva 1987, 1–16). The mythic histories echo Connor's "permanence of ethnic variegation," Smith's vitality of "ethnie" for national integration and disintegration, and Horowitz's "hierarchial yet parallel ethnicities."

Five legislative pieces enacted since independence changed conditions for each ethnic community. References to these highlight the interactive dynamic between internal ethnic politics and external political constraints within multicultural societies (Esman 1994).

The 1950s marked two significant national changes in Sri Lankan society, both of lasting importance. The Sinhalese Only Language Act was passed, ending the use of English in governance, and, more importantly, the dual tolerance/use of Tamil in official public activity. This had its greatest impact in political activity by restricting official documents to Sinhalese while, at the same time, encouraging increased Sinhala employment in government patronage and admissions to universities and schools. The second initiative, called the "internal recolonization" program, shifted Sinhalese populations into traditional Tamil northern and eastern districts through rice paddy land reforms.

Higher education saw another legislative change in 1970, through the Admissions Standardization Act. Sinhalese leaders charged that Tamil populations were disproportionately represented within Sri Lankan universities, despite the changes brought on by the Sinhalese Only Language Act. The law developed quotas for admissions according to total and district ethnic population percentages, which had the immediate effect of changing ethnic compositions and admissions quality standards between Sinhalese and Tamil applicants.

The late 1970s saw two changes—one constitutional and the other legislative. The 1977 elections brought the rightist United National Party (UNP) and its president, Jayewardene, into power with a campaign based upon Sinhalese ethnic dominance. The 1977 Sri Lankan Constitution provided special status to Buddhism, making it the nation's official religion and giving Buddhist representatives administrative responsibility within the Ministry of Cultural Affairs. The Prevention of Terrorism Act (1979), which gave police and legal institutions power to restrict constitutional guarantees in order to protect national interests, was initially directed at violence ascribing organizations such as the Tamil Liberation Tigers (formed in 1976) and the Sri Lankan Liberation Party (active in 1971). By outlawing any ascription to separatist ideology, the act had the effect of radicalizing the moderate Tamil United Liberation Front (TULF), which in 1977 had superseded Bandaranaika's Freedom Party and become the official opposition to UNP.

The following list of Tamil grievances extends from the above history:

- the loss of Indian Tamil citizenship in 1948;
- the Sinhalese Only Language Provisions of 1956;

- the necessity of Sinhalese for government patronage;
- continued internal colonization of traditional Tamil districts since 1952;
- development programs centered in the South and West;
- restructured discriminatory university admissions based upon district quotas and populations;
- the call for a semi-autonomous Tamil region (1972) and for a separate state of Eelam (1976);
- Buddhism as the national religion;
- the Terrorist Prevention Act of 1979 aimed at Tamils;
- the targeted destruction of Tamil businesses by Sinhalese separatist groups; and
- the banning of Tamil parties from Parliament. (Ponnambalam 1973, 3–4)

Does Sri Lankan history supply evidence that the above concerns relate to losses in participation, needs, and cultural acceptance and tolerance? In the Sri Lankan case, loss of participatory position for Tamil speaking peoples relates to three concerns: the use of Tamil for official purposes; the dilution of voting patterns in Tamil districts; and the closure of Tamil issues in public debate. As stated before, these concerns became *coding categories* for the study's content analysis on participatory loss.

A. Jeyaratnam Wilson's study on religious and ethnic changes in parliament from 1946–1977 verifies a declining position of power for Tamil political parties. Though Tamil representation remains nearly constant in absolute terms (20 Tamil delegates in 1946 and 21 delegates in 1977), significant increases in total parliamentary representation in 1956 and 1970 (from 95 seats to 151 and 168 respectively) decreased Tamil legislative capability. The percentage of Tamil representation declines from a high of 21 percent in 1946, to 12.5 percent in 1977. This decline in representation occurs as Tamil population growth moves from a little over 17 percent of Sri Lanka's population in 1946, to 20.5 percent in 1971. Historically acting as a balancing third party, the 1977 elections made TULF the opposition party in a UNP controlled, absolute majority parliament and further reduced Tamil influence (Wilson 1988, 35).

Studies done on the effects of recolonization policies show significant changes to demographic balances within traditional Tamil districts. Manogaran (1994) shows that years of internal colonization into eastern and northern electoral districts have changed solid Tamil population majorities into multi-ethnic pluralisms or Sinhalese majorities. Tamil governmental participation is lessened by the demographic shifts and by the reality that Sri Lankan political parties do indeed reflect the distribution of ethnic identities.

Though the 1979 Terrorism Prevention Act restricted the participation of Tamil separatist organizations, evidence for restrictions upon Tamil leaders and parties extends back through the four cases. The arrest of political party leaders (1958, 1971, 1977, and 1983), the removal of Tamil parties from parliament (1958 and 1983), or the inability for Tamil parties to participate in formal peace-building discussions (1977 and 1983) point to a history in which administrations representing Sinhalese controlled parties (SLDP and UNP) have excluded Tamil representatives. This restrictive trend in participation mirrors the Tamil development demanding increased autonomy—from autonomous regulation within a unified state in 1958 to the TULF platforms in 1977 and 1983 for a separate Tamil state.

The Sri Lankan context gives meaning to the concept of needs. For the most part, needs in Sri Lanka do not refer to the lack of food and adequate housing. Although any developing setting has some survival concerns, Sri Lankan needs refer principally to concerns about education and employment. Comments made by the Committee for Rational Development (1994, 180) suggest that the lack of a landed gentry and inadequate agricultural possibilities in Tamil regions made civil service and education the principal means for mobility and growth within the Tamil community. These means for growth met with traditional Sinhalese accusations, not all of them unfounded, that colonialism systematically favored Tamil aspirations to educational and governmental positions. Both communities, at differing times, charged the other with distributive injustice that was in need of systemic redress. Security needs—ethnic tolerance, safety, and the ability to pursue basic qualities of life—are central to the content analysis below.

Manogaran's study on the impact of educational change on ethnic communities shows declining Tamil opportunities in professional and university programs due to the Educational Standardization Act. Percentage changes of Tamil admittances to various university programs from 1970 to 1983 show declines of 27.6 percent to 23.4 percent in the physical and biological sciences, 48.3 percent to 28.1 percent in engineering programs, 48 percent to 22.1 percent for medical and dental programs, 53.6 percent to 45.2 percent in agricultural and veterinary sciences, and 34.6 percent to 11.5 percent in programs of law. Only in the arts is there an increase of Tamil university representation from 6.9 percent to 16.4 percent (Manogaran 1987, 120–125).

The Committee for Rational Development cites statistics that show by 1970 (on account of the Sinhalese Only Act) Tamils represented only 5 percent of the civil service labor force while, in 1978, none of those recruited for the civil service were from Tamil populations (The Committee for Rational Development 1984, 45–55). The history of foreign aid, especially water enhancement programs to develop new farm areas, indicates that from 1971 to 1981, no new industrial or agricultural development project went to Tamil regions, which helps to account for Jaffna's unemployment rate being the highest in Sri Lanka (The Committee for Rational Development 1984, 181).

The Cases

Three of the four cases—1958, 1977, and 1983—show similar results by relating the three loss categories to the expanding frequency and intensity of Sri Lankan social violence. The 1971 case differs significantly from the others and will be treated below as an anomaly within Sri Lankan protracted conflict. The incidents of violence were initially scored as present (1) or absent (0). Categories of violence were also given intensity rankings with absent being "0," protests "1," riots "2," sanctions "3," and deaths "4." Additively treating the rankings created a second violence indicator, violence level, and allowed for an ordinal scaling of 0–10. The size of the ordinal range enabled the use of OLS regression modeling of loss categories to the degree of violence to measure for model fit and the amount of variance in violence level accounted for by the loss indicators.

Coding questions identified the presence (1) or absence (0) of cultural, need based (economic and security developmental) and participatory indicators of loss. Familiarity with the Sri Lankan setting suggested relevant meanings for context specific needs. Cultural needs included references to either religious, historical, or language issues, and references to traditional homelands that included calls for separate states. Economically divisive issues included the availability or scarcity of civil service opportunities for both Sinhalese and Tamil populations, limited openings in higher education, and the placement of developmental assistance programs. Communities differed on their definition of security needs.

Tamil understandings drew attention to their safety in recognized traditional homelands, and in the physical security of Tamil property and communities. Loss to Sinhalese security took on a more national character by interpreting security loss as a loss of democracy, national security, freedom, and a way of life. Losses in participatory ability or, to use Burton's terminology, control, speaks to concerns of Indian Tamil involvement, minority party parliamentary concerns, and the physical arrest or assassination of party officials for either ethnic group.

A simple, symbolic, and potent illustration indicates how qualities of loss or gain distinguish the framing of common experiences across social identity groups and ultimately enter into the public dialogue over policy. February 1958 marked the tenth anniversary of Ceylonese independence from Great Britain. For the Sinhalese majority, the day was commemorated as a national day of celebration, accomplishment, and triumph. Tamil organizations and political parties used it as an official day of mourning to bring to light the losses and social decline experienced by their community at the hands of the Sinhalese.

Three analyses were done to examine the relationship between individual and collective loss indicators and the presence or level of violence. Simple frequency distributions were made to determine which loss indicators remained constant, grew, or declined across the four cases.

These losses (cultural, participatory, or perceived needs) were categorized simply as present (1) or absent (0) from the collected articles. Composite loss frequency counts identified how many of the statements recorded made appeals to one or more than one form of loss. Chi square tests examined whether any relationship existed between loss indicators and violence, as well as the significance of those relationships. Regression was used to determine model fit and to test significance of the individual variable coefficients.

Table 8.2 Presence/Absence of Loss and Composite Tallies

	1958	1971	1977	1983
"N"	40	31	21	51
CLF	32	4	20	41
PLF	23	1	13	26
NLF	12	29	12	32
Composite Loss				
3 Loss	4	0	8	19
2 Loss	18	2	9	14
1 Loss	18	29	4	14

Note: CLF: Cultural Loss Frequency; PLF: Participation Loss Frequency; NLF: Needs Loss Frequency

Table 8.3   Frequency Distribution and Chi sq. Values

	1958	1971	1977	1983
"N"	40	31	21	51
Crit Val	3.84	3.84	3.84	3.84
Cult Loss				
freq.	32	4	20	41
%	80	13	95	80
Chi	2.109	1.879	1.4	9.723
Part Loss				
freq.	23	1	13	26
%	58	3	57	51
Chi	2.723	2.526	.751	2.422
Needs Loss				
freq.	11	29	12	32
%	28	94	57	63
Chi	1.338	.456	3.646	3.063

Table 8.4   Regression Analysis on Model

	1958	1971	1977	1983
Cult. Coef.	1.232	1.413	2.541	2.203
p	.346	.554	.514	.040
Part. Coef.	2.061	−5.577	−1.260	1.557
p	.063	.361	.447	.066
Needs Coef.	−.172	−1.000	4.303	2.109
p	.886	.826	.015	.015
St. ErrorEst	3.230	3.898	4.046	2.777
R^2	.12	.074	.353	.336
R^2 adj	.047	—	.239	.293
F ratio	1.642	.718	3.096	7.910
p	.197	.550	.055	.008

General conclusions for the three related years include the consistent presence of cultural and participatory indicators of loss, especially by the Tamil community, and the increasing importance over time of economic and security needs (see tables 8.2 and 8.3 for presence of loss and frequency distribution). Using language, history, religion and homeland territory as indicators, the co-reported presence of cultural issues of loss with the presence of violence for three of the years were 52.5 percent, 57.1 percent, and 58.8 percent (1958, 1977, and 1983). The presence of perceived cultural loss excluding the manifestations of violence within the coded articles was even higher. Perceived and real losses in participation remained constant. The percentage of articles reflecting the presence of participatory loss and violence were 32.5 percent, 33.3 percent, and 37.25 percent across the years 1958, 1977, and 1983. The frequency of relating losses in needs with violence increased over the same three years from 12.5 percent, to 46.9 percent and 45.1 percent. The increase in needs based violence signals a bridge between communal identity issues and relative deprivation issues. A comparison of the composite tallies of loss across the case studies shows the increasing complexity and entanglement of Sri Lankan issues over time, especially in 1977 and 1983, where issue combinations of two and three issues of loss dominate the single issue concerns of 1958. This continuity amidst evolution is exemplified by the following selective yet representative events from Sri Lankan PSC.

Preceding the violence of 1958 was the passage of the Sinhalese Only Language Act of 1956, the efforts in the 1957 Chelvanayakam (Federal Party, Tamil) and Bandaranaika (Sri Lankan National Party, Sinhalese) discussions and agreement to clarify the meaning of "reasonable use of the Tamil Language," and the government's actions in 1958 to ignore the "C-B" pact. The pact allowed for dual language use and increased autonomy for Tamil homelands within a federal unified state, and a reduction of re-colonization efforts. The demise of the pact precipitated calls by the Federal Party for a national civil disobedience campaign, resulting in communally reciprocal, nation-wide acts of vandalism defacing Tamil and Sinhalese signs. As if to physically portray ethnic contempt, Tamil commercial interests in the capitol of Colombo, and public and governmental facilities (post offices, custom houses, and so on) in the northern and eastern districts were destroyed.

The loss to culture represented by the restrictive use of language and statements regarding the unique and accomplished Tamil history and the Hindu religion dominated the understanding of cultural need in 1958 (*The Times* February 4, 1958, 6). Though official Tamil party positions called for a federal unified state with additional autonomy for the Tamil provinces, the Tamil Independent Party parliamentarian, Suntharalingan, made the first call for the creation of a separate Tamil state (*The Times* July 3, 1958, 9). His call was promptly answered by the Sinhalese member of parliament, Rajartina, who rejected any reasonable use of the Tamil language, fearing the loss of rights, privileges, and jobs for the Sinhalese majority (*The Times* July 4, 1958, 9).

Cultural claims (history, language, and religion) of loss, victimization, or uniqueness have never been abandoned by Tamil party leaders. Cultural claims influence the understanding by Tamil leaders of the extent of their economic and developmental victimization, given gains within the Sinhalese community. The Tamil United Liberation Party (TULF) general secretary, Amirthalanigan, underscored the 1977 election landslide of Jayewardene's United National Party, which made TULF the official opposition, by saying that there was now a mandate to work for a Tamil separate state. The TULF Manifesto argued that the unique historical, cultural, and religious character of the Tamil people and the continuous history of decline since 1948 made such a change necessary (*The Times* August 4, 1977, 6). The consequence of a more separatist position seemed to harden the conservative UNP position as Jayewardene canceled an all-party conference to address Tamil requests, denied the validity of state separatist arguments, and refused to reopen the Sinhalese only language issue (*The Times* September 3, 1977, 5). The Tamil position favoring a separate state, which was made illegal by the Terrorism Prevention Act of 1979, remained the predominant understanding of Tamil parties in 1983 as TULF officials rejected President Jayewardene's demands for the loyalty of government employees and political parties, and as separatist organizations like the Tamil Liberation Tigers gained in popularity.

The above frequency tables, 8.3 and 8.4, also show considerable continuity in claims over real and perceived limits to participation within governance. The abuse in 1958 directed at Indian Tamils due to their lack of citizenship, was superseded by the arrest of Tamil party leaders, the banning of the Federal Party (Tamil) from parliament, and the restriction of Federal Party participation in national discussions regarding the ethnic violence crisis (*Christian Science Monitor* June 2, 1958, 1). These arrests and bans occurred in 1977 and 1983. Although heralded by TULF in 1977 as a mandate, the real consequence of the UNP landslide was the lessened ability for Tamil representation to balance one or the other of the major Sinhalese parties. Unique to the 1983 case are the Presidential Extension Act of December 1982, which extended Jayewardene's presidency for an additional six years, and his call for elections in May 1983 for those districts that supported TULF candidates in an effort to increase UNP's parliamentary majority (*The Times* March 21, 1983, 5). The seriousness of the attempt to rid Sri Lanka of Tamil opposition was emphasized in a statement by President Jayewardene; "Those seeking partition will lose their civil rights, cannot hold office, cannot practice their professions, join movements or organizations" (*The Times* July 29, 1977, 7).

Economic and security needs, which were low in 1958, increased in 1977 and 1983. A detailed description of economic and educational losses appears in TULF's 1977 Manifesto. TULF charged that the Sinhalese government — with education policy discrimination against Tamil students, massive human rights abuses, loss of government positions, programmed underdevelopment of Tamil districts, and through its recolonization program—had diluted Tamil political power making Tamil populations "second class citizens" in their own homelands (*The Times* August 4, 1977, 6). The turnaround of ethnic grievances is dramatically visible in that almost identical charges of educational displacement, job security, and favoritism were leveled by then President Bandaranaika in 1958 against Tamil/British exploitation of Sinhalese security and needs (*The Times* July 8, 1958, 8).

Tamil security needs were exacerbated in 1983. The riots and civil conflict created over 40,000 refugees in Colombo and caused hundreds of Tamil deaths including two massacres of Tamil leaders held under maximum security confinement, attacks by Sri Lankan (Sinhalese) military personnel and police units, the confiscation by the government of Tamil properties, and the targeted destruction of Tamil commercial and market facilities in southern and western provinces (*The Times* August 2, 1983, 6). The list of Tamil economic and educational grievances expanded from 1977 to 1983 to include human rights abuses, discrimination against Indian Tamils (charges not heard since 1958), and overt accusations of anti-Tamil politics against the president and his government and President Jayewardene was held responsible for Sinhalese violence against Tamils (*The Times* July 6, 1983, 6). Speaking for TULF, Secretary General Amirthalingen accused the army of willful violence against and negligence of Tamil communities in Trincomalee, and charged that "through its inaction, indifference and arrogant failure to mobilize international assistance [the government] expressed complete contempt for the life and property of Tamil people (*The Times* August 5, 1983, 1). In an interview, President Jayewardene acknowledged the Sri Lankan trauma, but accused foreigners, terrorist groups, and ethnic parties of promoting causes and actions unacceptable to the Sri Lankan state and its majority population (*The Christian Science Monitor* August 8, 1983, 24).

Chi square tests reveal that only in 1983 do relationships between loss indicators and the presence of violence satisfy .05 critical values for standards of significance. F tests on the 1983 regression model also reveal similar satisfactions with an empirical F value of 7.91, well beyond the .05 critical test value of 2.61. R^2 for the 1983 model accounts for 33.6 percent of the variance in violence levels. T tests on 1983 independent variable coefficients all lie above the critical value of 1.684, and tolerance levels for the three variables reveal sizeable independent impact of each independent variable upon the level of violence with only marginal multicollinearity (.878, .884, and .922 for 1983 losses in culture, participation and needs). Thus, the 1983 model confirms the hypothesized relationship of cultural loss variables to increasing levels of violence (escalation).

Though the model accounts for sizable variance in the level of violence for both 1958 (R^2=.12) and 1977 (R^2=.353), the null hypothesis of R^2= 0 in both years could not be rejected when using a .05 critical value for significance test. If the model in 1977 were tested at a critical level of .1, the null hypothesis could be rejected indicating that model difficulty might be due to small sample size. The hypothesis test for the "loss of needs" coefficient in the 1977 case, Beta=zero, exceeds the critical value of .05, and again, tolerance levels reveal sizeable independent impact by the independent variables upon the levels of violence. Less affirmative results are seen for the model in the 1958 case.

The 1971 case stands as an anomaly among the four cases. Cultural loss does not factor in as a significant independent variable. Security needs are frequently mentioned but from the point of view of President Bandaranaika and her ruling party No test statistic falls beyond a .05 critical test level and the model only accounts for 7 percent of the variance in violence levels. Though, of the cases studied, 1971 shows the highest degree of violence—over 5,000 deaths—it is *not between* ethnic groups. Civil war broke out between the Sri Lankan government and its security forces, and the Maoist influenced People's Liberation Front which sought to end capitalist domination in Sri Lanka. Here, joblessness and educational attainment factor into the violence, correlating to other theories of revolution and deprivation (*Christian Science Monitor* April 17, 1971, 18). The 1971 case emphasizes the difference between previous educational and professional opportunities and new realities. The Davies deprivation "J-curve" model descriptively fits the 1971 conditions more accurately than reliance on ethnic identity models. As became a rationale used in later cases, the government charged foreign powers, extremists, terrorists, and outsiders with plans to disrupt and end democracy, overturn the government, and assassinate the president (*The Times* April 17, 1971, 1).

Conclusion

This study sought to identify the relationship of loss and risk acceptance regarding cultural identity, human needs, and political participation as significant motivations for the resumption and escalation of protracted conflict. The study used four cases from Sri Lanka's post-independence experience of social and communal group identity conflict to ascertain such a relationship in hopes of establishing a point when conflict resolution mechanisms ought to be strengthened and more vigorously pursued.

The results of the study are mixed. Only one of the years, 1983, provided a clear example of the model's fit, where both the violence level was related significantly to all three independent variables, and each variable was associated with the presence of violence. The 1971 case stood out as an anomaly within the cultural conflict history of Sri Lanka, and can be better explained as an ideological revolt against governmental authority. The 1958 and 1977 cases failed to reject respective null hypotheses, yet, some independent variable coefficients (participation in 1958 and need in 1977) achieved significance, and the models accounted for moderately large variance in the levels of violence.

Loss of cultural identity and human needs does seem to explain and predict some settings of violent escalation within PSCs. The Sri Lankan historical background adds layers of confirmational information to the realities of loss experienced by Tamil minority populations over the course of independence and to ethnic and religious narratives frequently used to account for and justify the ongoing climate of violence. Given a meaningful evaluation of Sri Lankan violence, further application of prospect theory model building as a means of understanding and predicting protracted conflict cycles seems justified.

APPENDIX 8.1

Operational Questions to Determine Loss

1. Do stated issues reflect a loss to the communal group as they understand their cultural identity reflective of language, race, or religion?
2. Do stated issues reflect a loss to the communal group as they understand their history?
3. Do stated issues reflect a loss to the communal group as they are enabled to participate in governance? Do perceived solutions reflect a need for cultural separation?
4. Do stated issues reflect a loss to the communal group as they seek satisfaction of their human developmental needs?

5. Do stated issues reflect a loss to the communal group as they perceive their security?
6. Are reactions by leaders measured against some historical or changing benchmark reference of performance?
7. Do communal group leaders frame decisions, issues, or perceptions using categories of loss or gain?
8. Are decisions, issues, and perceptions framed by communal group leaders as zero-sum games between the conflicted groups?

Source: From Janice Gross Stein and Louis Pauly, eds. *Choosing to Cooperate, How States Avoid Loss.* Baltimore: Johns Hopkins University Press, 1993.

APPENDIX 8.2

Sample Case Evaluation Sheet

Issue _____

Article Title _____

Date _____

Domestic Violence Indicators	Present	Absent	How So?
Riots			
Protests			
Deaths			
Assassinations			
Sanctions			
Sanctions removed			

Loss Qualification Indicators	Present	Absent	How so?

(See appendix 8.1 for questions.)

Notes

1. The author contends that any regional study should include regional or local newspapers, such as, in this case, *The Times of India*. Time and lack of local availability prohibited its use.

2. Again, see Samuel Peleg's discussion of religion in this volume.

References

Azar, Edward. 1990. *The Management of Protracted Social Conflict*. Hampshire, UK: Dartmouth Publishing.

———. 1985. "Protracted International Conflicts: Ten Propositions." *International Interactions* 12 (1): 59–70.

Boulding, Kenneth. 1978. *Stable Peace*. Austin, TX: University of Texas Press.

Burton, John. 1988. "Human Needs versus Societal Needs." In *The Power of Human Needs in World Society,* ed. Roger Coate and Jerel A. Rosati. Boulder, CO: Lynne Rienner Publishers, pp. 34–58.

———. 1990. *Conflict Resolution and Prevention*. New York: St. Martin's Press.

Committee for Rational Development. 1984. *Sri Lanka, The Ethnic Conflict*. New Delhi, India: Navrang Publishers.

Connor, Walker. 1994. *Ethnonationalism*. Princeton, NJ: Princeton University Press.

de Silva, Chandra Richard. 1987. *Sri Lanka—A History*. New York: Advent Books.

Davies, James C., ed. 1971. *When Men Revolt and Why.* New York: The Free Press.

Esman, Milton J. 1994. *Ethnic Politics*. Ithaca, NY: Cornell University Press.

Gurr, Ted Robert. 1993. *Minorities at Risk*. Washington, DC: United States Institute of Peace.

Hellman-Rajanayagam, Dagmar. 1990. "The Politics of the Tamil Past." In *Sri Lanka: History and Roots of Conflict,* ed. Jonathan Spencer. London: Routledge, pp. 107–22.

Horowitz, Donald. 1985. *Ethnic Groups in Conflict*. Berkeley, CA: University of California Press.

Jervis, Robert. 1992. "Political Implications of Loss Aversion." *Political Psychology* 13 (2): 187–203.

Juergensmeyer, Mark. 1993. *The New Cold War?* Barkeley, CA: University of California Press.

Kearney, Robert. 1973. *The Politics of Ceylon*. Ithaca, NY: Cornell University Press.

Kripes, Steven. 1990. "J.R. Jayewardene, Righteousness and Real Politik." In *Sri Lanka: History and Roots of Conflict,* ed. Jonathan Spencer. London: Routledge, pp. 187–204.

Levy, Jack. 1992. "Prospect Theory and International Relations: Theoretical Applications and Analytical Problems." *Political Psychology* 13 (2): 283–309.

Little, David. 1994. *Sri Lanka: The Invention of Enmity*. Washington, DC: United States Institute for Peace.

Manogaran, Chelvadurai. 1987. *Ethnic Conflict and Reconciliation in Sri Lanka*. Honolulu: University of Hawaii Press.

———. 1994. "Colonialization as Politics: Political Use of Space in Sri Lankan Ethnic Conflict." In *Sri Lankan Tamil Ethnicity and Identity,* ed. Chelvadurai Manogaran and Bryan Pfaffenberger. Boulder, CO.: Westview Press, pp. 84–125.

Moynihan, Daniel Patrick. 1994. *Pandaemonium*. New York: Oxford University Press.

Nissan, Elizabeth, and R.C. Stirrat. 1990. "The Generation of Communal Identities." In *Sri Lanka: History and Roots of Conflict*, ed. Jonathan Spencer. London: Routledge, pp. 20–29.

Patin, Alan, ed. 1972. *What They Said in 1971*. Beverly Hills, CA: Monitor Book Company.

Ponnambalam, Satchi. 1973. *Sri Lanka: The National Question and the Tamil Liberation Struggle*. London: Zed Books.

Rogers, John D. 1990. "Historical Images of the British People." In *Sri Lanka: History and Roots of Conflict*, ed. Jonathan Spencer. London: Routledge, pp. 87–106.

Rubin Jeffrey, Dean G. Pruitt, and Sung Hee Kim. 1994. *Social Conflict Escalation, Stalemate, and Settlement*. New York: McGraw-Hill.

Smith, Anthony D. 1991. *National Identity*. Reno, NV: University of Nevada Press.

Stein, Janice Gross, and Louis Pauly, eds. 1993. *Choosing to Cooperate: How States Avoid Loss*. Baltimore, MD: Johns Hopkins University Press.

Tambiah, S.J. 1986. *Sri Lanka: Ethnic Fratricide and the Dismantling of Democracy*. Chicago: University of Chicago Press.

Taylor, Charles Lewis, and David A. Jodice. 1983. *World Handbook of Political and Social Indicators*, vol. 2. New Haven, CT: Yale University Press.

Wilson, A. Jeyaratnam. 1988. *The Break-Up of Sri Lanka*. Honolulu: University of Hawaii Press.

"Ceylon Take-Over Plot Foiled," *Christian Science Monitor*, April, 17, 1971: 18.

"A Political View of Sri Lanka's Violence," *Christian Science Monitor*, August 8, 1983: 24.

"Racial Friction: Tamils vs. Sinhalese," *Christian Science Monitor*, June 2, 1958: 1.

"Ceylon Inquiry Promised," *The Times*, London, July 3, 1958: 9.

"Ceylon Revolt Deaths Near 1000," April 17, 1971. *The Times*, London, April 17, 1971: 1.

"Ceylon's Point of No Return," *The Times*, London, February 4, 1958: 6.

"Colombo Acts to Appease," *The Times*, London, July 29, 1977: 7.

"Demand Grows for Tamil State," *The Times*, London, August 4, 1977: 6.

"Economic Basis for Ceylon Discord," *The Times*, London, July 8, 1958: 8.

"Jayewardene to Erase Poll Setback," *The Times*, London, March 21, 1983: 5.

"Language Policy Continuing," *The Times*, London, July 4, 1958: 9.

"Shortage of Food and Jobs as Sri Lanka Lies in Ruins," *The Times*, London, August 2, 1983: 6.

"Sri Lanka Rules Out Separatism for Tamils," *The Times*, London, September 3, 1977: 5.

"Sri Lankan Island of Terror," *The Times*, London, July 6, 1983: 6. "Tamils Shot by Soldiers, Leader Says," *The Times*, London, August 5, 1983: 1.

CHAPTER NINE

Protracted Conflict and Enduring Rivalry: India, Pakistan, and the Dynamics of Stalemate over Kashmir

Sangeeta Sharma

Introduction

This research effort has been an attempt to conduct what Arend Lijphart (1971) defined as an "interpretive theoretical case study," in order to examine the validity and applicability of established theoretical generalizations to specific cases of protracted conflict and enduring rivalry between states. Specific reference is made to the general theoretical propositions of status discrepancy theory as conceptualized by Johan Galtung (1964) in his conceptualization of "a structural theory of aggression," and further developed by Maurice East (1972) in his study on "status discrepancy and violence in the international system." These theoretical generalizations were then applied to two cases involving enduring rivalry leading to the outbreak of war between India and Pakistan over the disputed territory of Kashmir in 1965 and 1971. The focus of the study was to conduct a comparative study of the causal factors that increased the probability of war in each case. The time period under consideration is the 20-year period from 1957 to 1977, which encompasses both wars at relatively equal intervals, and whose end represents a period of relative peace and stability. The comparative method was chosen because limited resources and the small number of cases made extensive cross tabulation of the data for the period under study extremely difficult. Also, both countries (or cases)—India and Pakistan—are socioculturally similar, thus making them comparable. This sociocultural and ethnic similarity also puts them within the category of states considered by analysts like Azar as those most likely to face enduring rivalry, particulary over territorial matters.

The initial research puzzle was two-fold: (a) what factors contribute to long-term intractability and stalemate in an interstate boundary dispute between two neighboring states in a regional subsystem, and (b) what conditions lead to instability and aggression within such a system, thus disturbing the stalemate? The latter puzzle, (b), is the main focus of empirical analysis in this research, which was conducted in strict accordance with the conditions laid down by status discrepancy theory.

Based on the conceptual framework of status discrepancy theory, the research hypothesis proposes that there should exist a direct relationship between an increase in tension (dependent variable) just before each war, an increase in the gap in levels of socioeconomic development between India and Pakistan, and a rise in the insecurity of the Pakistani leadership as indicated by perceptual indicators of self-righteousness and of images of India as the enemy.

The focus of this study is thus primarily on Pakistan, with comparisons to India being conducted in order to determine the level of Pakistan's relative status discrepancy vis-à-vis the latter. The basic theoretical contention is that increased tension in the periods just preceding the two wars was caused by Pakistan's rising insecurity and frustration in the face of the increasing gap between the two states in terms of socioeconomic development, power, and prestige, which culminated in each case in an attempt by the Pakistani leadership to bridge this gap through the employment of violent means. This is thus a classic case of what has been defined as a "nonrealistic conflict" (Coser 1956) or "fight" (Rapoport 1960) between two states, whereby the need for tension release by one party over intangible issues involving self-identity and prestige is channeled into specific, violence-prone issues such as control over territory claimed by the other party. See Gil Friedman's chapter in this volume for an elaboration of the concepts of "nonrealistic conflicts" and "fights" between parties involved in protracted conflicts and enduring rivalries (see also Azar 1984, 1990).

The frontier territory of Kashmir, which has been claimed equally by both neighbors since their inception in 1947, has served as the focal point of the enduring rivalry between India and Pakistan. This is primarily because of its large size, its unique geographical position (bordering both nation states), as well as its particular ethnic composition (comprising both Hindus and Muslims), which serves to increase its strategic, ethnic, economic, and symbolic importance to both sides as a political manifestation of the age-old rivalry between the two religious groups for hegemony in the subcontinent.

The Underlying Dynamics of Stalemate

From a review of relevant literature, certain key concepts have been identified as useful in understanding the first part of the research puzzle: namely, what factors contribute to long-term intractability and stalemate in the case of an interstate boundary dispute?

A "conflict" exists when two or more people or groups of people (including nation states), wish to carry out acts that are mutually inconsistent. These acts may have their basis in purely practical wants, needs, or desires, or they may concern fundamental beliefs and ideologies. A conflict of interests can be resolved through the process of negotiation, which aims to prevent the actors from utilizing violent means to achieve their ends. War, an extreme utilization of large-scale violent means by nation-states to achieve their interests, is employed when other means to settle the conflict of interests (such as diplomatic persuasion and compromise) fail (Ikle 1971; Nicholson 1992; Cashman 1993). The aim of negotiation is thus to settle conflicts with means short of war, divert governments from the use of force, or terminate fighting before destruction becomes complete, based on the assumption that the conflicting parties share a common interest in survival, and hence will be willing to undertake the task of mutual problem solving. It may, however, be the case that the negotiating process leads to a compromise on marginal matters, while the central area of implacable conflict remains untouched.

One of the important elements in such a conflict of interests between nation-states has traditionally been the question of territory, which is essential for human beings in their collectivities as it serves the dual purpose of providing identification and security (Cukwurah 1967, Cashman 1993, Vasquez 1993). Within the realist conception of power, too, territory is an important component of a nation's power. This has been one of the main motivating factors for wars between nations in the past. Boundary disputes over contiguous territory between neighboring states are of a particularly explosive nature, since they provide both the opportunity as well as the willingness to resort to violent means to capture and/or retain it.

A conflict turns into a "dispute" when the parties involved are unable or unwilling to arrive at a private settlement on a bilateral (dyadic) basis, and place the matter into the public domain. Multilateral negotiation, characterized by the involvement of third parties in an agreed forum (such as the United Nations), thus begins. The outcome of negotiating activity can be of two types: a joint agreement on the terms for the issues in conflict, which, in the opinion of both parties to the conflict, are relatively satisfactory and better than no agreement; or a stalemate, whereby both parties see no way of arriving at mutually acceptable terms (Carroll 1969, Gulliver 1979, Duchacek 1972). In the latter situation, both conflicting parties refuse to accept the other's proposed alternative to the status quo. Each party's expectations remain divergent, and each is unwilling to shift its demands. Repetitive declarations of set positions lead to psychological ossification and consequently increased mistrust, anger, and anxiety, thus reducing the chances of future agreement and perpetuating the stalemate.

Such a stalemate is inherently unstable, since the basic conflict of interests continues to exist. The possibility of resorting to violent means is thus always present, despite relatively peaceful outward conditions. This is especially true in the case of stalemates in boundary disputes, in which extended periods of warlike peace are continually threatened by outbreaks of armed conflict along the border areas. The status quo that is established is thus characterized by a balance between conflict and harmony, and it is with the conditions leading to an escalation in the former that this paper is essentially concerned.

The Dynamics of Stalemate in India-Pakistan Relations over Kashmir

India and Pakistan emerged as independent nation-states in 1947 from the same political unit administered as British India for the previous two centuries. *Both states had their basis on different religious beliefs and political ideologies.* Pakistan justified its existence on the "two-nation" theory, which asserts that Hindus and Muslims are two separate peoples inherently incapable of living together peacefully, and hence should be separated into distinct political units. India, on the other hand, supported secularism, based on the belief that peoples of all faith could reside peacefully within the Indian Union. Pakistan, however, repeatedly stressed that the Hindu majority in India would always repress the Muslim minority.

When British India was divided in 1947, a number of semi-independent states ruled by local princes had the choice, based on the wishes of their people, of either becoming part of India or Pakistan, or of remaining independent. Most of the princedoms chose the former option, either because they were too small or because they were already surrounded by the land mass of the bigger states. Some princedoms, one of which was Kashmir, however, were large enough in terms of size and resources, as well as being geographically situated outside the land mass of each state, to be able to opt for independence.

Kashmir's special importance for both India and Pakistan lay in the fact that it borders other significant states in the region, such as Afghanistan, China and the former Soviet Union, and hence could act as a strategically important buffer region. The Kashmir situation was further compounded by the fact that the Indo-Pakistan borders were drawn by the British more as frontier zones than as borders of distinct political entities. This lack of formal delineation of territory was bound to create problems later.

At the point of independence in August 1947, Kashmir was ruled by a Hindu (Sikh) king, Raja Ranjit Singh, who had traditionally repressed the majority Muslim population of the state. In October 1947, Muslim tribesmen from neighboring Afghanistan raided Kashmir from its North-West frontier, ostensibly to aid their Muslim brethren in the valley by overthrowing the tyranny of the king. India charged Pakistan with aiding and abetting the tribesmen in their effort to invade Kashmir. Despite denials by Pakistan, India took the matter to the United Nations Security Council on October 26, 1947. In doing so, the matter was transformed from being a purely bilateral issue over territory between two neighbors, into an international dispute in accordance with the definitions adopted in the above section (and the U.N. charter).

Faced with an imminent threat to his life, Raja Ranjit Singh asked India for military assistance, in return for which he agreed to accede to the Indian Union. India then sent her armed forces into Kashmir in order to repel the raiders. Pakistan, faced with the possibility that India would occupy all of Kashmir, sent in her troops too, thus leading to the outbreak of the first Indo-Pakistan war of 1947. A cease-fire was eventually mediated by the United Nations, and a cease-fire line established between areas of Kashmir occupied by both states (with India occupying most of it). Security Council resolutions of January 20, and April 21, 1948, established that a final, peaceful solution to the dispute would be possible only if (a) both sides withdrew their troops from Kashmir, and (b) a free, impartial plebiscite be conducted to determine the wishes of the population of Kashmir as to the state to which they wished to accede.

India, while agreeing in principle to holding a plebiscite, however, claimed suzerainty over Kashmir due to the accession of Ranjit Singh to the Indian Union. Pakistan, on the other hand, claimed that the accession was obtained from the king under duress, and hence the Indian claim to Kashmir was fraudulent and illegal. Pakistan has therefore consistently asked for the withdrawal of Indian troops from Kashmir, as well as for a plebiscite, on the ground that the Muslim majority of that state will opt for union with Pakistan. It has also repeatedly blamed India for repressing the Muslim majority in Kashmir, a claim that India has repudiated as an attempt by Pakistan to inflame communal disharmony in the valley. The fact that India already has possession of a large part of Kashmir, moreover, presented a fait accompli to the rest of the world, and prompted Pakistani requests that the Kashmir dispute be settled on an equal basis between India and Pakistan. This, claimed Pakistan, could only be done through the auspices of the United Nations, since meaningful bilateral negotiations were impossible as long as India continued to be in a position of strength in Kashmir.

The enduring rivalry between India and Pakistan resulting in stalemate, thus, exists over issues of territory, religion, and, more fundamentally, over the question of equal treatment of both states in the formulation of a lasting solution to the dispute. India, as the party with the upper hand, was already well entrenched in Kashmir by the end of the 1940s, thus increasing Pakistan's sense of injustice and insecurity. This was the basis for the latter's repeated requests for multilateral intervention in the dispute through the 1950s and 1960s, while India maintained that the solution could be achieved bilaterally. The fact that India continues to have control over Kashmir can only bear testimony to the fact that Pakistan's claims do not carry the same weight as India's in the eyes of the rest of the world. Pakistan's relative status vis-à-vis India, thus is at a lower level, as far as Kashmir is concerned, a fact that can be extended to other areas of contention between the two within the theoretical constructs of status discrepancy theory.

Status Discrepancy Theory

Status discrepancy theory is essentially built upon the sociological notion of a stratified system consisting of a hierarchy of unequal positions, wherein one's position in that hierarchy determines one's behavior. It postulates that all nation-states of the world can be considered to constitute a great social system characterized by universal stratification. The elements of this social system interact with each other to occupy different positions within that system. These positions can be ranked according to a number of criteria, such as economic stature, power, and prestige, which constitute the "status" of a nation-state. Important indicators of status include military power, economic stability, productive capacity, technological sophistication, literacy, and diplomatic relations.

These rankings of status have a certain stability and continuity: that is, differential rankings will always exist, although the distance between them might vary. Also, elements within the system may cross each other in their rankings (due to technological development, for example), but the system as a whole will continue to possess a hierarchy of rankings.

Status discrepancy theory goes on to postulate that *the degree of status discrepancy (or rank-disequilibration) is a predictor of a nation state's tendency toward aggression or nonaggression,* where aggression can be defined as "drives towards change, even against the will of others" (Galtung 1964). While Galtung confined himself to status disequilibration within a nation state, East (1972) concentrated on status disequilibration between nation states themselves. This chapter adopts the latter conception, based on the assumption that if the nation-states of an international system are stratified along different dimensions as "topdogs," "underdogs," and those belonging to an intermediate level of status discrepancy, then it is the *last category of states that are most likely to exhibit aggressive behavior due to frustration arising out of their relative position within the system.* Total topdogs will be relatively peaceful since they already benefit from the status quo, and are satisfied with their privileged position. Total underdogs, though dissatisfied, nevertheless lack both the necessary resources and the motivation—in terms of "ideas, visions, acquaintances . . . social experience, courage to imagine oneself as a ruler, etc," in other words, they lack "opportunity and willingness" (Starr 1978).

It is, thus, only those states that are in a position of rank disequilibrium (where both topdog and underdog dimensions exist) that possess both the resources as well as the necessary motivation (opportunity and willingness) to instigate change in the system. This is because an entity in a disequilibriated state will constantly be reminded of its shortcomings by the differential treatment that it is exposed to by the other members of the global society.

As such, status discrepancy as a cause of aggression has two aspects: the actual, *objective* state of disequilibrium of an actor, and the actor's *subjective* perception of it, which lead's to the development of a kind of frustration-aggression mechanism. Extreme forms of aggression, such as war, however, are not resorted to, unless (a) other means of equilibration toward a complete topdog configuration have been tried, and (b) the culture has some practice in violent aggression. Both objective conditions of relative disequilibration, as well as subjective perceptions of oneself and those of the enemy have been combined to form the theoretical framework for the present research to examine the relations between India and Pakistan over the Kashmir boundary dispute.

Within the South Asian subsystem—comprised of Bangladesh, Bhutan, India, the Maldive Islands, Nepal, Pakistan, and Sri Lanka—India and Pakistan are the two closest nations competing for topdog status in terms of ranking of economic development, military capabilities, and status (to use East's classification). Nevertheless since its inception in 1947, India has consistently managed to retain a position of relative regional hegemony due to its large size and national resources and capabilities. Although both nation-states have risen in terms of absolute prosperity over the years, the "relative prosperity" of Pakistan vis-à-vis India continues to be perceived by the latter's leadership as being at a consistently lower level. Whether this perception corresponds to the actual state of affairs is one of the main questions that will be addressed below. Whether existing in reality or not, Pakistan's perception of India has led to feelings of insecurity, hostility, and hence aggressive tendencies on the part of Pakistan, thus leading to enduring rivalry between the two nation-states and compounding regional subsystemic instability and disequilibrium.

The theory propounded in this study is that objective indicators of socioeconomic development in Pakistan should show a perceptible gap from that of India in the period of two to five years (to use East's time-lag criteria) preceding each war. This gap should be reflected in perceptual terms in the statements of the Pakistani leaders, diplomats, and journalists, who will tend to be increasingly self-righteous and anti-Indian just before the outbreak of war. This should be reflected in the debates over Kashmir in the U.N. General Assembly and the Security Council. A further proposition is that the second independent variable, that is, the perceptual gap, is more important, though it occurs only in conjunction with the first independent variable as a causal factor leading to war.

If status discrepancy theory, as applied to the two cases of the outbreak of war between India and Pakistan over Kashmir in 1965 and 1971, is correct, then (a) the gap between indicators of socioeconomic development should show a steady increase (to the relative detriment of Pakistan) over a time lag of five years before each war, and (b) the insecurity of Pakistani leadership should correspondingly increase, as reflected in anti-Indian sentiments and expressions of self-righteousness in U.N. debates over Kashmir.

The causal relationship between dependent and independent variables in the research hypothesis was operationalized in the following terms:

a) $\Delta T \, \alpha \, \Delta D$

where ΔT is change (increase) in tension,

ΔD is change in gap in socioeconomic development between India and Pakistan,

$D = fn$ (economic, social-demographic indicators).

b) $\Delta T \, \alpha \, \Delta P$

where ΔP is change in perception (for example, increasing insecurity)

$\Delta P = fn \, (D, p), p = $ perception.

Data Collection and Method of Analysis

Primary data was collected for the purpose of analyzing both causal relationships. For examining the relationship between the outbreak of war and status discrepancy in terms of the widening gap in important social-demographic and economic indicators, existing statistics were collected from the *Yearbook of International Financial Statistics* (published by the International Monetary Fund, Washington, DC) and the *Statistical Yearbook* (published of the United Nations Commission on Asia and the Far East, Bangkok, Thailand). Statistics on 19 important indicators for both nation-states were obtained from each yearbook for the years 1957–1977 and then compiled in a time series. Most of the financial statistics (barring statistics on international liquidity and foreign reserves) were expressed in terms of the respective currencies of each state. The exchange rates in U.S. dollars for each nation-state were then collected for each year and used to standardize the statistics in terms of U.S. dollars. The compiled statistics on each indicator for the two nation states were then graphed against each other over the 20-year period under study in order to visually examine the trends in the gaps in levels of socioeconomic development between India and Pakistan. Finally, the percentage change in each indicator was calculated over the 20 years and graphed in order to examine the trend of these changes. The results for five years preceding each war (from 1961 to 1965, in the first case, and from 1967 to 1971, in the second case) were then tabulated for each indicator in accordance with Galtung's categorization of topdog or underdog status of each nation-state vis-à-vis the other. This was done in order to determine the relative status disequilibration of Pakistan with respect to India.

For examining the sense of insecurity in terms of the perceptions of the Pakistani leadership regarding their own status and that of India as the enemy, content analysis of their statements in debates over the Kashmir dispute in the United Nations was conducted (see Babbie 1995). Primary data in the form of the Official Records of the General Assembly revealed that the issue was not substantively discussed there, except for general statements of each side's position. It was presumed that Security Council Records would contain the bulk of the debate on the issue, as it was considered an issue of vital importance to the maintenance of peace and security in the region. Unfortunately, however, Security Council Records were not available for the years from 1962 to 68, and for 1971. Analysis was thus limited to an examination of the abbreviated records of the debates in the *UN Yearbook and Monthly Chronicles* for each year under consideration. These records, however, did provide a comprehensive review of the debate as it proceeded in important U.N. forums, including the Security Council, the General Assembly, the First (Political) Committee of the General Assembly, and UNESCO. They also provided important letters and messages of each state's leadership and their statements to their respective media.

The original research design was also revised in terms of the years for which the debates were examined. The original intention had been to examine the debates for every three years, starting from 1959, so as to be able to compare Pakistan's level of insecurity for each year in which war occurred (1965 and 1971) to the years characterized by relative peace and stability (1959, 1962, 1968, 1974, and 1977). However, since the debates for 1965 and 1971 were opened only after war had already commenced, they did not allow consideration of the level of Pakistan's insecurity just before each war. The years just before and after the year in which each war occurred (1964, 1966, 1970, and 1971) were thus added to the analysis to show fluctuations in the Pakistani stance on the issue just before and after each war. After 1972, there is no mention of Kashmir in U.N. debates, thus making 1972 the last year for which content analysis was performed.

Content analysis primarily focussed on the frequency of key words and sentiments (manifest, as well as latent content) expressing the anti-Indian bias and self-righteousness of the Pakistani leadership. The attitude of the Indian leadership was also analyzed during these debates. The results for both India and Pakistan were then compared in order to determine if the Pakistani sense of insecurity was higher than that of the Indians.

Results of Analysis

For analyzing the relationship between increase in tension (T) and increase in the gap in objective indicators of relative levels of socioeconomic development, the following indicators were selected for comparison between India and Pakistan:

I. *Important economic and financial indicators expressing level of economic prosperity and stability.*

  a) Gross domestic product (GDP), expressed in billions of U.S. dollars for each state (figure A.1 of appendix A) shows a steadily increasing gap between India and Pakistan in the five-year period preceding the 1965 war. Although the gap varies in absolute figures in the five years preceding the 1971 war, the relative gap between the two does show an overall upward trend. India thus retained its topdog configuration in accordance with Galtung's conceptualization throughout the period from 1957 to 1977.

  b) Gross national product (figure A.2) and national income (GNP less depreciation) (figure A.3), both expressed in billions of U.S. dollars, show a steadily increasing gap between India and Pakistan in the period preceding the 1965 war, while the trend varies in the period preceding the 1971 war. Nevertheless the gap continues to remain large enough for India to maintain its topdog status throughout the period.

  c) Total money supply (figure A.4), expressed in billions of U.S. dollars, too, shows a steadily rising gap between the two states. Although the gap does decrease in 1968 and 1969 (with no figure being available for Pakistan in 1970), the gap remains sufficiently large for India to maintain its topdog status.

  d) Balance of payments (figure A.5), expressed in billions of U.S. dollars, is interesting because it demonstrates the underdevelopment and relatively low financial stability of both states with respect to the world. Thus, although both are developing countries, the situation of Pakistan is much worse than that of India. This is particularly true for the period preceding the 1971 war, and could be due to the fact that Pakistan was depending heavily on the outside world (especially the United States) for aiding its development efforts, as opposed to India who has traditionally shown more reliance on development from within. This could reasonably be assumed to act as a contributing factor to Pakistan's perception of herself as lacking the requisite resources for development and hence necessarily dependent on external support, unlike India.

The above contention can be supported by examining the graph on government revenue and expenditure (figure A.9), demonstrating the internal deficit of each state. Pakistan's deficit is less than that of India's in absolute terms, but if one keeps in mind the correspondingly large figures on India's revenue and expenditure, then Pakistan's relative advantage vis-à-vis the low deficit is virtually lost. At the same time, this demonstrates the low level of financial resources available to Pakistan's government for development and defense purposes.

e) The graphs on total reserves (figure A.6), including gold, foreign exchange, and SDR reserve positions in the International Monetary Fund, and on gross fixed capital formation (figure A.7), expressed in billions of U.S. dollars, also maintain India's topdog ranking. The gap for both indicators is much wider for the period preceding the 1971 war, and demonstrate Pakistan's overall worsening position from 1957 to 1977.

f) The graph on foreign assets (figure A.8) is particularly interesting because it is one of the few indicators of financial stability that show Pakistan as possessing a topdog ranking relative to India. This is particularly true for the period before the 1965 war, though the period after 1967 shows an overwhelming increase in the foreign assets of the Indian Reserve Bank. Foreign assets, which are good indicators of the assets and liabilities of the national economic sector, thus demonstrate the growing internal economic and monetary liability of Pakistan vis-à-vis India over the period under consideration. The fact that its assets were once at a higher level than India's might be seen as a contributing factor to Pakistan's increasing sense of status discrepancy, particularly before the 1971 war.

g) The graphs on industrial and agricultural production indices (figures A.10 and A.11) also demonstrate the relative topdog status of Pakistan vis-à-vis India, particularly before 1965. In important sectors of domestic production, therefore, the growth rate for Pakistan was relatively higher than that of India in the years preceding the 1965 war. However, it must be remembered that these are index figures rather than actual figures of the actual industrial and agricultural production. Since index figures are percentages calculated against a country's own performance in a particular year (1963=100 for agricultural production, and 1975=100 for industrial production), their reliability for comparison between different states is limited. Nevertheless, they do demonstrate the internal growth rate of each country. Moreover, it could be contended that Pakistan's decreasing rate of agricultural and industrial production after 1965 led to its increased dependence on the importation of vital food grains and manufactured goods, which in turn increased its balance of payments and reduced its level of economic development further.

h) The graph on electricity (figure A.12), expressed in terms of both thermal as well as hydroelectric electricity generation for industrial and household purposes, is an indirect indicator of the level of industrialization and urbanization of each country. This is because increased industrial production and the establishment of urban areas require a greater supply of electrical energy. The graph shows an increase in electricity generation in absolute terms for both countries throughout the period under consideration, though India continues to maintain its topdog status.

i) Other indicators of the level of urbanization and general development of each country were expressed in terms of road transportation as well as shipping and airline activity. Also, since construction of motor vehicles and all the shipping and airline activity were under government control in both countries during that time, their activity was an indication of government involvement in trade and travel-related activities. Figures A.16, A.17, and A.18 once again demonstrate the topdog status of India, with the gap between the two countries being larger for the period preceding the 1971 war.

II. *Social demographic indicators*

a) Under the realist conception of power, population is an important component of a nation-state's power potential, comprising as it does, a significant part of the nation's work force and scientific/technological/academic intelligentsia. Figure A.13 demonstrates the power potential of India's population as being much larger than that of Pakistan's, with the gap between the population growth rate of each state steadily increasing.

b) Other indicators of a nation's power potential and general level of development are the level of education and freedom to develop one's opinion through the mass media. Figures A.14 (representing the number of educational institutions at the primary, secondary, and university level) and A.15 (representing the number of daily newspapers in circulation at all levels in each country) show the relatively low level of education and freedom of expression in Pakistan.

c) Finally, as an indicator of the relative accessibility of each country to foreign tourists and consequent income from tourism, figure

A.19 shows the number of international tourists who visited each
country from 1957 to 1977. Statistics for Pakistan were missing for
1968–1969, but nevertheless the trend (barring one year, 1964) was
one of an increasing gap between India and Pakistan. The relatively
stable gap before 1965 could be an indicator of the relative ease
with which international tourists could enter Pakistan before the
establishment of the authoritarian governments of Ayub Khan and
Zulfikar Ali Bhutto.

Of the 19 indicators of the level of socioeconomic development examined for each country over the 20-year period from 1957 to 1977, only
four—foreign assets, industrial and agricultural production, and number of
international tourists—showed the status discrepancy in favor of Pakistan
with respect to India. Despite the overall topdog status of India, however,
Pakistan's topdog ranking was in sufficiently significant categories to merit
its consideration as a rank discrepant state in the region, rather than as a
total underdog. Moreover, in accordance with the theoretical constructs of
status discrepancy theory, the *gap* between objective indicators of development did, in fact, show a *steady increase* over the time lag of five years before each case of the outbreak of armed conflict. Also, this gap was more
perceptible for the second case of war in 1971 than for the war in 1965.

The actual fact of an increase in the gap in objective indicators of socioeconomic development can thus be established for both cases of escalation from tension to war. This gap should be reflected in the rising
insecurity of the Pakistani leadership in their statements before the United
Nations.

Results of Content Analysis

The tabulated form of the results obtained from the content analysis of the
debates over Kashmir in the United Nations Security Council and General Assembly can be seen in appendix B. Both manifest content (frequency of key terms/words and phrases expressing hostility toward the
other's position) as well as latent content (underlying sentiment/meaning
behind spoken words/actions) of the statements of each side were analyzed.

a) What is the most important issue for each side? The most important
issue for each side concerned the status of Kashmir. India maintained that
Kashmir was an integral part of its territory due to legal accession by its
ruler to the Indian Union. Pakistan, on the other hand, claimed that the
accession was illegal and fraudulent and that Kashmir thus constituted a

disputed territory, the administration of which should be conducted under the auspices of the United Nations. This is the rationale behind its repeated requests for U.N. intervention/multilateral discussion of the issue. India, however, has consistently rejected the need for multilateral negotiation, preferring bilateral talks instead. It has also accused Pakistan of using the U.N. as a propaganda forum to further its own interests in the region.

It can, however, be contended that the repeated Pakistani requests for U.N. intervention for a peaceful solution to the dispute supports Galtung's theory that a status discrepant state does not resort to violence unless it has exhausted other avenues to resolve the dispute. Also, the fact that there is no mention of Kashmir in the records examined after 1972 might be said to show Pakistan's disenchantment with the efficacy of the U.N. as a forum to achieve its interests, particularly after its defeat in the wars of 1965 and 1971.

b) What was the basis for self-righteousness in the statements of each side? The statements of the Pakistani side consistently blamed India for planning and carrying out a long-standing "grand design" aimed at the destruction of Pakistan. This accusation was couched in terms of the hostility of India, as a Hindu majority power, to all Muslims in the region, even those in Kashmir. India was thus also blamed for repressing the Muslims in Kashmir in order to keep them from achieving "self-determination" (through union with Pakistan via a "free and impartial plebiscite"). India, on the other hand blamed Pakistan for stirring up communal disharmony in Kashmir, stressing that she had an inherent right to self-defense against all encroachments to her territorial sovereignty.

Latent content of the level of insecurity of each side was studied along a number of lines. The most interesting features examined related to the type of speakers/communicators expressing their side's viewpoint during the debates. While the Indian representatives took up the issue on their behalf most of the time, Pakistan's president, foreign minister, and deputy prime minister often addressed the Security Council on behalf of their side. This shows that the issue of Kashmir was far more important to the leadership of Pakistan than to the Indian leadership. A second interesting feature examined was the percentage of the debate taken up by the speakers of each side (operationalized as the percentage of total number of lines devoted to both sides in the records of the debates). The results clearly show that the Pakistani delegation devoted far more time to addressing the issue than the Indians.

The results of both manifest and latent content analysis of the records of U.N. debates over Kashmir clearly show the overall high anxiety level of the Pakistani side as compared to the Indian, both in times of relative stability as well as instability. This is also evident from the large number of empty cells showing the manifest content of Indian statements. Clearly, India, from its position of superiority over Kashmir, was relatively uninterested in discussing the Kashmir dispute in the forums of the U.N., except to repudiate Pakistani allegations. There is no substantial evidence, however, that Pakistan's level of anxiety/insecurity rose perceptibly in the period just before the outbreak of war. There is some indication, however, that its anti-Indian bias and feelings of self-righteousness, as expressed in the form of accusations of an Indian "grand design" against Pakistan, rose in the period just before each war. This is particularly true in the case of the 1971 war.

Conclusions

The results of this research effort provide support for the theoretical propositions of status discrepancy theory to the two specific cases of the outbreak of war between India and Pakistan over Kashmir under consideration. The original theoretical contention is that the perceptual, rather than the objective, indicators of status discrepancy/aggressive insecurity would prove to be the more significant causal factor behind increasing tension. However, the actual results prove the objective factors to be more important instead. Moreover, status discrepancy as a causal factor to the outbreak of war was more significant in the case of the 1971 war.

The main weakness of this research effort, apart from shortage of data, is in the estimation of the rise in tension. This has primarily been a psychological definition (mainly expressed in terms of the sentiments of the Pakistani leadership). The definition would have been greatly strengthened if objective indicators of tension (such as event based data on the number of military incidents between the two sides each year, for example) had been included. However, the constraints of time and resources did not allow such an analysis in this paper.

The main contribution of this research effort is in adding to the cumulative knowledge on the subject of the applicability of system wide, global concepts to particular instances of protracted conflict and enduring rivalry between nation-states. It is by no means a complete explanation of the causes leading to the outbreak of war in the two cases under consideration, but essentially an attempt to formulate and examine the conceptual framework within which the causal relationship between dependent and independent variables operate.

A1   Gross Domestic Product (GDP)

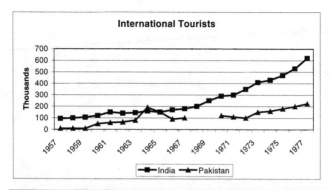

	Before 1965 War						Before 1971 War				
Year	1961	1962	1963	1964	1965		1967	1968	1969	1970	1971
India	T	T	T	T	T		T	T	T	T	T
Pak	U	U	U	U	U		U	U	U	U	U

Source: International Financial Statistics, IMF, Washington DC

T = Topdog Status
U = Underdog Status

A2   Gross National Product (GNP)

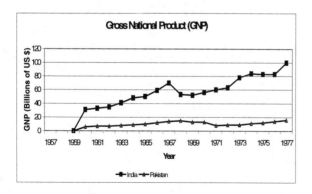

	Before 1965 War						Before 1971 War				
Year	1961	1962	1963	1964	1965		1967	1968	1969	1970	1971
India	T	T	T	T	T		T	T	T	T	T
Pak	U	U	U	U	U		U	U	U	U	U

Source: International Financial Statistics, IMF, Washington DC

T = Topdog Status
U = Underdog Status

A3   National Income

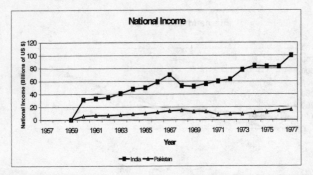

	Before 1965 War						Before 1971 War				
Year	1961	1962	1963	1964	1965		1967	1968	1969	1970	1971
India	T	T	T	T	T		T	T	T	T	T
Pak	U	U	U	U	U		U	U	U	U	U

Source: International Financial Statistics, IMF, Washington DC

T = Topdog Status
U = Underdog Status

A4   Total Money Supply

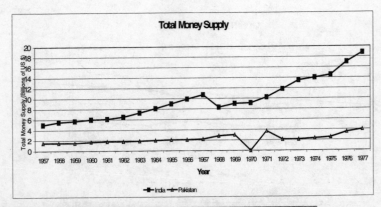

	Before 1965 War						Before 1971 War				
Year	1961	1962	1963	1964	1965		1967	1968	1969	1970	1971
India	T	T	T	T	T		T	T	T	T	T
Pak	U	U	U	U	U		U	U	U	U	U

Source: International Financial Statistics, IMF, Washington DC

T = Topdog Status
U = Underdog Status

A5   Balance of Payments

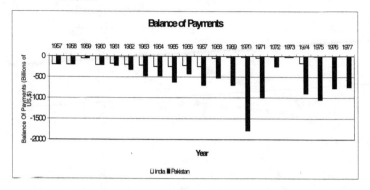

	Before 1965 War						Before 1971 War				
Year	1961	1962	1963	1964	1965		1967	1968	1969	1970	1971
India	T	T	T	T	T		T	T	T	T	T
Pak	U	U	U	U	U		U	U	U	U	U

Source: International Financial Statistics, IMF, Washington DC

T = Topdog Status
U = Underdog Status

A6   Total Reserves

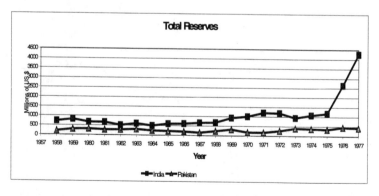

	Before 1965 War						Before 1971 War				
Year	1961	1962	1963	1964	1965		1967	1968	1969	1970	1971
India	T	T	T	T	T		T	T	T	T	T
Pak	U	U	U	U	U		U	U	U	U	U

Source: International Financial Statistics, IMF, Washington DC

T = Topdog Status
U = Underdog Status

A7   Gross Fixed Capital Formation (Billions Of US $)

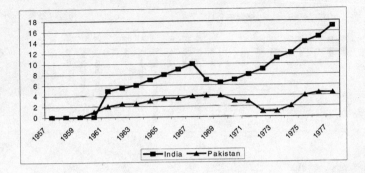

	Before 1965 War						Before 1971 War				
Year	1961	1962	1963	1964	1965		1967	1968	1969	1970	1971
% Diff	0.59184	0.54545	0.58333	0.57143	0.5625		0.61	0.42857	0.38462	0.57143	0.6375
India	T	T	T	T	T		T	T	T	T	T
Pak	U	U	U	U	U		U	U	U	U	U

Source: International Financial Statistics, IMF, Washington DC

T = Topdog Status
U = Underdog Status

A8   Foreign Assets

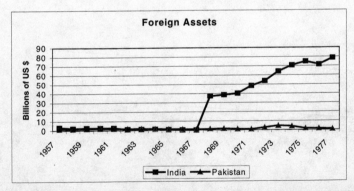

	Before 1965 War						Before 1971 War				
Year	1961	1962	1963	1964	1965		1967	1968	1969	1970	1971
% Diff	0.32836	-0.6216	-0.4729	-0.2143	-0.8293		-2.0294	0.96237	0.95349	0.97016	0.97876
India	T	U	U	U	U		U	T	T	T	T
Pak	U	T	T	T	T		T	U	U	U	U

Source: International Financial Statistics, IMF, Washington DC

T = Topdog Status
U = Underdog Status

A9   Government Revenue & Expenditure

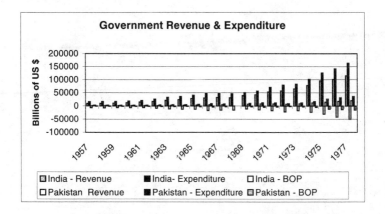

	Before 1965 War						Before 1971 War				
Year	1961	1962	1963	1964	1965		1967	1968	1969	1970	1971
India	T	T	T	T	T		T	T	T	T	T
Pak	U	U	U	U	U		U	U	U	U	U

Source: International Financial Statistics, IMF, Washington DC

T = Topdog Status
U = Underdog Status

A10   Industrial Production

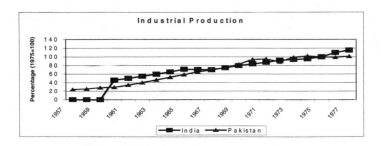

	Before 1965 War						Before 1971 War				
Year	1961	1962	1963	1964	1965		1967	1968	1969	1970	1971
India	T	T	T	T	T		T	U	U	U	U
Pak	U	U	U	U	U		U	T	T	T	T

Source: International Financial Statistics, IMF, Washington DC

T = Topdog Status
U = Underdog Status

A11 Agricultural Production

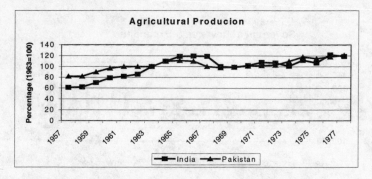

	Before 1965 War						Before 1971 War				
Year	1961	1962	1963	1964	1965		1967	1968	1969	1970	1971
India	U	U	U	U	T		T	T	T	T	T
Pak	T	T	T	T	U		U	U	U	U	U

Source: International Financial Statistics, IMF, Washington DC

T = Topdog Status
U = Underdog Status

A12 Electricity

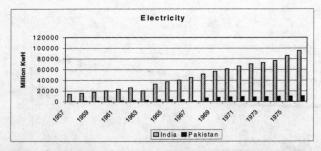

	Before 1965 War						Before 1971 War				
Year	1961	1962	1963	1964	1965		1967	1968	1969	1970	1971
India	T	T	T	T	T		T	T	T	T	T
Pak	U	U	U	U	U		U	U	U	U	U

Source: Statistical Year Book, UN Commission On Asia and the Far East. Bangkok, Thailand

T = Topdog Status
U = Underdog Status

A13   Population

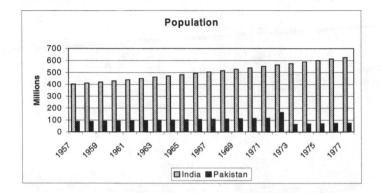

	Before 1965 War						Before 1971 War				
Year	1961	1962	1963	1964	1965		1967	1968	1969	1970	1971
India	T	T	T	T	T		T	T	T	T	T
Pak	U	U	U	U	U		U	U	U	U	U

Source: Statistical Year Book, UN Commission On Asia and the Far East. Bangkok, Thailand

T = Topdog Status
U = Underdog Status

A14   Education

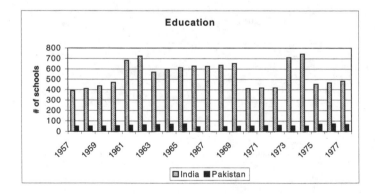

	Before 1965 War						Before 1971 War				
Year	1961	1962	1963	1964	1965		1967	1968	1969	1970	1971
India	T	T	T	T	T		T	T	T	T	T
Pak	U	U	U	U	U		U	U	U	U	U

Source: Statistical Year Book, UN Commission On Asia and the Far East. Bangkok, Thailand

T = Topdog Status
U = Underdog Status

A15 Newspapers

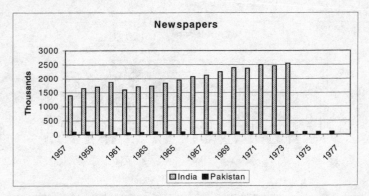

	Before 1965 War						Before 1971 War				
Year	1961	1962	1963	1964	1965		1967	1968	1969	1970	1971
India	T	T	T	T	T		T	T	T	T	T
Pak	U	U	U	U	U		U	U	U	U	U

Source: Statistical Year Book, UN Commission On Asia and the Far East. Bangkok, Thailand

T = Topdog Status
U = Underdog Status

A16 Transport (# of vehicles)

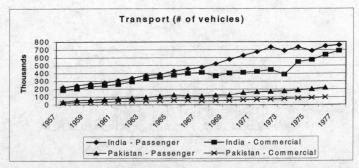

	Before 1965 War						Before 1971 War				
Year	1961	1962	1963	1964	1965		1967	1968	1969	1970	1971
India	T	T	T	T	T		T	T	T	T	T
Pak	U	U	U	U	U		U	U	U	U	U

Source: Statistical Year Book, UN Commission On Asia and the Far East. Bangkok, Thailand

T = Topdog Status
U = Underdog Status

A17   Transport (Kilometers)

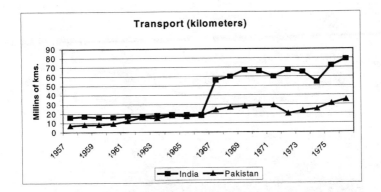

Year	Before 1965 War						Before 1971 War				
	1961	1962	1963	1964	1965		1967	1968	1969	1970	1971
India	T	T	T	T	T		T	T	T	T	T
Pak	U	U	U	U	U		U	U	U	U	U

Source: Statistical Year Book, UN Commission On Asia and the Far East. Bangkok, Thailand

T = Topdog Status
U = Underdog Status

A 18   Sea Shipping

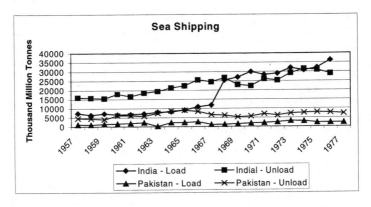

Year	Before 1965 War						Before 1971 War				
	1961	1962	1963	1964	1965		1967	1968	1969	1970	1971
India	T	T	T	T	T		T	T	T	T	T
Pak	U	U	U	U	U		U	U	U	U	U

Source: Statistical Year Book, UN Commission On Asia and the Far East. Bangkok, Thailand

T = Topdog Status
U = Underdog Status

A 19   International Tourists

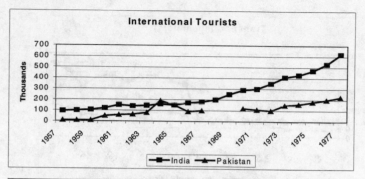

	Before 1965 War						Before 1971 War				
Year	1961	1962	1963	1964	1965		1967	1968	1969	1970	1971
India	T	T	T	T	T		T	T	T	T	T
Pak	U	U	U	U	U		U	U	U	U	U

Source: Statistical Year Book, UN Commission On Asia and the Far East. Bangkok, Thailand

T = Topdog Status
U = Underdog Status

B.1   Manifest Content: Frequency Of Key Terms, Phrases and Sentiments

	1959	1962	1954	1965	1966	1968	1970	1971	1972
Reference to UN Security Council Resolutions	7	13	10	18	1	2	4	6	1
JK disputed territory	2	1	5	4	0	3	3	3	2
Indian design for Pakistan destruction	1	2	3	16	1	3	1	20	3
Indian statements (actions) constituting grave danger in region	2	3	2	10	3	1	1	8	7
Indian denial of self-determination for JK	1	3	5	8	0	0	0	1	0
Fair/impartial plebiscite	2	4	4	7	0	0	3	1	0
Pakistan right to self defense	0	0	1	5	0	0	1	0	0
Failure of efforts at direct negotiations with India	0	3	2	2	0	0	0	1	1
JK constituent part of Indian Union	2	2	3	1	2	2	2	1	0
Need for bilateral negotiation	0	3	5	0	0	0	0	3	2
Pakistan attempts to use Security Council as a propaganda forum	1	1	1	2	0	0	0	1	6
Pakistan violations of Indian territory	2	0	1	1	0	0	1	0	1
Pakistan acts constituting threats to regional peace	0	5	3	1	1	2	2	8	2
Communal harmony exists in JK	0	1	1	0	0	0	0	1	1
Indian right to self defense	1	3	0	0	0	0	0	0	0

B.2   Latent Content
(Numbers in increasing order of insecurity levels)

1.   Importance of issue to leadership
Type of speaker / communicator
President (Pakistan) / Prime Minister (India) = 3
Foreign Minister = 2
UN Representative =1

	1959	1962	1954	1965	1966	1968	1970	1971	1972	Total
India	1	1	1	1	1	1	1	1/2/3	1	14
Pakistan	1	1	1	1	1	1/2/3	1	1/2/3	1	21

2.   Percentage of lines devoted to each country's speaker
. > 60% = 3
50 – 60% = 2
40 – 50% = 1
< 40% = 0

	1959	1962	1954	1965	1966	1968	1970	1971	1972	Total
India	1	0	1	0	0	0	0	1	1	4
Percentage (%)	44.8	33.73	44.83	34.6	33.97	30.14	35.96	45.28	45.55	
Pakistan	2	3		3	3	3	3	2	2	23
Percentage (%)	55.2	66.27	51.17	65.4	66.03	69.86	64.04	54.72	51.45	

3. Sense of urgency
Situations in JK "grave threat" to peace in region due to action of other party
= 1 x frequency of all

	1959	1962	1954	1965	1966	1968	1970	1971	1972	Total
India	0	5	3	7	1	1	2	8	2	29
Pakistan	2	3	2	10	3	1	1	8	7	37

4. Bilateral negotiations vs. multilateral / UN negotiations
Multilateral = 1 x frequency
Bilateral = 1 x frequency

	1959	1962	1954	1965	1966	1968	1970	1971	1972	Total
India	0	3	5	1	0	0	0	3	2	14
Pakistan	0	6	4	4	0	0	0	2	2	18
	14	26	20	36	2	4	8	12	2	124

5. Self righteousness (right to self defense)

	1959	1962	1954	1965	1966	1968	1970	1971	1972	Total
India	2	0	1	5	1	0	1	0	1	11
Pakistan	1	2	3	16	1	3	1	20	3	50

References

Azar, Edward E. 1984. "The Theory of Protracted Social Conflict and the Challenge of Transforming Conflict Situations." In *Conflict Processes and the Breakdown of International Systems,* ed. Dina A. Zinnes. Denver, CO: Monograph Series in World Affairs, University of Denver, pp. 81–99.

———. 1990. *The Management of Protracted Social Conflict: Theory and Cases.* Aldershot, UK: Dartmouth Publishing Company.

Babbie, Earl. 1995. *The Practice of Social Research.* Belmont, CA: Wadsworth.

Carroll, Berenice. 1969. "How Wars End." *Journal of Peace Research* 4 (3): 287–94.

Cashman, Greg. 1993. *What Causes War? An Introduction to Theories of International Conflict.* New York: Lexington Books.

Coser, Lewis. 1956. *The Functions of Social Conflict.* New York: The Free Press.

Cukwurah, A. O. 1967. *The Settlement of Boundary Disputes in International Law.* Dobbs Ferry, NY: Oceana Publications.

Deutsch, Morton. 1973. *The Resolution of Conflict: Constructive and Destructive Processes.* New Haven, CT: Yale University Press.

Dougherty, James, and R. L. Pfaltzgraff. 1971. *Contending Theories of International Relations.* Philadelphia, PA: Lippincott.

Duchacek, Ivo D., ed. 1972. *Discord and Harmony. Readings in International Politics.* New York: Holt, Rinehart and Winston.

East, Maurice. 1972. "Status Discrepancy and Violence in the International System." In *The Analysis of International Politics,* eds. James A. Rosenau, Vincent Davis, and Maurice East. New York: The Free Press, pp. 299–319.

Galtung, Johan. 1964. "A Structural Theory of Aggression." *Journal of Peace Research* 1 (1): 95–114.

Gulliver, P. H. 1979. *Disputes and Negotiations: A Cross Cultural Perspective.* New York: Academic Press.

Ikle, Fred Charles. 1971. *Every War Must End.* New York: Columbia University Press.

James, Patrick, and Michael Brecher. 1988. "Stablity and Polarity: New Paths for Inquiry." *Journal of Peace Research* 25 (1): 31–40.

Jervis, Robert. 1976. *Perception and Misperception in International Politics.* Princeton, NJ: Princeton University Press.

Lebow, Richard N. 1981. *Between Peace and War. The Nature of International Crisis.* Baltimore, MD: Johns Hopkins University Press.

Lijphart, Arend. 1971. "Comparative Politics and the Comparative Method." *American Political Science Review* 65 (September): 682–93.

Nicholson, Michael. 1992. *Rationality and the Analysis of International Conflict.* Cambridge, UK: Cambridge University Press.

Rapoport, Anatol. 1960. *Fights, Games, and Debates.* Ann Arbor, MI: University of Michigan Press.

Starr, Harvey. 1978. "'Opportunity' and 'Willingness' as Ordering Concepts in the Study of War." *International Interactions* 4 (December): 363–387.

Vasquez, John A. 1993. *The War Puzzle.* Cambridge, UK: Cambridge University Press.

Contributors

EDWARD E. AZAR was professor of government and politics, and director of the Center for International Development and Conflict Management, University of Maryland, at the time of his death in 1991.

GIL FRIEDMAN, is a doctoral student in political science at the University of South Carolina.

MICHAEL KUCHINSKY is a doctoral student in international studies at the University of South Carolina.

SAMUEL PELEG is a lecturer in political science at the Academic College of Tel Aviv-Jaffa.

PHILLIP A. SCHRODT is professor of political science at the University of Kansas.

SANGEETA SHARMA is a doctoral student in international studies at the University of South Carolina.

MARC V. SIMON is associate professor of political science at Bowling Green State University.

HARVEY STARR is the Dag Hammarskjold professor in international affairs in the department of government and international studies, University of South Carolina.

G. DALE THOMAS is a doctoral student in political science at the University of South Carolina.

Index